THE
DREAM

THE
DREAM

A Memoir

HARRY BERNSTEIN

BALLANTINE BOOKS / NEW YORK

Published in the United States by Ballantine Books, an imprint of The Random
House Publishing Group, a division of Random House, Inc., New York.
Published simultaneously in Great Britain by Arrow Books,
a division of Random House Group, Ltd.

BALLANTINE and colophon are registered trademarks of Random House, Inc.

All photographs courtesy of the author

Library of Congress Cataloging-in-Publication Data
Bernstein, Harry
The dream : a memoir / Harry Bernstein.
p. cm.
ISBN 978-0-345-50374-9 (acid-free paper)
1. Bernstein, Harry, 1910–Childhood and youth. 2. Bernstein, Harry, 1910–Family.
3. Bernstein, Harry, 1910–Homes and haunts—Illinois—Chicago. 4. Bernstein,
Harry, 1910–Homes and haunts—New York (State)—New York. 5. Authors,
American—20th century—Biography. 6. Jews—United States—Biography.
7. Immigrants—United States—Biography. 8. Depression—1929—United States.
I. Title.

PS3552.E7345Z46 2008
813'.54—dc22   2007043452
[B]

Printed in the United States of America on acid-free paper

www.ballantinebooks.com

2 4 6 8 9 7 5 3 1

First Edition

Book design by Susan Turner

Dedicated to Ruby,
whose love made the dream come true

THE
DREAM

Chapter One

DREAMS PLAYED AN IMPORTANT PART IN OUR LIVES IN THOSE EARLY days in England. Our mother invented them for us to make up for all the things we lacked and to give us some hope for the future. Perhaps, also, it was for herself, to escape the miseries she had to endure, which were caused chiefly by my father, who cared little about his family.

The dreams were always there to brighten our lives a little. Only they came and went, beautiful while they lasted, but fragile and quick to vanish. They were like the soap bubbles we used to blow out of a clay pipe, sending them floating in the air above us in a gay, colorful procession, each one tantalizing but elusive. When we reached up to seize one and hold it in our hand, it burst at the slightest touch and disappeared. That is how our dreams were.

Take, for instance, the front parlor. For years and years, as long as we had lived in the house, the front room, intended to be a parlor, had remained empty, completely without furniture of any sort, simply because we could not afford to buy any. The fireplace had never been lit, and stood there cold and gray. But that wasn't how it appeared in the dream my mother conjured up for us. It would, she promised, be warm and cozy, with red plush furniture, a luxurious divan, and big, comfortable chairs. It would have a red plush carpet on the floor too, and on top of all that there would be a piano. Yes, a piano with black and white keys that we could all play on.

Oh, it was a wonderful dream, and we used to pretend it had already happened and we were lounging on the chairs, with my sister Rose stretched out on the divan. She, more than any of us, gave vent to a vivid imagination, playing the part of a duchess and giving commands to servants in a haughty tone, with an imaginary lorgnette held to her eyes.

Then what happened? My mother must have done a lot of soul searching, and it must have cost her many a sleepless night before she reached her decision to do what Rose afterward, in her bitterness, called treachery. But what else could my poor mother have done? She was struggling desperately to keep us all alive with the little money my father doled out to her every week from his pay as a tailor, keeping the bulk of it for his drinking and gambling. She had to do something to keep us from starving, so she turned the front room into a small shop, where she sold faded fruits and vegetables, which she scavenged from underneath the stalls in the market.

A common shop, no less, to break that beautiful bubble. My sister Rose never forgave her, and indeed the bitterness and resentment lasted a lifetime, and she hardly ever talked to my mother again.

But that's how our dreams were, and it didn't seem as if the really big one my mother had would be any different. This was the dream of going to America. This was the one my mother would never give up. It was the panacea for all her ills, the only hope she had left of a better life.

We had relatives there—not hers; she had none of her own, having been orphaned as a child in Poland, then passed from one un-willing and often unkind household to another until she was sixteen and able to make her way to England. They were my father's rela-tives, his father and mother, and about ten brothers and sisters, a large brood of which he was the oldest.

At one time they too had lived in England, and in the very same house where we now lived, that whole family crowded into a house that was scarcely big enough for ours with only six children. No wonder they fought so often among themselves; it was for space, probably, they fought, although they fought with their neighbors as well. They were a noisy, unruly lot, I am told, and my father was the worst of them all when it came to battling. In fact, he terrorized his entire family with his loud voice and ready fists; even my grand-mother may have been afraid of him, and she was pretty tough her-self.

As for my grandfather, he played no part in any of this. He let my grandmother rule the house, which she did with an iron fist except when it came to my father. But my grandfather managed to keep pretty much to himself. He was a roofer by trade and he was away often, mending slate roofs in distant towns and enjoying himself im-mensely. He would sing while he worked, songs of all nationalities, Jewish, Irish, English, Polish, often drawing a large, appreciative au-dience below.

In an old cardboard box where my mother used to keep an as-sortment of family photographs I once found a sepia photo of my father's entire family, all of them arranged in three rows one behind the other, all dressed in their best clothes, smiling and looking like well-behaved, perfectly respectable children, far from the ruffians that they were. In the center sat the two parents, my grandmother heavy and double-chinned with a massive bosom and the glower on her face that was always there. Beside her sat my grandfather, a bearded and quite distinguished-looking gentleman holding a silver-knobbed cane between his legs, wearing a frock coat.

My father was not in that photograph, and for a very good reason: He was still in Poland.

The story, I have always felt, was somewhat apocryphal, yet older members of the family swear to its truth. At seven years of age my father had been put to work in a slaughterhouse, where he cleared up the remains of the animals that had been slaughtered for butchering. He worked twelve and sometimes more hours a day. At nine he started to drink. At ten he was defying my grandmother and a terror to all of them. He could not be handled. So one day while he was at work my grandmother gathered up the rest of her children and together with my grandfather they all fled to England, leaving my father to fend for himself. When he got home and found them gone, he almost went mad with rage. He followed them, however, and after many difficult weeks of travel finally got to England. He arrived at our street in the middle of the night, having learned from other Jewish people where they lived, and he banged on the door and demanded to be let in.

My grandmother was awakened along with the rest of the household. Peering down from her bedroom window and seeing who it was, she went to get the bucket that stood on the landing and was used as a toilet for the night. It was full to the brim. She carried it to the open window and poured it down on his head. He let out a yell of rage, but refused to give up and kept banging on the door until she was forced to let him in.

So now it was the same thing all over again, except that he was vengeful and more dangerous than ever, and my grandmother racked her brain for another means of getting rid of him. It was at this time, so the story goes, that my mother arrived in England and straight into the hands of my grandmother, who immediately saw the solution to her problem in this sweet, innocent young orphaned girl, who had no friends, no relatives, nobody in the world to turn to. It was not hard to promote the match between her and my father, so my mother, knowing nothing about him, fell into the trap of a marriage that brought her nothing but misery for the rest of her life.

That wasn't the end of the story. No sooner had this marriage taken place than my grandmother lost no time in putting as much distance as she could between her and her oldest son. Once again she packed her things, gathered her brood together, and took them off to America, and out of the goodness of her heart she arranged with the landlord for the newly married couple to take over her house.

In view of all this it would seem utterly useless for my mother to appeal to my father's family—my grandmother, especially—for help in coming to America. Twice they had fled from my father. What chance was there that they would spend their money to buy the steamship tickets that she always asked for and that would bring him back into their lives?

Yet, knowing this, knowing the terrible story of how they had abandoned him in Poland and the suspicion that it had been something similar when they went to America, my mother wrote to all of them just the same. By this time the children were grown up, and most of them were married and out of my grandmother's house, so there were many letters to write.

She could not write herself, since she had never gone to school; she dictated them to one of us. Through all the years this had been going on, the job was handed down from one to the other as we grew up, until finally it came to me, and I was the one who sat down opposite her at the table in the kitchen and dipped my pen in the ink bottle and waited while she thought of what to say.

At last she began: "My dear———," naming whomever this was being written to. "Just a few lines to let you know we are all well and hoping to hear the same from you."

Her letters always began this way, and eventually, after a few words of gossip about the old street—how Mrs. Cohen had had another baby, how this one across the street had been sick, how that one had lost a job—she would finally launch into her plea for the tickets. She never said the word *money*. She could not bear the thought of taking money from anyone. But tickets, steamship tickets, seemed better, and she would always reassure them that they would be paid for once we got to America and started working there.

They did not always answer. Sometimes weeks would go by and no letter came from America. The postman knew all about us and what we were expecting. Well, the whole street knew, but the postman especially. He was an elderly man with white hair sticking out from under his peaked hat, and he limped from a wounded leg he had got in the Boer War. He'd see me waiting at the front door while he limped his way down the street with his bag slung over one shoulder, and shake his head before he got to me and say, "Not today, lad. Better luck tomorrow."

We did get a letter from Uncle Abe. And it was an excited, jubilant letter. He wrote telling us how well he was doing, that he had three suits of clothing hanging in his closet. In his excitement his words got twisted a little, and one sentence came out as "I have a beautiful home and a wife with electric lights and a bathtub."

It was good for a laugh, but what about the tickets we'd asked him for? Nor did any of the others mention them. And as for my grandmother, the one letter she wrote in several years had a caustic touch. "What do you think I am," she asked, "the Bank of England? Or do you think I took the crown jewels with me when I left England?"

With all this you'd think my mother would get discouraged and give up writing letters. But that did not happen, and I don't know how many letters I wrote over the years, starting when I was about nine or ten. And then one morning when I was twelve, while we were all seated round the table at breakfast, there was a loud knocking at the front door.

"Go and see who it is," my mother said, addressing no one in particular. She was too busy serving the breakfast and trying to feed the baby, who was propped up in an improvised high chair made from an ordinary chair plus a wooden box and a strap.

For a while none of us seemed to have heard her. It was probably a Jewish holiday of some sort, for we were all home and my father was still upstairs sleeping. We were busy not only eating but
also reading, with our books and magazines propped up in front of
us against the sugar bowl, the milk jug, the loaf of bread, or whatever other support we could find. This was a regular practice of ours
at mealtimes. But the lack of response to my mother's request could
have been due to something else. Despite the absorption in our
reading, it could have been the thought that the knock might be
from a customer, and that would have been a good reason to ignore
it. We hated customers along with the shop, still not realizing that it
represented our very lifeblood.

And then my eyes lifted from the copy of *Treasure Island* that I
was reading, and my mother's gaze caught mine and she said, "You
go, Harry."

I got up reluctantly and went to the front door.

Chapter Two

It was not a customer. It was the postman. He was standing outside with his bag slung over a shoulder and a grin on his face, holding out a long, thick envelope. "All for you, lad," he said. "Sorry it isn't America. Maybe next time."

I took it from him and closed the door, wondering what could be in it. Yes, I was sorry it was not from America. A big thick envelope like that could very well have had tickets inside, and my heart had given a bit of a thump when I first saw it in his hand. But the postmark on this one was Manchester. It was addressed to the Bernsteins, no first name, simply the Bernsteins, and I was tempted to open it right then and there. However, I hurried in to give it to my mother.

Looking up from thrusting a spoonful of porridge into the baby's mouth, she too gave a start when she first saw it, probably thinking the same thing I had. But when I told her it was from Manchester the light that had sprung up in her face died out and she said, "It's probably an advertisement. Put it down and I'll look at it later."

"Maybe it's something important," I said. "Don't you want to open it now?"

"No, later," she said, and went back to feeding the baby.

But my curiosity was too great for me to be put off. "Can I open it?" I asked.

Impatiently she said, "All right, open it if you want."

I opened the envelope, saw what was inside, and the next moment I was yelling, "It's the tickets!"

At the table everyone looked up from their books. My mother stared at me with the spoon motionless in her hand. I'm not sure that she believed me. I don't think the others did either. But I was taking them out of the envelope. They were pink. Each had a name on it. There was one for each of us. There was the name of the boat we were to travel on: the SS *Regina*. There was the date: 22 June 1922. The departure point: Liverpool. The destination: Quebec, Canada.

I kept taking them out of the envelope and all the time I was yelling, and soon the others left the table and rushed over to see the tickets and to grab them out of my hand, and they too started yelling. My mother stood transfixed, not believing what she was hearing and seeing. At last she took one of the tickets from me and stared at it, unable to speak.

How does one feel when a dream comes true? When the bubble you grasp in your hand does not burst but remains there intact, as beautiful and rose-colored as when it was floating in the air? What does one say? My mother said nothing at first, nothing at all, and for a moment I thought she was going to burst into tears, so deep was the emotion I saw surging through her.

There were other things in that envelope that we would have to look at. There was a long letter from the travel agency giving us a mountain of instructions for packing, passports, photographs that would be necessary, vaccinations, but all of this could wait for later, when we had sobered up from that first moment's intoxication. The house was a bedlam with our shouts and yells of joy, and the baby crying from fright.

Then suddenly there was a voice saying roughly, "What the bloody 'ell's going on here?"

It was my father. He had come downstairs and into the kitchen without our noticing, and at once there was silence, save for the crying of the baby. Nobody dared move or say anything, all of us aware that we had broken the rule of maintaining absolute quiet in the house so long as he slept upstairs. His face was dark with anger, and he was obviously in the kind of mood that such noisy awakenings could bring on.

My mother had picked up the baby and was rocking him back and forth in an attempt to quiet him. "We forgot you were sleeping," she said. "But we couldn't help it. The tickets have come."

If she had expected that this joyous news could have a softening effect, she was mistaken. "Tickets?" he said, with no lessening of the anger. "What tickets you talking about?"

"To go to America."

"Who the bloody 'ell wants to go to America?"

He had said this before. He had made it perfectly clear that he had no intention of going to America. He had never shared that dream, and there was obviously no sentimental attachment on his part to the relatives in America, his father and mother, his brothers and sisters. Perhaps this was little wonder. They had abandoned him once in Poland. They had done the same thing here in England. Of that he was sure, and it rankled deep inside him. Things he had said before had indicated that.

There was unmistakable bitterness in his tone now. "What the bloody 'ell would I want to go to America for? To see that rotten bunch there? Do they want to see me? Like bloody 'ell they do. They can all rot in 'ell for all I care. You can go if you want. You can take your bloody little bastards and go. Do what they did. Run off. Go!"

"You mustn't talk that way," my mother said in a low voice. "I'm sure they all want to see you. The past is past. You must try to forget the past. This is our big chance. If they were as bad as you think they are, they wouldn't have sent us the tickets. It means they want to see you."

"Like bloody 'ell it does," he shouted back at her. "I'll bet you one thing. I'll bet you there's no ticket there for me. I'll bet you anything."

"Yes, there is," she said, louder now and more certain of herself. "I saw it. Here, see for yourself."

She took the tickets from me and handed them to him. But instead of looking at them he threw them on the floor, scattering them all over, and cursing: "You can stick your tickets up your arse. That's what I think of 'em. And you can go to 'ell, you and your little bastards, for all I care."

My mother had given a cry of horror as he threw them down, and I myself rushed to retrieve them, but as I bent down my father launched out with a foot and gave me a hard kick in the behind that sent me sprawling on the floor. Then he stomped out of the room and went back upstairs.

My mother helped me to my feet, and the others, who had remained silent and shocked by all this, joined in picking up the pink steamship tickets. Then I, with a sore behind and hatred in my heart, went outside. I must have walked for miles trying to drive it all away, but thinking all the while that someday I was going to kill my father.

One good thing came out of this: the thought that since my father was not going with us we would be free of him forever, and all the fear and hatred for him that had hung over us ever since I could remember would no longer be there. It gave me a feeling of immense happiness, and because I knew the scene that morning had thrown a shadow over my mother's joy, I talked with her about it later in the evening.

She had decided that the first thing she must do was write a letter of thanks for the tickets, so I was sitting in my usual position at the table in the kitchen opposite her, the writing pad and the ink bottle in front of me and the pen in my hand, when I brought it up. "You must tell them he's not coming," I reminded her. We always referred to him as "he" or "him," never as "Father" or "Dad" or any of the other familiar terms that children use for fathers.

My mother, deeply buried in thought about what she was going to say, looked up at me and stared for a moment. "Why do you say he's not coming?" she asked finally.

I was a bit surprised. "He made it plain enough this morning," I said, and rubbed my behind a bit ruefully. It was still painful.

She saw me and understood. "He's your father," she said.

"Does that give him the right to kick me in the arse?" I asked.

"He can't help it, I suppose," she said. "He's been treated roughly himself from the time he was a little boy, younger than you are now. It's the only way he knows."

"I don't care," I said. "He's got no right to kick me like that. And I'm glad he's not coming with us to America."

"I wouldn't be too sure about that," she said.

I looked at her, surprised and with a faint disappointment settling inside me. "He said he wouldn't go."

"He says a lot of things that he doesn't mean."

The disappointment deepened. "Then he's coming?"

"We'll have to see."

That was all she wanted to say about it, so we turned back to the letter and I dipped my pen into the ink bottle once more. "Dear———" she began, and halted.

"Who are we writing to?" I asked.

She was puzzled. "Who did the tickets come from?"

"A travel agency in Manchester," I reminded her.

"I know that. But didn't they tell us where the money for the tickets came from? Look in the envelope. There was a letter from the travel agency. Maybe it's in there."

I looked. I took out the tickets, the letter, all the other literature the agency had sent us with information about the trip we were going to make. There wasn't a single word as to who had sent the money.

We began to conjecture. Not Grandma—she was not the Bank of England, nor had she had the crown jewels when she left England. With this caustic statement still fresh in our minds she was eliminated from the start. And if not Grandma, then certainly not Grandpa, for he would have less to do with anything than anybody. So who, then? Uncle Abe, who had three suits of clothing hanging in the closet and a beautiful wife with electric lights and a bathtub? But he with his boasting surely would have let us know that he was paying for the tickets. What about Uncle Morris, who was such a nice man and wrote such pleasant letters when he did reply, and his wife, Leah, who sometimes wrote in his place and gave us such a cheerful picture of their life in America—though never saying a word about the tickets? Or Aunt Sophie, who was nice too and had recently married a barber named Sam, who was supposed to be quite well off? Hadn't she once said that she'd love to see us all? And Uncle Barney, the comedian of the family, who wrote such funny letters, once suggesting that we all take swimming lessons and maybe swim across the Atlantic Ocean to America?

Name after name came to us. Uncle Joe, Uncle Harry, Aunt this, Aunt that, until we'd eliminated virtually every one of the ten members of the family, including their spouses, without coming up with one that we knew for sure was our benefactor.

It was a complete mystery, and the letter had to be put off until we found out, so I put my pad of paper and ink bottle and pen back in the drawer of the dresser, and my mother went back to her clothes washing in the scullery.

Chapter Three

THERE WERE NO SECRETS ON OUR STREET. MOST OF THE PEOPLE had been living there a long time and knew everything there was to know about everybody else. It was, after all, just a small, cobble-stoned street with only two long rows of houses facing one another, all the houses on each side linked together under a common slate roof, with short, stubby chimneys sticking up at the top of each roof in a straight line.

The street looked like any other street in the poor section of a Lancashire mill town, with the rows of brick houses all the same, but there was a difference about ours because it had two distinct sides, one occupied by Christians, the other Jews. There was an invisible wall, the imaginary barrier that separated the two sides.

And yet despite that, despite the cultural differences and an-cient enmities, the two sides got along quite well, and when news got out that we had received tickets to go to America there were al-

most as many Christians as Jews who came over to shake our hands
and clap us on the back, to congratulate us and tell us how lucky we
were.

There was a great deal of excitement throughout the entire
street. After all, how often was it that any family left the street? On
the Christian side, especially, there were families whose houses had
been passed on from generation to generation. The Jews had come
later, after being driven out of Poland and Russia and a few other
European countries, and they had found refuge here on this little
street.

But to be able to go to America! Others may have shared my
mother's dream. Certainly there was envy among them, and it only
doubled my mother's happiness and caused her cheeks to flush with
pride at being so fortunate—for once in her life.

Among the people who came over from the Christian side to
congratulate us were the Forshaws, and I'm sure that when they
came my mother felt the same awkwardness she had been experi-
encing for a long time at their presence on the street. They shook
hands and chatted a little, they too perhaps concealing their embarrassment, and when finally they had gone, my mother took a deep
breath of relief. She liked the Forshaws; everybody on the street did.
They shared their gramophone with the whole street on summer
nights, leaving their door open while it was playing so that everyone
could hear. They did things like that, and my mother could not have
had anything against them. Except that they were Christians, and
their son was married to her daughter, and there was a grandchild
who was half Jewish and half Christian.

A secret romance between my sister Lily and Arthur Forshaw
had carried on for years, and there had been a secret marriage at a
country inn called the Seventeen Windows. When my mother had
found out she collapsed from grief and went into mourning, for a
Jewish person who marries outside his religion is considered dead.
We all sat shiva, which is the ritual for mourning the dead, and re-

quires that you sit every day for seven days in a darkened room in your stocking feet and say certain prayers.

Eventually my mother relented and went to see the baby that was born to Lily and Arthur, and we, together with the Forshaws, even gave a party for the whole street to celebrate the birth. It was one of those rare times when the two sides of our street came together as one, and it was really a very wonderful thing. But then things got back to normal again and once more there was that distance between the two sides—the invisible wall—separating us. For my mother there was constant embarrassment knowing that the Forshaws, who lived directly across from us, were relations—and Christians. I have wondered if this did not add to the urgency of her desire to go to America. I am sure, however, that she must have felt tremendous relief knowing that she would not have to be faced with this awkwardness again.

But we were not going yet. When all the excitement had died down and we were able to think more soberly, the realization came that there was more involved in travel to America than just steamship tickets. There was the rail trip to Liverpool and the much longer one from Quebec, where our ship would land, to Chicago. There were numerous other expenses: the fee for the passports, the cost of taking pictures for the passports, and above all, clothes.

"We can't go to America looking like beggars," my mother said.

She would remember those words later and the irony they contained. But she could not have thought of it then, and there were other things on her mind. She worried day and night. Where were we to get the money to pay for all the things we needed? Our benefactor, whoever he or she was—we could not seem to find out from the travel agency—had given no thought to this problem, and my mother was at her wits' end to know where to get the money. There was no use asking my father. He wouldn't have given it even if he had had it, and he still would have nothing to do with going to America. So what was she to do? Totaling up the amount we needed, it came to pounds and pounds.

For a while it looked as if the dream, so close to fulfillment, was to be snatched out of our hands. But my mother would never have let that happen. She had faced other adversities before this and had overcome them. She would do it again.

What she did was a desperate move, and one that elicited wails of protest from us and roars of anger from my father, but it was the only way out for her. She began to sell what little broken furniture we had, together with all the ornaments and everything possible that somebody might want. With still one month to go before our departure, we found ourselves without a table to eat on, without chairs to sit on, without our beloved sofa, torn and flattened but precious to our comfort. Cups, saucers, even the teapot—they all went, as did the clock with two angels clinging to either side, which had been on the mantelpiece for as long as we could remember.

We cried and protested, but what could she do? My father stormed and cursed America and all his relatives there, but that was nothing yet. He would soon be without a bed to sleep in and would have to sleep on the floor. We would all have to do that. The house emptied itself out bit by bit. Our neighbors from both sides of the street bought most of it, and I think that in many cases it was an act of charity on their part rather than need.

I recall one time when my brothers and I were carrying a dresser across the street to the Forshaws' house. They had bought a number of things from us before this, and my mother had been surprised that they had chosen the dresser, since it was in such poor condition, with drawers that did not open or close and the paint worn off here and there. But they had bought it, saying it was just what they needed, and now we were carrying it across the street to them, the three of us sweating a little with its weight, when in the middle of the street the back fell off. And there in the doorway were Mr. and Mrs. Forshaw looking at us. We came to a halt, not knowing what to do, the broken back lying on the ground.

Then the next moment Mr. Forshaw was approaching us, pipe

in his mouth and a hammer in his hand. "Don't worry, lads," he said to us cheerfully. "We'll get this thing straightened out in a minute."

He had brought some nails with him too, and it took him just a minute to get the back of the dresser into place again, this time more securely than before. Then he helped us carry it into his house, with his wife once more exclaiming, "This is just what I've always wanted."

But in spite of all the help we got from our neighbors it still wasn't enough for the clothes that we had to buy, and the shoes, and then to have a little left over when we got there so that we didn't have to borrow money from the relatives, from my grandmother especially. Yet there was nothing else to sell—except the shop.

Perhaps this had not occurred to her before. Maybe, if she had given any thought to it at all, she had resisted parting with what had meant so much to her. It had saved our lives once. Could it do so again? I do not know what was in her mind, but one afternoon, when I was in the shop helping my mother clear out what was left of the rotted fruits and vegetables of her stock, Mrs. Abrams, who lived a few doors away, came in with two young and rather small people, a man and woman.

I was big for my age, taller even than either of my two brothers, so the couple who followed Mrs. Abrams into the shop may have seemed smaller than they were. They looked like a boy and girl to me, but they were a married couple, and the man was Mrs. Abrams's nephew. They were from Manchester, Mrs. Abrams explained, and they were recently married and were looking for a place to live and set up a bakery. The man was a bagel maker, so he was looking for a Jewish area, and he thought our street might be the right place for him.

I saw my mother's face light up. "My shop is just right for you," she said. "I have mostly Jewish customers and they'd all want bagels. Where can you get bagels in this town?" This was true. I myself hardly knew what a bagel was.

My mother added that she herself would give anything for a bagel, especially one that was hot and fresh and just out of the oven. Mrs. Abrams agreed with her. This was a good street for them. Even the Christians might learn to eat bagels.

As this talk went on, the couple grew a little excited, the man especially. He was an excitable person to start with. He began to talk, quite rapidly, and to jerk his head around as he did so, like a rooster pecking away at the corn on the ground and the hens around him. Mostly his talk extolled the virtues of bagels. He believed they were healthy, good for you, but more than that, he believed they were a symbol of Jewish unity, that they brought Jews together and reminded them of their heritage. Furthermore, he went on, English Jews had been deprived of bagels for generations, and he felt it was his religious duty to bring bagels to them.

On and on he went, and my mother's cheeks began to flush with hope; perhaps in that moment she saw the shop as a solution to her problem. She interrupted the little man to cry out, "So then you must buy my shop. It's the perfect place for you. It's more than a shop. It's like a club room. All the Jewish women come in here to sit and talk and drink my sour milk. Isn't that right, Mrs. Abrams?"

Mrs. Abrams, huddled in her shawl, nodded vigorously. "It's like a shul in here sometimes. I come myself, especially on a rainy day, and when the fire is lit it's nice and cozy, and we sit and talk for hours."

"Do you have a good oven?" the baker asked.

"Do I have a good oven?" my mother cried. "I have a wonderful oven. I bake a lot of cakes myself, and bread too. Come and see it."

She led them into the kitchen, and I followed. The little man was more excited than ever when he saw the oven. It was big and black, the door well polished. My mother had baked some wonderful cakes here, especially for the holidays. The house would be filled with their aroma, which would spread even to the upstairs, and you could smell it as you went to sleep.

There was no question that the baker was impressed, and he began to jerk his head about this way and that, looking around the kitchen, opening and closing the oven door, peering inside, looking at the fireplace, peering up into the chimney, no doubt sizing up the place as a future workroom.

I saw his wife pluck at his sleeve and take him aside to whisper in his ear. I have very acute hearing, so I heard what she said: "Don't be such an idiot. Stop liking everything. She'll only charge you more."

My mother would not have charged more than what it was worth. Back in the shop they began their haggling. The little baker, mindful of what his wife had said, began to disparage things, saying the shelves looked warped, the hinges on the bin doors were rusted, the counter sagged a little, the scales didn't seem to be accurate. He found fault with everything, even the window, which looked too small to display his bagels. "My bagels," he said, "need plenty of space to show off their beauty. I have a secret recipe that has been handed down through my family for over a hundred years. There aren't any bagels like them in this whole world. They deserve to be shown off."

Then, still mindful of his wife's whispering in his ear, he came to a sudden decision. "I tell you what I'll do," he said, "I'll give you five shillings for the whole lot."

I saw the shock go through my mother. Her face began to turn red from anger. "I could get more than that if I sold it for firewood," she said.

The little man and his wife pretended to start turning away, with Mrs. Abrams shaking her head under her shawl. But the couple wanted the shop, and so there was a bit more haggling before it was settled. The money my mother got for the shop was not quite as much as she needed, but it would do, and it left her triumphant and happy once more. I do think, however, there was a lot of sadness inside her at parting with the shop. It had served her well through the hardest of all the years, and she would never again have the feeling of independence that it had given her, and the warmth that came on those afternoons when she sat enthroned behind the counter with all the women gathered around her, gossiping and sipping the sour milk that she had made, the fire blazing behind her, throwing a dancing light on the bent figures huddled in their shawls.

Chapter Four

WE LEFT ON A WARM, SUNNY DAY IN JUNE. BOTH LILY AND ARTHUR came to see us off, bringing their baby. They walked with us to the railroad station, Lily carrying her baby, my mother carrying hers, side by side, with the rest of us straggling behind, each of us carrying a piece of the secondhand luggage my mother had bought for the trip.

My father, though, was at the head of the parade, walking a bit faster than the rest of us, as if he wanted it to seem that he had nothing to do with us and was not going to America himself.

The whole street had come out to their doorsteps as we left, and they were all waving and shouting, "Ta-ta. Good luck in America!"

We answered with little waves of the free hand that was not carrying luggage and shouted back to them, "Ta-ta!"

I remember that Mrs. Humberstone wept a little as she stood on her doorstep waving to us. There was weeping too from my mother and Lily, and hugs and handshakes from Arthur, when we were at the railway station and the train had pulled in and it was time to say goodbye. We kept waving to them from the windows as the train started to move, and we did not know then that we would never see them again.

But we quickly forgot about them in the excitement of the journey. Until that day I had never been outside the town, even the street itself, other than for an occasional ramble to Bramhall or Marple and places like that.

It was the same with my brothers and my sister, so we saw England for the first time through the windows of the train that took us to Liverpool, and watching the landscape flash by, seeing farms and fields and cows and sheep and strange towns with strange-looking buildings, held us fascinated for the entire trip.

But that was nothing compared to Liverpool and our first sight of the ship that was to take us to America. We had seen ships before only in pictures in books and magazines, but never a real one like this huge vessel resting at the side of the dock, its three funnels slanting lazily and the name on the bow telling us that this was the SS *Regina*. There was something awesome and frightening about it, and when the time came to board I don't think any of us felt comfortable. We clung close together and followed a steward down to our cabins. Once we were there the fear soon vanished, and after days of eating without a table or a chair to sit on or a bed to sleep in—those last terrible three nights when we slept on the floor—we began to appreciate the luxury of an ocean liner, the kind of life that may have belonged in our dreams, certainly not in the harsh reality of a Lancashire mill town.

There were three cabins reserved for us by our still unknown benefactor—one for my parents and the baby, one for my sister, a third for myself and my brothers—and for the first time in our life each of us had a bed to himself. There were no feet at my head, no wrestling for space, no bumping into one another during the night and angry shouts. There were also startlingly clean white sheets and warm blankets. And then there were meals prepared for us in a dining room, where the tables had white tablecloths for every meal, three times a day, with an extra supper added at night if you wanted it. And there was entertainment: someone playing a piano, couples dancing, a movie once.

"I'd like to stay here forever," I said to my mother.

She laughed. She was very happy herself. Wasn't this the dream come true? A preliminary taste of what America was going to be like? "Wait till you get to America," she said. "You'll like it even better there."

"Will I?" I said. "What will I be doing there?"

"You'll be going to school."

"What about Joe and Saul?" I asked. "Will they be going to school too?"

"No," she said. "They're too old to go to school. They'll have to find jobs. But you'll go to school and you won't have to take a scholarship exam. Everybody your age goes to school in America, and you've got a chance to become something."

"What?" I asked.

"You'll decide that when you get older. But you can be a doctor, or a lawyer, or an engineer, or anything you want. That's one of the reasons I always wanted to go to America, so you could have a chance to become something."

I remember that talk we had while we were sitting on the deck. The ship was rocking slightly from side to side, but not so that it was unpleasant. The sun was shining, and the sea was quite calm and blue like the sky. We had wonderful weather like that all through the voyage. And I don't think my mother ever experienced such happiness. What made it still happier for her was my father. I'd had some bitter regrets about his coming, a decision he had made at the last moment and only after a lot of pleading on the part of my mother, something I had not been able to understand, thinking that she would seize the opportunity to be rid of him. But such was not the case, and I could never understand why.

He seemed to have changed, though, and I myself could not deny that. The trip forced his presence on us every moment of each day. This was something new to all of us, for until now he had always been like a boarder: he came and went, he ate his meals alone, and after coming home from work and eating he rushed out to the pub or to his club for a game of cards. But there was no opportunity for him to avoid us while we were on the ship, so we saw him constantly, and ate with him, and spent the evenings with him, and with a touch of amazement we could see how well he seemed to get along with other people. We had always wondered about that—was he as much of a loner in the pubs as he was in his home? The answer we got here was no. He was quite sociable with others. And several times we saw him laugh. That was stranger than anything else. We had never seen him laugh before. When he did he threw his head back a little and opened his mouth wide so that you could see all his teeth, and the gold one in the center of the top row.

We knew the story of this tooth. Our mother had told it to us once, somewhat bitterly but with a lot of sadness that I did not understand. She had been suffering from a bad toothache for days before she plucked up the courage to ask my father for money to go to a dentist and have the tooth pulled. There was not the slightest sympathy. Instead, he made a joke out of it. Jeering, he said, "I'll make it easier and cheaper for you if you want. I'll knock the tooth out for you with my fist."

Several days later, still suffering from the toothache, she heard from people that he'd made a killing on a horse he'd bet on. And then she noticed the gold tooth in his mouth. He'd used his winnings to have a perfectly good tooth extracted and a gold one put in its place for purely cosmetic purposes.

I hated my father more than ever after I heard this story, but I wondered a great deal about the sadness in my mother's tone when she told it to us. And afterward I wondered why she had urged my father to come to America with us. Why?

These were things that I did not understand then, but I do know that my own negative feelings toward my father lessened somewhat during the days of our voyage across the Atlantic, and that my mother seemed almost incredibly happy that whole time. Perhaps this was due to the fact that my father scarcely did any drinking, which in turn was because it was expensive to buy liquor on the ship and he did not have any money, and my mother managed to keep the little she was hoarding away from him.

But then, suddenly, everything seemed to change as the voyage began to come to an end and the ship, pulled by two tiny tugboats, sailed slowly up the St. Lawrence River toward Quebec. My father became his old self again, sullen and bad-tempered, cursing, the familiar dark, angry figure we had always known.

The worried look came back onto my mother's face. The baby seemed to be doing a lot of crying, and this added to my father's vicious temper. "Shut that little bastard up," he snarled, "or I'll throw him overboard."

We were standing on the deck of the ship among other passengers getting ready to disembark as the ship approached the landing dock, and I saw heads turn and shocked looks on the faces of people who had heard my father's outburst. There were also some sympathetic looks cast at my mother, who was rocking the baby back and forth to silence it.

Then, finally, we stepped off the ship and into an oppressive heat that we had never experienced before in the mild climate of England. It struck us like a blow in the face and left us a little dazed. Luckily, we were able to escape the ordeal of Ellis Island, the usual entrance to America for immigrants. The customs and immigration examinations at Quebec were swift and simple, though one officer, half joking, or perhaps seeking a way of showing his thoroughness, pointed to my father and asked me, "Is this man your father?"

I don't know why I hesitated, but I did, and I looked at my mother, as if for the answer.

I saw the look of fury on my father's face. The officer was laughing. "Not sure, eh?" he said, winking at the other officers, who were laughing too.

"Of course he is," my mother said, speaking up for me at last in an indignant tone.

Our passports were stamped and we were able to leave, out into the heat once more, with all of us sweating and blinking against the blinding sun. We were lucky again in that the railroad terminal was only a short distance away and a train was already waiting there. We checked our luggage and climbed onto it. The seats had high backs and were red plush, hot from baking in the sun. We would soon find out how prickly and uncomfortable they were. It didn't take long for other passengers to board and for the train to get under way, and a short time later the conductor came in and we heard the click of his puncher as he collected tickets.

My mother had bought the tickets for us at the terminal, paying for them out of the purse she kept attached to a string and tucked in her bosom. She was holding the baby in her lap and she gave the tickets to my father. He was still glowering from that business with the immigration officer, and I've no doubt he was thirsty. It was no ordinary thirst—he had been without a drink for a week and the heat added much to it.

When the conductor came alongside, my father thrust the tickets at him roughly, and they would have fallen to the floor if the conductor hadn't grabbed them quickly. He gave my father a sharp look but said nothing. He began to punch the tickets, then halted and asked, "Who's the half rate?"

My mother pointed to me and said, "He is."

The conductor looked at me. I was sitting in the seat in front of her with Saul and Joe.

"How old is he?" the conductor asked.

"Twelve," my mother replied, rocking the baby, who was crying again. "They said it was half rate for twelve and under."

"Son," said the conductor, addressing me now, "how tall are you?"

I didn't know. I looked at my mother for the answer. She gave it, having only recently measured me for clothes. "He's five feet six inches," she said.

"And you say he's only twelve?"

"Yes. Is there something wrong?" my mother asked, beginning to worry.

"Lady," said the conductor, "if he's twelve, then I'm twelve."

It was at this point that my father decided to intervene. I heard a familiar cough from him that always signaled a coming outburst that was still under control. He rose from his seat and faced the conductor. "Are you trying to call my wife a liar?" he asked.

The conductor looked back at him steadily but coolly. "I'm not calling anybody a liar," he said. "I'm just saying this boy doesn't look twelve years old."

"And who the bloody 'ell are you to know how old he is or isn't? Are you looking for a fight? Because if you are, here I am, willing and ready to give you one."

Other passengers were staring now, and my mother had risen in alarm and was plucking at my father's sleeve to get him to sit down. He shook her hand away savagely. He was in the mood for a fight. He wanted one badly.

For a moment the two stood eyeball to eyeball, then the conductor punched the ticket he had been questioning, handed the stubs back to my mother, and walked on.

My father hitched up his trousers, coughed, and returned to his seat, but not before he had cast a glare at me that revealed the hatred he felt toward me, still not forgetting the episode in the immigration office and the question of whether he was my father.

Chapter Five

I<small>T WAS A LONG, HOT, DUSTY RIDE ON PRICKLY PLUSH SEATS THAT</small> soon became filled with debris from the food we ate, its wrappers, the magazines we read, clothing, and all sorts of other things that accumulated throughout the endless hours of the day and through the night when the seats became our beds. Sometime during the night the train halted and we had to get out, dazed and half asleep, and stumble our way through another customs and immigration questioning. It was the American border, and there was another train to take, this time on stiff leather seats that were harder than the others and made even worse beds for the rest of the night.

We were tired and worn, and we complained bitterly—to our mother, of course. She bore with it patiently, assuring us it would soon be over, and she rocked the baby, who seemed to cry steadily, while my father cursed.

Loud enough for all the other passengers to hear, he shouted,

"So you had to come to America. England wasn't good enough for you? But you see what you're getting. Wait! There's worse coming for you and your bastards." She said nothing, just kept rocking the baby and speaking softly to him and feeding him with a bottle.

The train swept on, and the seats grew harder and harder, and the landscape flashed by in a never-ending chain of fields and forests and houses and farms. Grit flew in through the open window and got into our eyes, and we complained about this too to our mother, who was so tired herself that she could hardly keep her own eyes open, but did nevertheless what she could to take care of us, and never complained herself and was always patient.

Until at last, finally, thank God, the train began to slow down, and the rails spread out to form a maze of tracks that grew wider and wider with freight cars parked on them and an occasional engine puffing slowly along them. Then suddenly it grew dark and we were in a tunnel, and then there was a long platform sliding past us and the conductors were shouting, "Chicago! Chicago!"

Collecting our things, we lined up behind our parents and stumbled off the train, still dazed, still half asleep, hardly knowing where we were or where we were going, but following like sheep. Then we were out on the platform and once more trailing after them, with other passengers surging past us and porters bent over carts filled with luggage. We passed the stilled engine, which was hissing out clouds of steam, on our way to the baggage room, where we picked up our worn, secondhand luggage. Each one of us carrying a suitcase, we emerged into the bright lights of the waiting room, putting our luggage down and standing in a group wondering what next.

It came quickly. From a distant group of waiting people came the shrill cry of a woman: "There they are!"

Two people were running toward us, a tall, thin man with a grin on his face and a tall, thin woman; it was she who had uttered the cry. I heard my father mutter, "The lovers."

Everybody in my father's family had a nickname. That of the approaching couple was more complimentary than the ones given to the others. It was "the lovers." Theirs had been a forbidden love, as they were first cousins. The two families from which they came had tried to put a stop to it. But it was no use. So infatuated with Leah was Morris, one story goes, that once he spent his entire week's wages riding on the Dobby horses in Vernon Park with her. His mother gave him a sound beating when he got home payless, and then she went to Leah's family and did battle with them. But nothing could stop it. The two were married. They had three children now, and I knew them well enough from the letters I had written to them.

My father's fears over the kind of reception he would get from his family may have subsided somewhat as they descended on us with hugs and kisses and excited chatter. They had been delegated by the family to meet us, and there couldn't have been a warmer greeting, which included my father as well. He was reassured enough even to joke a little in his jeering fashion, asking, "So how's the hand?"

It was a reminder that went back to the years when my father had still been living with his family and he'd broken Morris's wrist in a fight they'd had. It had never mended properly, and the wrist was still slightly crooked.

Morris held no grudge against my father for it. He grinned amiably now and said, "It's doing well."

"Well enough to pick a few pockets?" my father shot back.

Morris laughed and said nothing further about the matter. It was true, however. He had picked a pocket or two in his youth and had been caught once and narrowly escaped being sent to jail. But that was all in the past. He made raincoats for a living and was a respectable family man, and he and Leah were still lovers and a pleasant couple to be with. I had always liked their letters, and my mother had too, and she had considered them the most promising of all the

family to help us get to America; they were the first who had come
to her mind when we were speculating as to who might have sent us
the tickets. She had been thinking of that for some time, and probably couldn't wait to ask what she did now. "So who bought us the
tickets? Did you and Morris?"

The answer never came, because Morris decided we had to
hurry. There was a cab waiting for us. We followed him and Leah to
the taxi stand outside, and there it was, a Checker cab, and the
driver waiting impatiently was Louis, my aunt Ada's husband, a tall,
heavily built man with worried-looking eyes and very much in a
hurry to get away.

He wasted very little time on greetings, explaining that the cop
on duty had warned him twice already about being parked too long,
and he'd get a ticket in another minute or two if he didn't move his
cab. He packed our luggage into the trunk, some of it on the top of
the cab, then helped push us all inside, and how we all managed to
squeeze in I'll never know. But we did somehow, with several of us
including me sitting on laps, and Louis finally took off.

As he did so another taxi, a Yellow cab, drove off from behind at
the same time and tried to cut in front of him.

The two cabs came to a screeching halt inches away from one
another. Louis's temper had been frayed long before this, what with
nearly getting a ticket for parking, then having such a big load to get
into his cab, plus the fact that he was not getting paid for this trip,
since it was for family. There was something else. Recently there had
been a taxi strike in which he had been involved as a striker. The Yellow cabs, however, had refused to join the strike. Now this one had
nearly run into him.

Louis's temper exploded. He leaned across through the open
window and yelled, "You dirty Yellow scab. I'll cut your balls off."

"Go fuck yourself," the other driver yelled back.

"Louis," Leah shrieked, "there are women and children in this
cab!"

Louis ignored her. He leaned sideways a little more and spat, catching the other driver right in the eye. And then, quickly, Louis drove off and the rest of the drive was peaceful. But it was not what I would have wanted. I did not mind having to sit on somebody's lap, but I would have liked to see the city as we drove along. My view, however, was blocked by heads and shoulders and backs, and I could not see anything through the window.

I was glad when it was over, and so were all the others. It was just as hard getting out as it had been getting in. We tumbled out stiffly, and I found myself on a sidewalk alongside a building that had a high stoop. I scarcely saw the other buildings on the street, and we were led up the stoop carrying our luggage once more, then up two dark flights of steps until we got to the top, where an open door let out a volley of noise that came largely from the chatter of voices.

It was the family in there, all gathered to greet us, to welcome us to Chicago, the aunts and uncles, the cousins, the in-laws. Scarcely had we stepped inside than they were all over us with hands round necks, wet kisses, shrieks, cries, a confusion of faces and voices that left me bewildered. The names too added to the confusion. I do not know if there was a shortage of names in those days, but so many of them in my father's family were the same as the ones in our family. There was even an Aunt Lily, the same as my older sister, though she looked nothing like our Lily. She was taller and heavier, and she was several years older.

But I only caught snatches of people then. There were simply too many of them to be able to take in each one separately. Faces were a blur, coming one moment to smile, say a few words, then disappear. I do remember wondering where my grandfather was. More than any of the others on that old sepia photo, his face stood out in my memory, with its dignified beard, the distinguished look on him, the silver-knobbed cane clasped between his legs. But he did not seem to be here. My grandmother was, however, and quite prominently too in the midst of all this noise and confusion, seated on a high-backed chair that was a bit like a throne, saying very little, a heavy, hulking woman, as I remembered from that same photo, with double chins, a huge bosom that had a necklace dangling from it, and yes, much jewelry on her hands and wrists.

She could not have been missed. I had been brought up to her, as had my brothers and sister, and she had moved her lips a little but said nothing that could be heard. Her bejeweled hands were clasped in front of her and did not move to touch a hand or pat a head or anything like what you might expect from a grandmother.

My mother had gone up to her almost as soon as we had entered, and she had stayed near her several moments, saying something to her that I did not hear. Then it was my father's turn. He seemed to have hung back for a little, as if afraid to approach her, which undoubtedly he was, and the entire room grew silent for a moment as this was taking place, everyone probably wondering what sort of greeting this was going to be.

Well, it amounted to nothing at all. He too murmured just a few words and she said something to him, but there was no rebuff, nothing to indicate that he was not welcome, and the room became noisy again and perhaps even livelier than before with the relief they all felt, including, unquestionably, my father.

It was very hot in the house. It had been hot outside, but here it was stifling. Some of them were fanning themselves with their hands, sweat showing on their faces. The two windows were wide open, but no air came through. I noticed a chair empty near one of them and went up to it, grateful to be away from the crowd for a while, and also because it could give me a chance to look out and see the America I had missed thus far.

Nobody saw me as I sat down and leaned forward with my hands on the sill. There was not the slightest breeze coming from outside, and a rank odor rose from below that reminded me of the smell that used to come from the middens at the back of our house in England. I looked down and what I saw was vastly different from what I had been expecting, different from what we had seen of America in the picture shows, the columned houses with gardens surrounding them, and swimming pools and everything very beautiful. What I saw was a narrow alley with garbage cans lined up at intervals, some of them without lids and the garbage overflowing onto the ground. It was from these that the smell had come.

Across the alley were backyards with clotheslines strung across and washing dangling from them. And rising above were layers of back porches all piled on top of one another like egg crates, some with people on them lazing in chairs and gazing blankly across at me. There were steps zigzagging down from one layer to another, reaching the ground.

My eyes wandered back to the alley, and on top of one garbage can I saw something move. It was a rat, a large gray one, and it was feasting on the garbage.

I would have turned away anyhow. I felt sick. But just then a violent shout rose in the room behind me. It was my father's voice, and he was shouting, "Where's me father? Where the bloody 'ell is 'e?"

During the time I had been sitting at the window, another one of my uncles had arrived. It was my uncle Abe, the one who'd written telling us that he had three suits of clothing hanging in his closet and was doing so well, with a beautiful home and a wife who had electric lights and a bathtub.

As I turned round at the outcry from my father, I saw Abe sitting among them, and he did not look prosperous. He wore shabby clothes and his tie was hanging loose from the collar of his shirt. There was a bottle on the table beside him.

This was the bottle that Abe had brought with him, and with the loose, uncontrollable laugh that came from him, showing broken yellow teeth in his mouth, I gathered that he had already sampled much of what was in that bottle. Yes, he had brought it in a brown paper bag, and it came from the closet where he was supposed to have three suits of clothing. Well, things had changed a bit since then. He had lost his job, and the wife with electric lights and a bathtub who had already given birth to three children was threatening to leave him. The three suits had gone. The closet now held a barrel of what they called moonshine. Abe had struck a deal with a bootlegger to store the barrel in his closet in return for the rent on the house. It had saved him from being evicted with his family, and it had also given him a free supply of what he liked best: whiskey. The bootlegger would never know if he helped himself to a bottle now and then, though it was more than a bottle. Abe had never been sober since he made the deal.

The bottle, which was almost empty by this time, had livened up the gathering still more, and especially my father, who took to what was in the bottle like a man dying from thirst. By this time my father's brain was sufficiently inflamed by the raw liquor to give him the courage he needed to make himself heard in my grandmother's home once again. Despite the haziness that must have come with the drinking, he had noticed what had struck me also: the absence of my grandfather. He had asked them in less violent tones but had not been able to get an answer, and now his patience was gone and he was demanding it in the way the liquor inside him commanded.

Hearing it as I turned round, and thinking of what I had just seen, I felt with a sinking sensation that we were back to what we had come from. I cast a look over at my mother, seated among them. Her head was bent, and I knew that she was thinking virtually the same thing. I saw also that my grandmother's face had tightened, and she too may have been having similar thoughts in regard to her own experiences with my father back in the days when he'd terrorized them all with his fists and his voice.

His fist came crashing down on the table, and once more he demanded to know where his father was. This time Barney answered him.

Barney, the humorist of the family, was a short man. His nickname was "the Dwarf," and he was close to being one. So was his wife. Sitting beside him now, she was as short as he was, but plump. Barney was never without a five-cent White Owl cigar in his mouth, making him look even smaller, somehow, than he was.

With that huge cigar sticking out of his mouth, but also with a slight twinkle in his eyes, Barney now gave him the answer: "He's in New York."

My father swung glaring eyes to him. "What's he doing in New York?"

"He's there on business." The twinkle was even more noticeable as he spoke, and I saw his wife touch his arm, as if to warn him of something.

My father's eyes remained on Barney. "What the bloody 'ell are you talking about? What business? Since when was roofing a business? It's a job, not a business."

"Who said anything about roofing?" Barney asked calmly, puffing slightly on the big cigar. Once again his wife touched his arm, and I thought I detected an uneasy stir go through the assemblage, people looking at one another.

"Dwarf," said my father, beginning to grit his teeth as he always did when his rage mounted, "are you trying to be funny with me? Because if you are, you know what's going to happen. I can knock your eye out too."

This last was a reference to Abe, whose nickname was "Cock-eye," the result of a bad injury to one of his eyes that had never been corrected and had been caused by my father's fist during an altercation when they were boys.

Barney was about to say something when his wife put a hand over his mouth. At the same time my grandmother rose from her throne. There followed then a scene that I would witness quite often in the future at gatherings of the family, when my grandmother had reached the limits of her endurance with the family and what there was of her generosity as a hostess had been exhausted.

Rising with some effort and finally getting her heavy body on her feet, the jewelry resettling on her, the immense bosom lifting with her, she waved both arms about and shouted in a hoarse voice, "Go home! Go home, all of you! I've had enough of you already. Take your things and take your children and get out of here and leave me in peace. Go, go, go."

The obedience was swift and prompt, and it was accomplished mostly in silence. In a few moments they were all gone and the house was strangely silent. My grandmother gave one last look at us before she left the room. It was a look that seemed to imply she wished we had joined the exodus.

We were all silent for a while longer. Even my father seemed subdued and said nothing.

It was my mother who spoke finally. "We mustn't stay here long. We'll have to get a place of our own, and you must get jobs as soon as you can. Tomorrow you'll start looking. We'll be all right. At least we got to America."

Chapter Six

I was lucky. I did not have to look for a job. In the fall I would be going to school. Meanwhile, I had to find some way of passing the time. I missed my friends back in England, the games of cricket or footer on the rec. I had no friends here. But I was not lonely. There was plenty for me to do. There was a whole new city for me to explore.

On the day after we arrived in Chicago, I set out from my grandmother's house to see what I had not been able to see from that window. The heat was intense and the sun beat down on me mercilessly, but I didn't mind. I would perhaps have liked to do my sightseeing on one of the trams I saw going by in an endless stream, or better yet from the window of one of those elevated trains that roared overhead and showered dust on my head every time I walked under an iron trestle. But that cost money, seven cents a ride, and I didn't have seven cents. I was a good walker, though. I liked to walk, and everything I saw filled me with wonder. I had never seen anything like it before: the long busy streets with their ceaseless flow of cars, so many of them, and a few clip-clopping horses and rattling carts, and shops of all kinds with large windows that displayed all sorts of things and kept me glued to them for longer periods, especially those with wax models in them that looked as if they were alive, real people who'd start walking and talking any minute. It was like Alice in Wonderland and all the crazy things she saw after she fell down the rabbit hole. I went on, but I paused once more at a street corner where a large crowd was gathered around a man who was standing on a ladder demonstrating something he had in his hands that he called a radio. I'd never seen one or even heard of one before.

It was a black box with dials in the front and a handle to hold it. When he turned one of the dials music started to come out of the box, and the man, who was tall and skinny with a long neck and spoke with a voice that was hoarse, probably from a lot of talking, was saying, "Folks, that music you hear is coming from a thousand miles away, from New Orleans, Louisiana. . . ." There were murmurs of amazement in the crowd, and people edged closer to get a better look at this magic box. "It's a radio, folks, and the time isn't far off when every home in the country is going to have one. I can let you have one right now for the unbelievable bargain price of . . ."

The price was ridiculous for me. I would have given my right arm for one of those radios, but I didn't even have seven cents for a streetcar. I continued my walk, and my mind was soon distracted by other things that I saw. Eventually I came to the Loop, and here my mouth really opened wide with amazement as I looked up at the clusters of tall buildings that seemed to reach up into the sky. Back where I had come from the tallest building in the town was the jam works, four stories high. So you can understand how I felt when I saw my first American skyscrapers. It was sheer fantasy to me.

But then after walking through the Loop and coming to Michigan Boulevard and seeing beyond that, stretching incredibly before

me, Lake Michigan—a sea as wide and as blue as the one I had
crossed a few days ago—I realized that Chicago had not only the ug-
liness that I had seen from the window but this beauty also.

I would come back after that day. I could not get enough of
Chicago. I walked and walked every day during that hot summer,
and I saw the city's beaches and its parks and the river that flowed
through the city, and I would come back to my grandmother's
house, exhausted but exhilarated, my shirt damp with sweat, my feet
tired, but my mind filled with all the things I had seen.

The heat never seemed to lessen and in fact grew still more intense as the summer went on, and all of us suffered from it. The
nights were perhaps the worst, when the heat became even more oppressive and no air stirred. The house inside was like an oven, and
when night came we stayed outside as long as we could, sitting on
the stoop and slapping at the mosquitoes that buzzed around us—
another of the tortures that we had never experienced before. And
in addition to all this an evil, fetid odor crept over us and over the
entire city, coming from the stockyards on the South Side, where
thousands of animals were slaughtered every day.

We went upstairs to bed at last. We had to. We were all tired and
somehow, despite the sweating and the mosquitoes, we managed to
get to sleep. Except this one night. I slept in the dining room with
my two brothers—once again in the same bed (which was a davenport, as sofabeds were called in those days) and once again at their
feet. It may have been an involuntary kick from the feet of one of
them in his sleep, or perhaps the heat and the mosquitoes, but I
awoke sometime during the night, sweating and hearing that familiar buzzing around my head. I lay for a while uncomfortably, slapping a few times, and then I thought I heard a sound of murmured
voices coming from the kitchen. My grandmother slept in the bedroom that led off it, and I wondered if she could be in the kitchen
talking to herself. But there were two voices. And then I heard a
strange clinking sound, like coins being jingled.

I waited, listening further. There was light showing in the cracks of the door that separated the dining room from the kitchen, and I knew for sure now that people were in there. It was none of my business, but my curiosity got the better of me—I couldn't sleep anyhow, and that clinking noise intrigued me. I got out of bed, making sure I did not wake my brothers, and went softly to the door. I opened it just an inch or two and peeped in.

Yes, there were two people sitting there at the table. One of them was my grandmother in a robe, her hair down at her shoulders. The other I did not recognize at first. It was a man, a bearded man wearing shabby clothes, looking almost like a tramp. In front of them were stacks of coins of different sizes, and scattered there too were other coins through which they were sorting with heads bent close together.

I must have made some sort of noise with the door, because instantly their heads rose and my grandmother called out sharply, "Who's there?"

I thought of turning and running back to bed, but I knew she'd come after me, so I opened the door wider and stepped in. Blinking against the strong light and rubbing my eyes, I stood there not knowing what to say.

The man spoke. "Is that Yankel's son?"

"It's the younger one," my grandmother said, and I could tell from her tone that she was angry. "What are you doing here?" she demanded.

An excuse had come to me quickly. "I'm thirsty," I said. "I came for a drink of water."

"Then go to the sink and take it," she said. "And then go to bed." And I heard her mutter in a low tone, "They're all a damned nuisance."

I went to the sink, poured a glass of water and drank some of it, and was about to leave, but the man said in a kindly tone, "Come here."

I went over to him and he put an arm round me and drew me closer. "Do you know who I am?" he asked.

"No," I said.

"I'm your grandfather."

I said nothing. I could not somehow see him as the distinguished-looking man in the sepia photo, with the neatly trimmed beard, the cutaway coat, and the silver-knobbed cane clasped between his legs. This man was ragged in comparison. The beard was scraggly and gray; he needed a haircut too. The rest of the face not covered by the beard was red and weather-beaten. But it did have a pleasant, half-amused smile.

"He's a big boy," he said. "How old is he?"

"Twelve," snapped my grandmother, and then to me, "Go to bed."

In the meantime she had done something strange. She had taken a cloth from a drawer and spread it over the coins on the table. She had just finished doing it as she snapped at me, and the old man chuckled. "What are you afraid of," he said, "he'll steal it?"

"Be quiet," she said angrily, then once more to me, "Go on, go to bed."

"Let him finish his drink at least," my grandfather said. "What's the rush for bed? Let him stay up for a while longer. I want to talk to him." Then he asked me, "Do you like toffee?"

"Yes," I said.

"Does Mrs. Turnbull still have her toffee shop on your street?"

I nodded and sipped at my glass, only pretending to drink, and at the same time kept a careful eye on my grandmother. She was getting angrier by the second.

My grandfather chuckled. "You must miss her shop," he said. "But you'll find plenty of toffee shops here. Buy yourself some." He dipped his hand under the cloth and brought out a quarter. She tried to snatch it away from him, but he managed to avoid her hand and thrust the coin into mine. Then he said, "Now you can go to bed."

I went hurriedly, clutching the quarter, aware of the glaring eyes of my grandmother on me. I closed the door after me and slipped into bed, still clutching my quarter.

I heard the murmur of their voices again, my grandmother's still sounding angry, and there was more clinking of coins before I finally fell asleep.

I SLEPT LATE. WHEN I awoke they were all at breakfast. The kitchen door was wide open and their voices came to me loudly, along with the rattle of crockery and the smell of coffee. It was a Sunday morning. Everybody was home. I could distinguish some of the voices: my brothers', my sister's, Aunt Lily's, Uncle Saul's, and the hoarse one of my grandfather. I remembered it from last night, along with the chuckle he gave occasionally. I did not hear my father's voice, though, and gathered that he was still in bed.

It gave me more incentive to join them. I hurried to dress and went into the kitchen. They were all seated round the table talking animatedly, and my entrance was hardly noticed, save by my mother, who hurried to serve me as soon as I had slipped into a seat among them. My grandmother, who was helping with the serving, frowned darkly at me, evidently remembering last night and the quarter I'd been given.

My grandfather seemed to be doing most of the talking, and I gathered that what he was saying amused them all, because there was considerable laughter. His own face was wreathed in smiles, and he gave vent to his chuckles now and then. He seemed to be enjoying himself tremendously, as was everyone else. Uncle Saul once reached out a hand across the table and pressed his father's hand in a gesture that showed his affection. Aunt Lily seemed to have the same feeling toward him. They were two of the three in the family who were unmarried and still living with my grandmother. There was a third, Eli. He was missing, and I should not have been sur-

prised. In the two weeks or so that we had been living here we
learned that Eli was often not home, and if he was, he slept until all
hours of the day. He had never worked, and when he came home
from the nights and days that he was away he was bleary-eyed and
still sodden with drink, and could barely make his way to his bed. He
had been an alcoholic since he was fourteen. He was the youngest
member of the family of ten.

After my grandfather finished with what he had been telling
them, he turned to me and said, "Ah, here's the night owl. Did you
buy your toffee yet?"

"No," I said, although the quarter had been the first thing I
thought of when I awoke. It was safely tucked away in a pocket of my
trousers. I was sitting close to him, already spooning the oatmeal my
mother had put in front of me.

He reached out with a hand and ruffled my hair. "He's only
twelve," he said. "But already he's as big as a man. Soon you'll be getting married, I suppose."

I said nothing and went on eating. My mother smiled. "He's not
ready for marriage yet," she said. "He still goes to school."

"Ah," said my grandfather. "And what is he going to be? A lawyer
too, like his uncle Saul?"

Uncle Saul grinned. "I'm not a lawyer yet, Pop," he said. "I'm just
hoping I'll be one."

Uncle Saul was the only one of the family who had graduated
from high school in America. He had planned on going further and
studying law, but my grandmother had thought differently. He now
worked as a door-to-door salesman selling magazine subscriptions.
Now and then, evenings, I used to see him buried in a big thick law
book, but those evenings had grown fewer and fewer, and he spent
his time more often at the basement club to which he belonged, or
taking girls out.

My grandfather nodded at his comment and said, "Yes, yes, you
will be one," and for a moment he seemed to sober and the laughter

died out. But he quickly recovered and turned to my brothers. "And you, Joe, and you, Saul? What are you going to be?"

Joe answered promptly, "I'm going to be a journalist." It was something he had wanted to be in England when he was younger than his present sixteen. Despite the fact that he had been thrust right into one of the tailoring shops after he left school, he had continued to have this ambition.

Uncle Saul, who was sitting next to him, clapped an arm affectionately round his shoulders. He had taken quite a fancy to Joe and had introduced him to his basement club friends—the Rover Boys—and to some of the girls who frequented the club.

"Don't you worry about Joe. He's going to be all right. I'll see to that. Tomorrow I'm going to break him in to selling subscriptions. He'll make a good living until he becomes a journalist."

"And you?" my grandfather said, turning to my brother Saul, who had been sitting there uneasily with his eyes cast down, fearing the question because the answer would make people laugh at him.

It was my mother who answered for him: "Saul is going to be a rabbi." She said it with pride, her face lighting up. It had been talked about before. Saul had always been devoutly religious. Since his bar mitzvah he had taken to wearing tzitzit, a prayer shawl with long fringes that stuck out of the tops of his trousers, and every morning when he rose he put on tefillin, small leather boxes that contained prayers and fastened round his forehead and one arm with straps. He held a siddur, a prayer book, in his hands, and rocking to and fro, he said the morning prayers.

We had sometimes ridiculed him for it, but he persisted, and evidently it meant a great deal to him. The tzitzit fringes showed quite clearly now, and my grandfather was looking at them and nodding, as if he approved.

"The rabbi business is very good," he said. "People commit so many sins, there is a great need for rabbis to give advice and forgive. I too wanted to be a rabbi once."

"You!" cried Uncle Saul and Aunt Lily, and they both burst into laughter.

"Yes, me," the old man said gravely. "Why not? I had a good start, a beard. And I knew all the prayers. My father taught them to me and he beat me if I didn't say them, first thing in the morning, before every meal, after every meal, at night before going to bed. That was not counting the prayers I said in the synagogue. I was a regular prayer man."

It was hard to tell whether he was serious or joking. Only his eyes seemed to have a glimmer of amusement in them. My grandmother gave a sound of what seemed like contempt and I heard her mutter, "He should live so! A rabbi, no less!"

But now, suddenly changing the subject, my grandfather turned to Rose, who was sitting opposite me with that distant look on her face that she always had when she was among us. There was a touch of haughtiness mixed with it that separated her still further from us. She had affected that look, along with an upper-class British accent, ever since the days when we played at being rich in our empty front room that became a shop. Very little had changed with her since then, and it was obvious that she did not like the attention suddenly focused on her.

"So how about you, young lady? What are you going to be now that you're in America?"

"I have no plans that I care to discuss," she said stiffly, then rose immediately from her chair and went out of the room with her head held high. There was a brief pause, then my mother said, "She's trying to get a job as a dressmaker."

"And is that so hard?" asked my grandfather.

"For her, yes," answered my mother. "She won't work in an ordinary dress shop. She's turned down a few jobs already because they were in what she calls low-class places with low-class workers and customers. In England she worked in a fancy dress shop that catered to rich women. And that's what she wants here. High class."

My mother spoke sadly. Rose was still a problem to her, refusing to talk to her most of the time and apparently still bearing a grudge against her for having turned the parlor into a shop. "I just don't know what to do with her," she said.

"Don't worry," Aunt Lily put in. "She'll get over it. She'll meet some fellow soon and that'll be the end of her silly ideas. Give her time."

"What about you?" my grandfather asked. "Have you met a nice fellow yet?"

This was an old story, Aunt Lily being without a fellow, considered an old maid already. She was the only one of the girls in her family who was not married. But things had changed. I noticed that Aunt Lily and Uncle Saul exchanged a swift glance. That glance was full of meaning about something the old man did not know. Nor did we ourselves have any inkling of what lay behind that look.

Just then my father came striding into the room. He ignored everyone, including my grandfather, whom he had not met yet. He seated himself at the table and spoke to my mother in his rough tone. "If there's an egg in this house, fry it for me, and don't take all morning."

It was not an unusual sort of greeting for him and it did not surprise anyone, though it cast a damper over the table and everyone became silent. My mother hastened to comply, and my grandmother scowled and showed her displeasure by turning her back on him.

My grandfather had been watching him with an amused expression on his face. He spoke first. "Yankel," he said, "don't you know your father?"

My father's face was twisted sideways. He was not looking at him. "Since when," he said, "do I have a father?"

The old man laughed. "When were you without a father?" he said. "From the day you were born you had a father."

"So where have you been all the years since I was born? I don't remember ever seeing you. Where were you to greet me when we came from England? Were you there? They tell me you were in New York. What the bloody 'ell were you doing in New York? Isn't Chicago good enough for you anymore?"

The old man laughed again softly. "Yankel," he said, "you haven't changed."

My father ignored this comment. He was quite obviously in a bad mood. "They tell me you were in New York on business. What sort of business have you got there? You don't fix roofs anymore?"

"I'm too old for roofs," my grandfather said, "but roofs aren't the only way to make a living. Here in America there are plenty of opportunities. They call it the land of opportunity. So why should I go crawling up roofs?"

My father's curiosity was sufficiently aroused for him to ask in an almost normal voice, "So what is it then you do?"

My grandfather let out a chuckle this time. His eyes had narrowed and taken on an almost cunning expression. "Ah," he said, "I do what is best for me to do. I make a living. That is the most important thing for any man to do."

The normalcy hadn't lasted long. The anger surged out of my father in a sudden eruption. He banged a fist on the table and a milk jug spilled over. "So what the bloody 'ell is it you do?" he shouted.

My grandmother had swung round, and fury came over her face when she saw the milk spilling all over the table. "Madman," she shouted. Perhaps she would have intervened in any event, but this may have given her the excuse she wanted. Her voice roared out, louder even than his. "Who the hell do you think you are? You think this is your house? You can do anything you want here? Did you buy that milk? Did you buy the egg your wife is frying for you? Did you buy anything here? I took you and your whole family in and gave you food to eat because you had no other place to go, but I can kick you out just as easily, and you dare open your big mouth once more and knock over my milk again and that's what will happen, out you'll go!"

It was a storm that my mother had been dreading, had seen coming in the collisions the two had already had, and with horror on her face she looked up from the stove where she had been frying my father's egg. This was what she had been fearing since the day we'd come here. She had been warning my father: if he kept on getting into arguments with his mother, she would throw us all out. And where would we go? Was this the moment my mother had feared would come?

Perhaps it would have been if my father had answered my grandmother. But he didn't, strangely; my mother's warnings may have had some influence at that particular moment. He remained silent, and when my mother placed the fried egg in front of him on a plate together with some toast he wolfed it down, eating as he always did with head bent low over the plate and shoveling the food into his mouth fast with little grunts and noises. The rest of the table remained silent, my grandmother too, and soon everyone got up and left, and my father strode out too, and we heard the front door bang after him, and that was almost like the days in England when he would be striding off to his pub. Except that now he did not have any money to buy drink and would have to go to Uncle Abe, where in the closet there was plenty of what he wanted and, yes, perhaps needed badly.

In the days that followed my grandfather came and went, and we saw little of him. He was on the same mysterious business that took him to New York for long periods at a time and we still did not know what it was. The others knew, but there was obviously a conspiracy of silence among them to keep it from us. My father stopped asking. He was having trouble finding a job, and he slogged his way around the city daily hunting for a tailoring job, the only kind of work he knew. Both my brother Saul and sister Rose were having the same sort of trouble, but Joe was beginning to learn the business of selling magazine subscriptions with Uncle Saul's tutelage, the two going out together every morning and coming back in the evening, sometimes exhilarated with the luck they'd had, sometimes gloomy when they hadn't made a single sale all day.

The little money that Joe earned he gave to my mother, who tucked it in the purse she kept on a string inside her dress. But it was still not enough for us to get a place of our own, and that was what she wished for now more than anything else, for the threat of my grandmother hung over us constantly, and you could never tell when the next clash would take place between her and my father.

As for me, I kept on exploring the city of Chicago, always finding something new—another beach, another park, a zoo that I had never seen before. For several days I kept the quarter I had been given in my trouser pocket, not allowing myself the toffee for which it had been intended by my grandfather. I did not quite know what to do with it, until suddenly it occurred to me that now I could afford a ride on an elevated train. I had always wanted to do that, and now I had the means for it.

That morning, instead of setting out on another exploration trip on foot, I headed for the nearest 'L' station, which was several blocks away from the house. With a feeling of excitement in me, clutching my quarter to give to whomever you paid for the fare, I mounted the steps along with a number of other people. Everybody was hurrying, and I hurried with them, anxious to get on the first train that came. I could already hear the distant roar of one heading toward the station.

In fact, as I climbed upward I tried to get ahead of those in front of me in order to be able to catch the train that was coming in. However, there was a sudden blockage. Several of those in front were coming to a halt momentarily and delaying my passage. As I struggled impatiently to get past them, I saw the reason for it. There was a landing just before the last flight of steps, and seated on the landing was a blind beggar wearing blue glasses. He was holding out a tin cup and people paused to fish in their pockets and toss some coins into the cup.

I was a bit annoyed and would have managed to get past them if the beard hadn't caught my attention. The beggar's scraggly gray beard reminded me of someone I knew. Then I saw the weather-beaten face fully behind the blue glasses, and with a violent shock I realized that this old beggar was my grandfather. Nor could I mistake the croaking voice that was singing.

I came to an abrupt halt and this time it was others behind me who fought to get past me. I stood and stared, incredulous. There was no mistaking it. This, then, was the mystery that they had been keeping from us.

He saw me as I stood there not wanting to believe what I saw, and it seemed to amuse him. I heard the familiar chuckle escape from him. He waited for two more people to go by, one of them tossing a coin into his cup, and then he spoke to me. "Hello, Harry," he said.

"Hello," I said.

"Are you surprised?" he asked.

I nodded.

"What could I do?" he said. "American roofs are not like English roofs. I didn't know that. So I slipped and fell off one. I hurt a leg. That meant I could never fix roofs again. But I could sing. And so I sing to make a living. It's not so terrible."

I didn't say anything. More people came and went. More coins were tossed into the cup. The train had come and gone. It didn't matter.

"Are you going to tell them?" he asked.

I still didn't say anything.

"About your father I don't care," he said. "But I like your mother. She is a very nice woman."

"Grandpa," I said, "I've got to go."

"Where are you going?"

"Just for a ride on the 'L.' "

"Then go and enjoy yourself."

I went up the last flight of steps and got on the next train that came in, but I didn't enjoy myself.

It was a week before I told my mother. I could no longer keep it to myself. She was terribly upset. She wanted to know if I was absolutely sure that it was my grandfather. I said I was quite sure. I told her we had talked a bit and he knew my name, so there couldn't be any doubt. She didn't want to believe it. I knew that. I knew how she felt about things like begging and taking charity. Even in the worst of times she would not have accepted any kind of help from anyone.

I remember one time, when things were very bad for us and the shop was not making any money, she inadvertently overcharged a customer by a halfpenny. It was night and it was raining and blustery outside, but she put on her shawl and took an umbrella and ran to where the woman lived, a goodly distance away, to return the halfpenny. She was that way about money, and to find now that her own father-in-law was a common street beggar must have been a terrible blow to her.

But to make matters worse, while we were still talking about it, my father came in. He had just returned from job hunting yet again, with no results, and was in a dangerous mood. It should have been a warning to my mother, but in her disturbed state she felt she had to tell him. As he listened his face darkened still more. Then, after she had finished, without a word he swung round and walked out of the room.

Instantly my mother followed him, crying, "Where are you going?"

He didn't answer her but kept on walking straight to the kitchen. She followed him, knowing what he was about to do now and begging him not to. I ran after her.

My grandmother was sweeping the floor in the kitchen and looked up, startled, as we all came in. Even when she did housework my grandmother wore her jewelry. She had on a brilliant necklace and a thick gold bracelet. My father pointed to them and through gritted teeth demanded, "Where did you get that jewelry?"

She was obviously taken aback by the question. She stared at him for a moment, then, recovering a little, snapped, "I bought it. What business is it of yours?"

"And where did you get the money from?" he demanded, his teeth so tightly locked that the words came out with difficulty.

She didn't answer him. She simply stared.

"I'll tell you where you got it from," he continued. "You got it from a beggar, from a street beggar who pretends to be blind and *will* be blind when I get done with him. So that's the respectable business he's got in New York. Or is that just a branch of the business he's got here? I'm surprised you didn't send me out to beg for you when I was five years old instead of to a slaughterhouse when we were in Poland. I'd have made more money for you, and then you wouldn't have had to run away and leave me all by myself when I was still a boy. Now you send out an old man to beg for you so you can buy yourself all that fine jewelry and bring shame on the rest of us." He was breathing hard, and the spittle was coming from his mouth as he spoke.

By this time my grandmother was fully recovered from the surprise attack he'd launched on her, and the fury was mounting inside her massive bosom. She struck back hard, shouting, "Shame? Is that all you get from it? What about the money? When anybody's short of money—for the rent, for a new pair of shoes, for a set of teeth from the dentist, for a doctor's bill, or for steamship tickets to come to America—where do they come? They come to me, and when I give them the money they need they don't feel any shame. They know where it comes from and they take it and they're glad of it. And you? How do you think you got here? Where did that money come from? I'll tell you one thing. I didn't want it. I didn't need a madman like you on my hands again. I'd had enough of you. In my old age I wanted a bit of peace. But your father wanted it. He wanted to make it up to you, he said, for leaving you in Poland. So he sent you the tickets."

I heard my mother give a little cry. She knew now where the tickets had come from, and my father knew also. He threw a look of fury at my mother and said, "Good for you! This is what you deserve. England wasn't good enough for you." But he wasn't done yet with my grandmother. "If you think I wanted to come to America, you're mistaken. As far as I was concerned, you could have taken those tickets and shoved them up your big fat arse. I came here because she wanted to come, not because I wanted to see you or the blind beggar. And I'll tell you right now, nothing can make up for what you did when you left me in Poland to be by myself. As far as I'm concerned, you and him too can both go straight to 'ell."

"Then get out," my grandmother shouted. "Go back to England. Go wherever you want. But get out of my house, all of you. Pack your things and go."

My father strode ahead of us, his face murderous. I had to help my mother out. She was stunned. The very worst that she had feared had happened. On top of everything else, we were being kicked out of my grandmother's house. And where could we go?

Chapter Seven

IT WAS JOE WHO SAVED THE DAY FOR US. MY OLDEST BROTHER'S handsome face with its winning smile and large brown eyes, along with his touching plea that he was working his way through college, charmed the housewives who answered his knock, and got them to buy annual subscriptions to such leading magazines as *Collier's, Liberty,* and the *Saturday Evening Post,* along with *Popular Mechanics,* which they did not read or want.

Joe was starting to make money, and all of this was thanks to his mentor, Uncle Saul, whose face shone with glee as he told us of his pupil's success. He was simply crazy about Joe. They were together day and night, they went to dances together at the Rover Boys club, they double-dated together. Joe was sixteen and, thanks to Uncle Saul, already had a string of girls that he took out.

He gave my mother enough now for us to get a place of our own, and we lost no time doing it. It was not a great deal of money for a whole family; my mother still had to pinch pennies, and she had to find the cheapest place possible for us to live in. She found it only a short distance away from my grandmother's house—on the same street, in fact. And, both ironically and sadly, it was a place that was pervaded by the smell of rotting fruits and vegetables, exactly like the one we had come from.

This must have struck her immediately when she stumbled on it, wandering blindly the very next few moments after my grandmother had ordered us out. My father had gone to seek consolation with Uncle Abe and his barrel of moonshine. My mother went alone, half frantic with fear that we might all have to sleep out on the street.

There, only a few doors away, was an old frame house that had somehow been overlooked when the developers came to build their tenements and those balloonlike brick houses with three floors whose fronts swelled out like pregnant women, one of which my grandmother lived in.

The house that my mother saw probably should have been knocked down years earlier. It leaned so badly to one side that we could never fill a bowl of soup or a cup of coffee or tea to the brim, or the liquid would spill over. But there was a For Rent sign in the landlord's window and my mother went in to inquire.

She caught the smell immediately, and it reminded her of her little shop back there in England. But she did not know quite where it came from at first. All she knew was that the bearded, hoarse-voiced landlord made it cheap enough for us to be able to live off Joe's earnings.

It was only after we had moved in, after borrowing some furnishings from relatives and buying some on credit at payments of a dollar a week, that on our first morning we were awakened at dawn by the rattling of chains and the sound of a horse snorting, and we discovered then that the landlord was a peddler of fruits and vegetables. He had a stable in the backyard where he kept his horse and also stored his produce, some of it rotting before he could sell it and giving off the odor that was so familiar to us.

It was almost like going back to where we had come from, as if we were starting all over again, as if our dream had never come true. My mother was not happy. None of us was. But my mother especially must have had a heavy heart through that whole time we were there, the smell coming through the cracked windows to taunt her.

Yet I don't think she ever gave up. Whatever feelings she might have had she kept to herself, but to us she was as optimistic as ever, still promising better things, still making up dreams for us.

"Things'll get better, you'll see. Everybody will get a job. It's just a matter of time. As soon as everybody is working we'll look for another place to live, and it'll be nicer than this one and in a better neighborhood. Barney, who lives on the Northwest Side, tells me there are lots of apartments there for rent."

My father was listening to her along with the rest of us, and when she had finished he said, "What about him? Will he get a job too?"

His gaze was directed at me, and it was filled with hatred. But this was something he had been harping on before, and my mother was prepared for him. "Harry is going to school," she said.

"School? What for? He's twelve already. He looks like sixteen. What's wrong if he goes out and looks for a job like the rest of us? Who is he around here, Lord Muck?"

"I want one, at least, to have an education and become something." Her tone was firm, and on this she would never budge. It meant so much to her. It was part of the dream that had brought us here to America.

And despite the hostility she had to contend with from my father, when fall came I went to school.

IT WAS A LATE FALL that year. The heat did not want to give up the deadly grip it had on the city, and it continued well into September, when school had already started. This made it easier for me as far as comfort was concerned, because I was wearing the short pants that all English schoolboys wore, with bare knees and long stockings. A white flannel cricket shirt went with my outfit, one that my mother had been proud of when she bought it in England for our trip to America.

However, it drew stares and laughter from both pupils and teachers when I first appeared at the grimy red-brick building of the grade school that was just round the corner from where we lived. Boys then wore knickerbockers with the bottoms tucked into long woolen stockings, without knees showing. And in addition I was taller than any of the other pupils, taller than some of the teachers, and that added to the ridicule.

But there was worse yet in store for me. Nobody seemed to understand what I was saying. As soon as I entered the yard filled with yelling, screaming kids racing about prior to the ringing of the bell, a large number of them gathered around me, astonished at my dress and my height. The neighborhood on Chicago's West Side was made up of recent immigrants from Russia and Poland, and many of these kids spoke with a strong foreign accent. But mine was different from theirs, and it had them puzzled.

"From vere you come?" one boy asked.

"England," I said, and it seemed to me there was only one way to pronounce *England* and I had done it.

But the boy said, "Vere?" and others echoed it.

"England," I repeated.

"Aingland? Vere is Aingland?"

Where was England? I knew very little of the globe, so I said what I knew. "It's near Manchester."

"Vere?" They were getting more and more puzzled, and the crowd around me was increasing. None of them had heard a Lancashire accent before. Nor had they ever seen any boy wearing short pants. The questions came one after the other. A teacher finally rescued me. She led me off to the principal's office, asking a few questions on the way and seeming just as puzzled as my earlier inquisitors by my answers.

The principal was a tall, frowning woman with gray hair piled thickly on her head. She sat at a desk and looked me over with the frown deepening.

The teacher who had brought me in spoke. "I can't make out much of what he says," she said. "It does and it doesn't sound like English, and his name he says is Arry or something like that, I'm not sure where he's from. I asked him and I thought he said England, but his speech can't possibly be English. I think he might be from Egypt. We had an Egyptian boy who talked a bit like that."

"Well, then," said the principal, "let's put him in the foreign-speaking class to learn English. How old is he?"

"He claims he's only twelve."

"Twelve?" She stared. "He can't be any less than fifteen."

"That's what I thought."

"Well, he'll have to bring a birth certificate next time he comes. There's something very strange about all this. Why is he wearing such short pants? I think his parents are trying to make him look younger than he is for some reason. I don't like this at all." She was very annoyed, very irritated, and very busy. It was the first day of school and there were many things she had to do. "In the meantime," she snapped, "take him to Miss Richards's class. Let her get started on his English."

Miss Richards was the teacher in charge of the foreign students, and I entered her room objecting inwardly to what was happening to me and ready at any moment to rebel openly. The room was filled with children of all ages who had only recently come to the United States with their parents, mostly from countries in Europe. On the blackboard were such carefully lettered words as *cat, dog, stick, man, woman.*

The class had been reciting these words as I entered, but immediately they halted and all eyes turned to me. Miss Richards too stared. But I would have better luck with her than with the principal or the teacher who had escorted me here. She was younger and she could smile. She averted her eyes from my short pants and bare knees and said, "What country are you from?" pronouncing each word carefully, as if I might not know the English language too well. And when I said England she had no difficulty understanding me, and seemed startled. "Then what are you doing here?" she asked.

"They said I couldn't speak English."

"Oh, what nonsense!" she exclaimed. "Of course you speak English. It's just your accent they don't understand. I've traveled through England and I've heard lots of people speak like you do, especially up in the north. Are you from Yorkshire?"

"No, Lancashire."

"Lancashire. That's right. That's near Manchester, isn't it?"

I nodded.

"They speak a bit differently in every area you go to, and sometimes they don't understand one another. It's no wonder the principal was puzzled. But I'll straighten it out with her, and in the meantime you stay here for today and help me teach these other children the English language. Is that all right with you?"

"Yis," I said.

"Yes," she corrected. "Can you say it that way?"

"Yes," I said, for the first time in my life.

So, THANKS TO MISS RICHARDS, I was spared the humiliation of having to join the foreign-language-speaking class and learn the English language all over again. And eventually, thanks to Miss Richards again, I got rid of some of my Lancashire accent and began to speak in a more American way. My short pants and bare knees still brought stares and remarks, but there was no money for knickerbockers. Nor could there be any hand-me-downs from my older brothers. They had both been wearing long pants since they left school to go to work, always a sign on our street that you were grown up and ready for work.

We tried asking my grandmother if there weren't any leftovers from my uncles—things that had been patched up a bit since we had moved to our own place. She did a little searching in her closets but came up with nothing.

It was truly a desperate situation for me because the cold weather was coming on and I was already beginning to freeze in the chill winds that came off the lake. Then one day, when I had come home from school with my knees purple from the cold, my grandfather came in carrying a package. He had never been to see us before this, certainly not when my father was present, and his arrival took my mother by surprise. I was surprised too. It was the first time I had seen him since the day I had bumped into him at the 'L' station.

His face was very red from the wind and cold, but he was chuckling as he greeted us, and he put his package down on the table and said nothing about it, although both my mother's and my eyes were on it and we were wondering what it contained.

He had come, he said, to say goodbye. He was going back to New York. My mother made him welcome, even though she may have had reservations about the visit and would have preferred that he not come. Very little had been spoken about him all these past weeks since we left my grandmother's house, and I don't think my mother felt comfortable.

She offered to make him a cup of tea, and he accepted with alacrity. He was rubbing his hands to thaw out from the cold and did not take off the worn overcoat that he had on, nor did my mother ask him to. In New York, he said, it was less bitter, but it was cold there too.

"So why do you go?" my mother asked politely.

He chuckled, but there was no amusement in it. "Why do I go?" he said, and shrugged. "What else is there for me to do?"

The question didn't seem to require any answer, and my mother said nothing. We all knew by now how unwelcome he was among his family; save for Uncle Saul and Aunt Lily, he was a pariah among them. The other uncles and aunts had stayed away from my grandmother's house while he was there, and once they knew that we had discovered the old man's business they had asked us not to tell their children. They did not want them to know that their grandfather was a street beggar, and they were all uneasy while he was in Chicago.

My mother had made the tea, pouring it for him in a glass and handing it to him with a lump of sugar. He took it gratefully, nibbled off a bit of sugar, took a small sip, and sighed with pleasure. He looked across at me and asked, "So how is school?"

"Good," I said.

He nodded, holding the glass in both hands and blowing on it slightly. "He'll be a big man someday," he said.

"Yes," my mother agreed. "He's doing well at school. He gets good marks. They put him in the top grade, and next year he'll go to high school." She spoke proudly.

"You'll not be sorry that you came to America," he said.

"I'll never be sorry for that," my mother said. "The only thing I'm sorry for is that you sent me the tickets to come. If I had known who sent them, I would not have come."

"And what is wrong with who sent them?"

"Father"—it sounded strange to me to hear her call him that, but what else could she have said?—"I must tell you, I must be honest. I can't find fault with you, I know you are a good man, but it is the way you make your money that is not good, and I want to tell you that I will pay back every cent of what you spent on the tickets."

"I can't help the way I make my money. I used to be a roofer. From the time I was ten years old I mended roofs. In Poland, then in England, then America. I was a good roofer, but no matter how good you are, age has the last say. I fell off a roof and I was in the hospital four months. My roofing days were over. So what was left?

My voice was left. So I sang songs, and people liked it and they gave me money. What's wrong with that? People go on the stage and sing for a living. I could not go on the stage, but I could sing, so what is terrible about that?"

"I didn't know about that," my mother said with genuine sympathy in her voice. "I didn't know you fell off a roof and were in the hospital for four months. They never wrote to us about that. You must have been hurt real bad, and I'm sorry. But it's the way you dress up with those blue glasses and pretend you're blind and hold up a tin cup to them and they toss money into it. That's begging, Father."

My grandfather sipped his tea and thought for a moment. "So what do people do when they're on the stage?" he asked. "They dress up in all sorts of costumes and pretend they're somebody else. Even Caruso puts on a costume." He laughed. He could not be serious for long. "Of course, I'm not Caruso, although when I was younger I used to think I was as good as he was."

But my mother was not laughing. "What they do on the stage and what you do on the street are two different things," she said.

He did not argue the point. He thought for another moment, sipped a little more, then said slowly, "Ada, do you know why I sent you the tickets?"

"Why?"

"Because of you."

"Me?"

"For years it's been bothering me, and more and more as I got older. When you get old you look back and see things the way you never saw them before. So now I could see you when you came from Poland, a sixteen-year-old girl, so innocent, with nobody in the world to turn to. And you fell into our hands and that is what's been bothering me so much, how we caught you like a spider catches a fly, and we married you to my madman son. I could never forgive myself."

"You shouldn't talk like that," my mother said, speaking softly but, I could see, with a lot of emotion. "You didn't trick me into it. Nobody did. One day we went for a walk. We went to the park. We sat on a bench. There he told me the whole story. How you went off from Poland and left him behind to be all alone. He cried when he told it to me. My heart broke for him. I promised he would never be alone again. So you see, nobody tricked me into marrying him. I made the decision."

But the old man was shaking his head and chuckling. "You believed that old story, that we ran away from him and left him there to be alone? Sarah did some bad things with the children. She used to give each one a spoonful of cordial to put them to sleep so she could go out to play cards with the neighbor next door; she taught them to be drinkers before they were five years old. But to run off and leave one behind just to get away from him? No, that's a *bubbe meise*—a fairy tale. There were other reasons for leaving, the pogroms especially, and I could get so little work because I was a Jew. The truth is, she wanted him to come, but he wouldn't. That's what she told me, and I believed her. No, Ada, he lied to you."

My mother was silent, and I do not know what she was thinking or whether she believed him.

The old man continued after a moment, "So it was bothering me all those years. Then I heard about the letters you had been sending and how much you wanted to come to America. Sarah, of course, paid no attention, and the others, if they felt anything for you at all, never had any money. So I thought maybe this was how I could make up to you for what we had done to you. I arranged with a travel agency in Manchester to send you the tickets, and because I knew you would think it strange if you knew the tickets came from me and you'd start to ask questions, I told the agency not to tell you who sent them."

There were tears in my mother's eyes by the time he finished, and she wiped them with a handkerchief and said, "It was very good of you to do what you did, but I want you to know that the money has to be paid back, and I'll do that as soon as they all start to work. If I'd known about it then, I would have sent the tickets back."

He sighed and said, "Well, you must do what you think is best, just as I do what I think is best. But I have to go now." He had finished his tea, and now he rose, getting out of his chair with the slow, difficult movements of an old man.

"You mustn't forget your package," my mother said.

"It's for you," he said.

"For me?" She was startled. Who had ever given her a package before?

"And for Harry."

I was startled too. Who'd ever given me a package before?

He kissed us both before he left, and his beard was rough against my cheek. He gave me an extra pat on the head and said, "You're going to be a real mensch."

We waited until he'd gone before opening the package. Inside were a pair of thick woolen gloves for my mother and a pair of knickerbockers for me.

Chapter Eight

THE WINTER CAME EARLY THAT YEAR, AND IT CAME HARD AND
bitter, with driving winds off the lake and heavy snows that covered
streets and made walking impossible in spots, and freezing cold that
nipped ears, stung eyes, and numbed feet and hands.

It was a cruel experience for us after the relatively mild winters
of England, and we were totally unprepared for it with our clothes.
We lacked the heavy overcoats, the earmuffs, the thick woolen
gloves, and galoshes that were so necessary to fend off the sharp
thrusts of the freezing weather and to plow our way through the
drifts of snow that piled up on street corners.

We came into the house gasping for breath, holding the palms
of our hands against our stung ears, stamping our feet to help thaw
them out, and at night we cried with pain from the chilblains that
had formed on our toes. We needed warmer clothes, but we did not
have the money to buy them. My mother was scarcely able to stretch

what Joe was bringing in to meet all our needs, and so we all suffered that winter.

I was lucky. I had the knickerbockers that my grandfather had bought me, and my mother gave no thought to refusing them and the gloves he had bought her, ignoring for the time being where the money had come from. But the knickerbockers were hardly enough to keep me warm as I went to and from school. Making my way through thick snow and getting my feet wet, I'd forge ahead as quickly as I could in order to get into the warmth of the school. I'd do the same going home, running up the steps of the leaning house to burst in and thrust my hands out to the potbellied stove that was red hot from the burning coal and stamping my feet on the linoleum floor, trying to catch my breath.

I was luckier than my two brothers, my sister, and my father too, who had to be out in that bitter cold: Joe selling magazine subscriptions, the others still searching endlessly for work. Their clothes were not much better. How we ever got through that winter I will never know. And yet, in spite of everything, even on those bitterly cold nights, we trudged through the snow over to my grandmother's house.

All was forgiven there now that we had our own place, and a truce had been declared between my grandmother and my father. We were invited over there one Saturday night, and we came in shivering and feeling surprise at all the noise that greeted us, and even some lively piano playing together with some other instruments, but especially from where all this was coming.

Blinking in the lights and stamping the cold out of our feet, we realized that it was all taking place in the front room, a sanctified area usually sealed off from the rest of the house by a sliding door except for some special occasion. This room, sometimes called the parlor, contained my grandmother's best furniture, which she considered too good to be sat on, and most treasured of all was a piano, a big, hulking upright that could well have been an antique. I think it was Barney, the humorist, who commented that if she allowed anyone to play on it, it was with the understanding that they were to play on the black keys only, since the white keys could get soiled.

Nevertheless, Uncle Saul had taught himself to play on it quite well, and he was thumping out a jazz piece now, together with Eli, whom we scarcely ever saw and who was now swinging about holding a harmonica to his mouth. There was also a short, pudgy man with a jolly grin on his face, whom we had never seen before, strumming on a mandolin.

All the relatives were there, including the young cousins, who were adding to the din by running about wildly and yelling and screaming at one another. But no one, not even my grandmother, stopped them or seemed to be objecting, and there was a general air of gaiety throughout the room.

Obviously, this was a special occasion of some sort. Was it perhaps to celebrate my grandfather's departure? That did have a lot to do with it, as we discovered later. But there was more to it than that, and we learned what that was all about when Uncle Saul crashed out the last chord and the music stopped.

Then Aunt Lily, dressed as we had never seen her dressed before, in a low-cut black party gown that displayed a bosom we had never suspected existed before—the everyday plain clothes she wore gave her a flat-chested look—approached us, leading by the hand the short, pudgy man who had been playing the mandolin. He was still holding the instrument in his hand and the jolly look was still on his face. "I want you to meet Phil," she said, and there was a smile on her face too, and she didn't look a bit like an old maid.

SEVERAL WEEKS BEFORE WE CAME to America, Aunt Lily was coming home from work in the corset department of the Mandel Brothers department store and was stepping off a streetcar when she slipped and fell. A car that had been racing alongside the tram screeched to a halt just inches away from where she lay sprawled on the ground.

The panic-stricken driver, thinking he had knocked her down, rushed to help her. Fortunately, she was not badly hurt, but he put her in his car and drove her home—and fell madly in love with her at first sight, and saw her every day thereafter.

Phil was younger than Aunt Lily by several years, and much shorter, but he was quite a catch. He was in the Victrola business and had an office and a showroom in one of the skyscrapers in the Loop, where he displayed all the latest models of the new machine that had replaced the gramophone and were all the rage now.

He was obviously quite well off. He had this business, and a brand-new lemon-colored sports car, a Nash. Moreover, he came from a rich family, the Falks, who lived on the South Side among such people as the Loebs and the Leopolds and the Franks, who would become quite prominent in the newspapers in the near future.

But perhaps this was the only drawback, because when Phil's parents learned whom he had fallen in love with and planned to marry, a girl who was a corset saleswoman in the Mandel Brothers store—they knew the Mandels quite well also—and who lived on the West Side, where all the poor Jews lived, they wanted him to give her up.

Phil refused, so there was trouble between them. They declined to let him bring her to the house to meet them, and Phil had to cook up excuses to Aunt Lily for not introducing her to them, especially now that he had proposed and she had accepted and they would soon get married. At the same time Aunt Lily was terrified that Phil would find out about her father and how he made his living. During the time that my grandfather had been in Chicago she had not allowed Phil to come at all, making the excuse that her mother was ill and could not have visitors.

Now that the old man had gone, all restraints were cast aside, and the Saturday night that we came was Phil's first visit since the ban had been imposed. The family had met him before and liked him, and little wonder. He was a jolly fellow, he could tell jokes, and he could play an assortment of stringed instruments, including the violin, the harp, the guitar, and the mandolin he had just been playing along with Uncle Saul and Uncle Eli.

He greeted us warmly. He had heard about us and had wanted to meet us before, but Lily had given him the excuse that we were exhausted from the voyage and wanted to rest and get oriented to our new surroundings before meeting new people.

"And so we finally meet," he said, shaking hands with me, my brothers, and my father. My father quickly wrenched his hand away, muttered something indistinguishable, and went off to join several other uncles who had gathered at the table in the dining room around the bottle that Abe had brought. Eli had also joined them.

But Phil never stopped smiling. He kissed my mother, then tried to kiss Rose, but she froze, turned her head aside, and immediately went off to the bedroom that she had shared with Aunt Lily when we lived here. There she shut the door after her and remained inside for the entire evening.

The men at the dining room table called out to Phil to come and drink with them, but he shook his head, laughing, not wanting to hurt their feelings. He didn't drink anything except tea. Besides, right now he had something to do, he told them.

What he had to do was sweep Aunt Lily up in his arms and kiss her long and passionately, and while he was doing that everyone cheered and applauded.

It would happen again throughout the evening. Phil would amuse us with his mandolin and his singing, and he could dance too, a Russian dance, with legs crossed and arms folded across his chest, and he would fly about with Uncle Saul playing fast music and all the watchers clapping hands in time with the music. And then, as soon as he had finished his performance, he went up to Lily and once more swept her into his arms for a long, passionate kiss, bending her so far backward that her head almost touched the floor, with the entire room cheering him on—all except my father, who growled, "Why the bloody 'ell don't they go in the bedroom and get it over with?"

Suddenly there were shouts of protest among the men at the table. My father swung his head round in time to see Eli tilting the bottle to his lips. He was going at it hard, sucking like a baby on its bottle. My father jumped up and swung a fist, knocking the bottle out of Eli's mouth. Someone grabbed it quickly enough to keep most of the liquor from spilling out.

In the sacred front room they saw none of this and heard nothing. Phil was performing for them again, to their great enjoyment, this time with his mandolin, strumming and singing a song that was a great favorite all over America. And we joined in, with Uncle Saul grinning, thumping out an accompaniment on the piano. I remember that song:

> *Barney Google, Barney Google,*
> *With the goo-goo-googly eyes*
> *Barney Google, had a wife three times his size . . .*

And now that I think of it, in spite of all the fierce quarrels that often took place there, sometimes fights breaking out among the men if they were drunk enough, and despite the usual outbursts from my grandmother toward the end of the evening ordering everyone out, we did have some good times at my grandmother's house.

Chapter Nine

IT WAS 1923, A YEAR AFTER WE HAD COME TO AMERICA, AND IN
August of that year a tall, taciturn man by the name of John Calvin
Coolidge became president of the United States. All the country
seemed to be benefiting—times were getting better, and people were
working and buying the newfangled radios that let you hear voices
from thousands of miles away, and the Victrolas that made voices
sound as if they were right in your living room, and cars too, more
and more of them, little black Fords and Nashes that could go as fast
as forty miles an hour. The roads were full of them, even becoming
congested in spots.

For us it was becoming more like the America we had always
dreamed of. All the family members were working now. Joe, still
maintaining that he was going to be a journalist, just as Uncle Saul
insisted that he was just marking time until he became a lawyer, kept
on selling magazine subscriptions door-to-door, along with Uncle

Saul, growing more and more proficient at it and making enough money—as my mother proudly put it to the relatives—to get married.

Saul, despite the fringes of his prayer shawl sticking out at his waist and refusing to take off his hat, which had always discouraged prospective employers from hiring him, at last found work as an order picker for Sears, Roebuck and Co. My father too found work tailoring with an equally large company: Hart Schaffner & Marx, a leading clothing manufacturer. And Rose got her wish, a place at Madame LaFarge's high-class dressmaking establishment. The wages were so low that she barely had enough for the carfare after all the expenses were taken out, but it didn't matter. The fact that the wife of the secretary of the treasury came from Washington to have her dresses made there, along with a number of prominent socialites and a very famous actress, made up for everything, and she held her head high and was more aloof than ever, and her high-class English accent grew more and more affected and less understandable.

But there was much more to add to it for her, and a chance for my mother to make up to her, however belatedly, for the loss of the parlor in England—and to us as well. It had been in my mother's mind all these years as part of the dream of coming to America, and now that they were all working and bringing money to her she lost no time in fulfilling the promise she had made to us.

First we moved out of the leaning house, away from the stable and the smell of rotting fruit and vegetables mixed with that of horse manure—away from all that forever, my mother vowed—and we found a new place on the Northwest Side, near where Barney and Rose lived, near Humboldt Park, near streets that were clean and quiet, near heaven itself.

Compared to where we had lived before, this was a high-class neighborhood. True, the building in which we rented a third-floor flat was very much like the one in which my grandmother lived, three-story brick with a front that curved out like a pregnant woman's stomach, with a high stoop. But then, half the apartment buildings in Chicago were like that, as if the same architect had designed them all, and ours had been freshly painted and the steps were swept clean every day by our Polish landlord, who lived on the floor below us.

The rooms were big and light and airy, and there were electric lights, of course, and a bathroom with a toilet and a bathtub and a sink. And what's more, the previous tenant had had a telephone, which was still there, though disconnected, and after much argument with my father—who saw no bloody reason why we needed a telephone, why anybody needed one—my mother prevailed and we kept the phone and had it connected. Every time you wanted to make a call you put a nickel in the coin box and that's how it worked.

My mother was simply trembling with joy. A telephone, no less! She had me write a letter to Fanny Cohen on our street back there in England, telling her of our new acquisition. In England no one would have dreamed they would have a telephone in their lifetime. The only one we had ever seen in the whole town was in the jam works. We used to see it through a window, and we'd stare at it for a long time and wonder what it was like to hear a voice come over one of those big black things. And here we had one to ourselves, although it took a long time before we dared use it.

The first to do so was Joe, and it was to call a girl he had met to ask for a date. That first time was a big event in our lives. We all gathered round him as he sat down to make the call, with no thought of giving him privacy. He didn't want it anyway. He was so nervous at making this first call and needed the support of our presence.

He tried to put the nickel into the box with a hand that shook a little, and he missed the slot at first, but found it the second time. Then, all of us listening with open mouths, we heard him say shakily, "Hello. Is this the Friedmans' house? . . . Can I speak to Janice—I mean, Frieda?"

In his nervousness he had asked for the wrong girl. But that was corrected. And finally he spoke to her and everything worked out well. He had the date. He turned away from the phone, his face flushed with triumph, and we all shared that triumph.

Well, everything was big and new and important for us during those heady days when America became the kind of place we had always dreamed it would be. There was this new flat still smelling of paint, with electric lights and a telephone and everything, and there was all this new furniture that we had bought on time payments, two dollars a week, from Michael's Furniture Emporium on Division Street. Best of all for me, it included a davenport that was my bed at night, giving me a bed to myself and relieving me of having to sleep at the feet of my two brothers in one bed and fight for a bit of space.

But it also included the parlor that my mother had once promised us. It was not exactly the same. It did not have red plush divans and a red plush carpet. Michael's didn't have that kind of furniture—my mother had asked for it, wanting so much to make every little thing she had promised come true—but the furniture she bought was good, solid stuff: big, comfortable chairs and matching sofa, a floor lamp with fringes on its big shade, and the carpet— my grandmother had been consulted about the furniture, advising my mother to get one that was the color of dirt so that when people walked on it nothing would show, but my mother chose a light brown color to match the furniture, even though she knew she took the risk of offending Grandma. But it was as close as she could come to red plush, and the whole thing delighted her. But wait, the pièce de résistance was yet to come.

One day, passing a piano store on Division Street, she halted to look in the window. She had looked before but had seen only pianos that cost a fortune. She could never afford one, even though she wanted to add a piano to her parlor more than she wanted anything else in the world. And there, that day, right in the center of all the other pianos that were being displayed, was a big, bulky upright piano with a large price tag plastered on it that said twenty-five dollars. She could hardly believe it. It was still a lot of money to have to spend, but not for a piano.

She hurried in, and the salesman tried to draw her attention to other, more expensive pianos—better-looking ones, certainly. "Who is the piano for?" he asked her.

"My daughter," she answered. Of course—whom else could the piano be for? And in her mind was the thought that a piano more than anything else could change Rose's attitude toward her.

The salesman looked aghast when she told him whom it was for. "My dear lady," he said, "I wouldn't mind if it was for a man or a boy who wants to pound out some jazz. But a girl, a young lady! How would she look sitting at that piano playing some Chopin? It would never look right."

My mother didn't know that the old upright in the window was what is known as a "come-on" and was there simply to lure people inside so that the salesman could sell something more expensive. But she resisted all his efforts, and finally she had her way and the piano was delivered soon afterward, hauled after a mighty struggle by two brawny men up our stoop and two flights of stairs and into our parlor. And there it was, big, heavy, ugly, but the great pride and joy of my mother.

She could hardly wait for Rose to come home from Madame La-Farge's high class dressmaking establishment. My sister came in as she usually did, without any greeting and heading immediately for her room. But my mother stopped her. I was home at the time. I saw Rose's face stiffen as my mother spoke to her.

"Come and take a look at something," she said.

I thought for a moment that Rose was going to ignore her and continue walking to her room, but after some hesitation she followed her into the living room and saw the piano.

There was no comment from her. She simply stared at it for a long time, then to our surprise she sat down at it on the bench that my mother had persuaded the salesman to give her along with the piano, and plunged both hands down on the keys with a thunderous discordant sound. Again and again she moved her hands along the keyboard to create other, equally loud, and even more discordant sounds.

We would see this often later. She would sit there crashing out deafening noises that she may honestly have believed was piano playing, and she would sit erect and with a dreamy look on her face, as if she were a great concert artist performing before a huge, silent, spellbound audience. Then she would leave and go into her room, which was what happened that evening, without any comment to my mother.

It did nothing to change her attitude toward Ma, which remained as frozen as it had always been, and would never change. But my mother derived some comfort, I am sure, from knowing that she had kept her promise to us, that she had finally given us our parlor and a piano to go with it.

It called for some letter writing to England, to Fanny Cohen again telling her of the piano and to my sister Lily, with whom we had been corresponding steadily since our arrival in America. Fanny Cohen had kept us abreast of the latest gossip on our street, telling us that the bagel maker had made a great hit with his bagels. Even people like Mrs. Turnbull and her boarders and the Greens and the Humberstones were buying them, and people had come from all parts of town to buy the bagels. The very smell of the bagels when they came out of the oven in the mornings was enough, she said, to drive you mad.

My mother laughed when she read that. She was glad that the little man she had argued with over the shop had made such a success out of the place. But in America, she wrote back, bagels were nothing new and people ate them just as often as they ate bread, and what's more, they had cream cheese and smoked salmon on their bagels. There was a bit of rivalry going on in the letters. I could see that. But I said nothing as I wrote. I was still the letter writer, except

that now in America writing to England, I no longer used an ordinary pen but one of the new fountain pens that were made by a
company called Waterman, one of which I had received as a gift on
my thirteenth birthday from my mother.

I boasted to Lily about my new pen in the letter to her, and she
wrote back saying that she too had one and they were beginning to
sell them in England. She had much more than that to tell us, mostly
about little Jimmy and how he was growing fast and able to walk
and talk. My mother smiled and nodded when I read that to her, and
in turn, in her answer to that letter she told Lily about how her baby
was growing up fast too and how little Sidney could now walk and
talk also.

But there was something she could not write to Lily about,
though she did put it in the letter to Fanny Cohen. "There are so
many good things here to tell you about—I only wish you were here
to share them with me—but best of all, we don't have anybody
across the street to call us 'bloody Jews.' . . . Here there is no such
thing."

She couldn't have written that to Lily because Lily was married
to a Christian and could well have been upset by it. But I was thinking of something else as I wrote it for my mother. I was thinking of
an experience I'd had a short time before. I had been walking along
Division Street into an area where I had never been before, an area
that I would later learn was one that Jews did not go into. It was very
much like Back Brook Street near where I had once lived in England,
only this one was known as Little Poland. As I walked, suddenly I
found myself surrounded by a bunch of Polish kids all yelling,
"Dirty Jew, Christ-killer!" Then they sprang on me, knocking me to
the ground and kicking and punching me. There was nothing I
could do. They rifled my pockets, took the bit of change I had in one
of them, and finally let me go. I didn't want to upset my mother and
said nothing about it, and to explain my rumpled clothes and some
marks on my face said that I had slipped and fallen.

Thinking of that now as I wrote what she was dictating—"Here there is no such thing"—I was tempted to tell her, but then decided against it. I did not want to spoil the illusion she had. She would soon find out for herself. But at least it was not right across the street from us. The only Polish people around here were our landlord and his family, and we couldn't have had nicer people for neighbors— the friendship that developed between us lasted as long as we lived there.

A FEW MONTHS AFTER WE had settled in our new home, when things were going so well for us, I entered high school. I had chosen to go to Lane Tech, an all-boys school that I had picked because they gave a four-year architectural course. I had decided to become an architect after reading an ad in the back of *Popular Mechanics* that showed a picture of Chief Draftsman Dobe wearing an artist's smock bent over a drawing board. The ad offered a free ruler to anyone who sent for information about Chief Draftsman Dobe's course in architecture. I sent for it, received the ruler and the information, and discovered it would cost more money than I would ever have. It was a blow for me, but at least I had the ruler. Then I learned about Lane Tech, and their four-year architectural course, which wouldn't cost anything except the daily streetcar fare to and from the school.

I lost no time going to the grimy old red-brick building on a distant part of Division Street, where the school was located in those days, with its mixed smells of baking, machine oil and various other things because it taught other vocations as well, such as bakery, printing, and auto mechanics, in addition to the regular academic subjects.

It was a big day for my mother when I enrolled there. "Now I feel sure that at least one member of the family is going to become something," she said. It was something to boast about, and she did so to everyone she knew—to our Polish landlord and his fat wife, to the blind man who lived in the basement apartment, to all the relatives, and to people in England, including my sister and her husband, Fanny Cohen, and even Mrs. Humberstone, who had lived across the street from us on the Christian side. "My son is now going to high school and is studying to be an architect," she wrote to each one, her face flushed with pride and excitement as she dictated her letters to me.

They all wrote back congratulating us, but it was my sister's letter that I remember most clearly: "I am so glad to hear that Harry is now in high school and is going to become an architect. I wish I'd had the opportunity that he is having. I almost did, didn't I? But it didn't quite turn out for me. . . ."

No, it didn't. I remembered that terrible time, how she'd won a scholarship—top of the list, too—and how she'd put on her pretty white dress to go to the grammar school for her interview, and how my father had refused to let her go and had dragged her by the hair, screaming, through the streets to the tailoring shop, and how we all stood on the doorstep in horror listening to her voice fading in the distance, screaming, "I won't go! I won't go!"

I had never forgotten it, and I thought of it again when I read her letter, and knew how lucky I was. My mother thought so too. Her eyes filled with tears when I read it to her, and perhaps it spoiled her pleasure over me for a while.

But she was too elated to let that sad bit of memory ruin it completely. Besides, she knew that Lily had found a great enough happiness in her marriage to Arthur to make up for everything that was in the past. So had she herself, through me and the great future she saw in store for me, found a happiness that made up for all the bitter moments she had endured in the past. That dream she'd always had was surely coming true.

I realized that, and because of it I did not have the heart to tell her of my architectural drawing teacher's reaction to the first house plan design I attempted. The entire freshman class had been given the assignment, obviously in an effort to ferret out any hidden talent that might exist among them.

We had spent a week working on the drawing, then each in turn went up to the teacher's desk for his review and criticism. Some came off quite well—especially those who'd had foresight enough to take a book of house plans out of the library and borrow ideas from that. There may also have been some genuine talent among them, and there also could have been inspiration from the fine houses some of the wealthier students lived in. The boys at the school came from all social classes—the rich ones from the higher-class North Side, the middle-class ones from the Near North Side, the poorer ones such as myself from the West or Northwest side.

And what did I know about houses? I had lived in a row house in England, in a railroad-style flat with my grandmother, in the horrible leaning house that was as much a stable as a house, and finally the one we lived in now, which was an improvement over the others but by no means an inspiration to a budding architect.

I had struggled hard over my drawing, depending more on my imagination than anything else, and it was with some trepidation that I approached the teacher's desk when my turn came. I had always been afraid of him.

He was a sickly-looking man with a pallid complexion and a chronic cough that brought up phlegm that he spat into the wastebasket at his side. He did that now as I waited for him to acknowledge me. He straightened up from the wastebasket, took the drawing from my hands, and scanned it slowly. My heart beat a little fast as I waited.

Finally he lifted his head from my drawing and spoke. But it was the class, not me, that he addressed. "Let me have your attention," he said, and they looked up from their drawing boards. He held up my drawing. "I want you all to look at this and see something that has never been seen in this classroom before. What you are looking at is the worst drawing I've ever had to check in my whole career as a teacher."

Now he turned to me. "Are you planning on staying at Lane for the entire four years?"

"Yes, sir," I said.

"Well, then, take my advice. When you're in your senior year, if you ever get there, file an application with the Sanitation Department and get yourself a job on a garbage wagon."

No, I couldn't tell my mother that. I never did. But I knew then that I was not going to become an architect. It would have to be something else, but I didn't know what, and I don't suppose it really mattered.

Chapter Ten

I was not quite fourteen when I entered Lane, and at close to six feet tall I still towered over the other freshmen. But now I wore long pants that made life a bit easier for me. I had made friends. I had joined a club of boys and girls in the neighborhood, and I had discovered girls' legs and knees. Skirts were getting shorter. I went to parties and played a game called Spin the Bottle, which sent me into a dark room to kiss some sweaty, giggling girl. I was very busy with my schoolwork and my social life, but not too busy and not yet too old to be going places with my mother, to visit relatives mostly, and to help carry Sidney, who was now well able to walk but preferred to be carried.

On some occasions my father and my two brothers went along with us. These would be the times when we all needed haircuts, and it would be to visit Aunt Sophie, whose husband, Sam, was a barber and a good-natured man who didn't mind devoting his weekend to cutting hair for the relatives, with never any talk of payment. Several families in addition to our own would sometimes descend on them on a Saturday and on occasion stay overnight, with beds on the floor, and not only would Sam be busy cutting hair, but Sophie would be bustling about preparing the mountains of food needed to feed this army.

There was never any shortage of food. Sam saw to that because he had sufficient forethought every Friday after his week's work was over at a large barber shop in the city to stop off and buy several salamis, pounds of frankfurters, corned beef, pickles, and loaves of rye bread, and bringing it home with him in a sack that he carried over his shoulder. He never knew how many people would come or how long they would stay after the haircut, but he took no chance of having a hungry horde on his hands.

Perhaps if the house that Uncle Sam, Aunt Sophie, and their two daughters lived in had been closer to the city, it would have been even more crowded on the weekends than it generally was. But it was situated in an area that was difficult to get to, a new development called Elmwood Park, a virtual wilderness in those days. We took a streetcar to the end of the line first to get there, then walked about five miles before we reached their frame house, which had a run-down look to it.

Sam had bought the house sight unseen from a customer in the barber shop where he worked. He had not known such a place as Elmwood Park existed before he bought it, nor how far it was to the streetcar terminal. But behind all that lay a story that the family never got tired of telling, always with much laughter.

It was chiefly on account of Aunt Sophie that everything happened. She was a very beautiful woman, with glowing healthy cheeks, sparkling dark eyes, and a lush figure. Sam fell madly in love with her back there in England, when Sophie lived with my grandmother on our street and Sam was just learning the barbering trade from Mr. Dargan, the barber on King Street, who also taught the violin.

But Sophie was quite a neurotic when it came to noises. She

couldn't abide the slightest noise around her. They had already moved from apartment to apartment because of noisy neighbors when they came to one where the people who lived above them practically drove Sophie insane with noises night and day. Sophie had tried talking to them, begging and pleading with them to tone things down and at least to wear slippers when they walked across the carpetless floor. But to no avail. They told her to go jump in the lake. In a great rage, Sophie countered with a noise barrage of her own to give them a taste of their own medicine. She placed a tall ladder in a spot that was directly beneath their bedroom, mounted a portable record player on top of the ladder with a record of a popular song called "It's Three o'Clock in the Morning," and set it on automatic, so that starting at three in the morning it played steadily over and over, with the volume set at the loudest.

When the upstairs couple complained, Sophie was delighted. She told the woman what she had told her, to go jump in the lake. They took Sophie and Sam to court, and a judge fined them $150 for malicious mischief.

It was at this point that one of Sam's customers told him a sad story of needing a thousand dollars for an operation on his eye, otherwise he would go blind and he would lose his job, and his five children would starve to death. His only possession of any worth was the house in Elmwood Park and he had been unable to sell it. Sam was softhearted and, even without Sophie's problem and the fine they'd just paid, he might have done what he did then. Before he had finished cutting the man's hair he had bought the house. Sophie, he had figured, couldn't find a quieter place.

They wasted very little time moving out to Elmwood Park and, as Sophie explained later, she had certain misgivings when she saw the wilderness that was spread out before them as they arrived. She wondered then if perhaps there wasn't such a thing as too much quiet. But nevertheless they began unloading their furniture into the new house and they were busy doing that, and marveling at the quiet and serenity around them, with no other houses in sight for almost a mile, when suddenly that blessed stillness was shattered by the whistle blast of an approaching train. The roar grew louder and louder until it was absolutely deafening and seemed as if it might go right through the house, and when the startled couple recovered from the shock sufficiently to look through a window, they saw an express from the Chicago, St. Paul & Minnesota Railroad racing past on tracks not more than fifteen feet behind the house.

The story has it that Sophie went wild with anger and beat Sam with her fists, and for a long time afterward she used to throw stones at the trains as they raced past. Sometimes she hit the engineer in the locomotive, and he learned to duck as he went by. But apparently, given enough time, you can get used to anything; when we were there and a train went by and we had to stop talking until it had passed, there was no look of annoyance on Sophie's still-beautiful face, and she even smiled until it was quiet again. She had also developed a friendly relationship with the engineer at whom she had previously thrown stones, and now they waved to each other.

Altogether, the move to Elmwood Park seemed to have done her a lot of good, and she now had a tolerance for noise that she'd never had before. Certainly there was plenty of it inside the house when we were all there. There were never enough chairs, so people had to stand while they were eating. And there was always eating going on, with mounds of food on the table, as everyone talked and kids ran wildly about. Sophie didn't seem troubled by that. She loved company. And I suppose Sam did. He was busy the whole time cutting hair. It was like a barber shop, with people waiting their turn and the constant *snip snip* of scissors.

We left there with our stomachs full, our breath reeking of garlic and our heads shorn. Among the men the smell of garlic was mixed with that of liquor. Sam knew a good bootlegger, and always provided a bottle. The only bad part about these visits was the five-mile trek to the streetcar terminal.

My father once cursed Sam out for buying a house so far from where we got the streetcar. "Didn't you have enough brains in your head to pick out a house where your guests didn't have to walk so much to get to you and to get away from you?" he said.

"I'm sorry," Sam said quietly. He was a gentle man with a big heart and a great love for his wife and children. He was rather short, with a dark complexion and sad eyes. I never knew him to shout or lose his temper with anyone. He didn't take offense when my father cursed him out. Eventually he bought a car, so he'd pick us up at the terminal and drive us to his house, and then he'd drive us back. The only thing my father had to grumble about now was that he hadn't bought a bigger car so that we didn't have to pack into it so tightly. Sam didn't say anything then, but sometime later he did exchange his car for a bigger one, and it was in that one he came into the city to drive us to my aunt Lily's wedding.

Chapter Eleven

PHIL'S PARENTS HAD FINALLY AGREED TO ATTEND THE WEDDING, and with that and with my grandfather safely out of the way there was no longer any need to put off the marriage that Phil wanted so badly. Aunt Lily had wanted it to be a very formal affair, with a full ceremony in a big synagogue and then a fancy reception and wedding feast in a fashionable hall, not only to please herself but to impress Phil's wealthy parents.

But when my grandmother heard what it would cost, she asked, "Who do you expect to pay for all this?"

"We have to," Lily said. "It's the bride's family that pays for the wedding when a daughter marries."

"Is it?" my grandmother said. "Well, then you'd better get yourself a gun."

"What are you talking about, Mama?" Lily asked.

"Because you'd have to put a gun to my head to get me to spend that kind of money. Even then I wouldn't do it. Ten thousand dollars! Who d'you think I am, the Princess of Wales?"

"Mama, do you want us to look like a bunch of schnorrers in front of Phil's parents?"

It was then that my grandmother slapped her face, because Lily had trodden on dangerous ground. The word *schnorrer* meant "beggar."

Aunt Lily cried, but eventually she gave up, and the wedding was planned for my grandmother's apartment. It was good enough, my grandmother said. All the other girls, Ada and Sophie and Dora, had been married in her house, and what was good enough for them was good enough for Lily, and if Phil's parents didn't like it, they could go kiss her ass.

So it was settled and the invitations were sent out. We received one, and it set my father to grumbling and cursing because it meant that we'd have to buy a present. But there was more than that. I would need a suit to attend the wedding. All I had was my pair of long pants and a sweater that I wore to school. A suit, such as both my brothers had, was as important as a present in order to attend a wedding.

My father gritted his teeth and threw malevolent looks at me as he raged, "What the bloody 'ell does he need a suit for? Where's he going, to the king's ball? Who the bloody 'ell will notice the difference what he wears? And why should I have to spend my money on him? He doesn't bring a penny into this house. All he does is waste his time in a school when he should be working and earning money like everybody else."

He carried on like that for quite some time. My mother said very little. But I know what was going through her mind. These were no longer the days when she waited trembling on a Saturday afternoon for him to dole out to her what he decided was enough from his pay. She no longer had to depend on him. There were my two brothers and sister contributing money to the house. In the end he

may have realized that himself, and he stomped off, cursing but de-
feated.

There was only one place to buy clothes, and that was Maxwell
Street, where there were bargains galore, two rows of pushcarts lin-
ing either side with peddlers hawking all kinds of goods, edible and
nonedible, and garments of all kinds for men and women. And
there were stores where suits of clothes hung outside dusty windows
in lieu of signs to indicate this was a place where clothing could be
bought cheap. Outside some of them were "pushers-in," men who
tried to inveigle you into their particular store, urging, grabbing
your arm as you went by, almost forcing you to come in and try on
a suit—cheap, cheap, cheap, a next-to-nothing price you couldn't
beat anywhere. They were sometimes difficult to get away from. You
had to pull your arm free and keep walking.

My mother seemed to know where to go. She had been here before with Saul and Joe to buy suits for them. There was one place
where she could depend on getting clothes at the cheapest possible
price. There was no pusher-in at this store that we finally came to.
But before we went in, we halted and my mother said in a low voice,
"If you see something you like particularly, don't let the man know.
Try to seem as if you aren't sure about it."

There was a technique for buying clothes on Maxwell Street,
and my mother was well versed in it. She'd had a lot of experience
before, buying our clothes in the market in England, and there was
not much difference. My mother knew immediately the moment we
entered the store that we had come at the right time. It was empty
save for the man who was standing behind the counter with a
gloomy look on his unshaven face. It lit up at the sight of my
mother. He remembered her from the last time she'd been there.
The gloom vanished. "Ah!" he cried. "How are you? How good to see
you again. How are your two boys? I see you've brought another
one. So you have three boys. Well, well, well." All this in one effusive
greeting that pleased my mother considerably.

"I have four boys," she said.

"Four! So where is the other one? Why didn't you bring him too? You know I have the best suits for boys here at the cheapest prices."

"He's too young to need a suit. You'll have to wait a few more years."

"So I'll wait. I've got plenty of time. Right now I'll bet you want a suit for this one. You're in luck. I just got in a new shipment of boys' suits at bargain prices."

"I wasn't thinking of buying," my mother said. "I'm just looking in case I should need one for him sometime in the future."

I was alarmed. I thought she really meant it. I did not know that she was playing a game according to the rules. The man knew. He did not seem disturbed. He shrugged. "Go right ahead and look," he said. "That's what my store is for, so people can look. Who said anything about buying?"

He then started to pace up and down behind the counter with his hands clasped behind his back, ignoring us as if we were not there. My mother began to look. There were clothes hanging on racks and she went through them, with me at her side. I thought they were all good. I'd have taken any of them. But she apparently had her own ideas. She took one after another off the rack, brought it out to the light, examined it closely, tugged here and there at the cloth, looked at the linings, put it back on the rack and took off another, going through the same process, sometimes having me try on a jacket.

It must have taken about an hour before she came to the brown one and whispered to me, "Do you like this one?"

I'd have said yes to any of them, but this one I really did like and I said, "Yes."

She put a hand to her lips and looked over at the proprietor. He had his back to us and was looking through the window. I had spoken rather loudly and I didn't say *yis* anymore. I said *yes* the American way, and very clearly. He must have heard me. But it didn't really matter. The game was being played out. It was now up to my mother to put it back on the rack and start leaving.

The proprietor turned away from the window. "So you couldn't find anything you liked?" he asked.

"Not this time," my mother answered. "Perhaps next time I'll see something for him that I like. . . ." She seemed ready to go, and I followed her, still puzzled and disappointed. I had liked that brown suit. It was double-breasted and very much like one Joe had bought, which I had admired when I saw him wearing it.

But then my mother, seemingly on the way out, halted and said casually, "By the way, how much is that brown double-breasted suit?"

"Which one?"

She went back to the rack and took it off and showed it to him.

He examined it carefully and finally said, "For you, seeing that you're an old customer, sixteen dollars."

"Come, Harry," my mother said to me, "let's go."

"How much do you want to pay?" the man asked quickly.

"I told you," my mother said, "I'm not buying. I'm just looking. There's another store down the street I want to look at."

"How much would you want to pay for the brown suit if you were buying?"

"Seven dollars," my mother said.

"Goodbye," the man said, turning back to go behind the counter again and look out through the window.

We actually went out. My disappointment was keen. The less chance there seemed of my getting the brown suit, the more I wanted it. I walked beside my mother and was about to voice my disappointment when I felt a hand on my shoulder from behind. I had not heard the footsteps. Perhaps my mother had. She did not seem surprised when she saw it was the man from the clothing store halting us.

"All right," he said, "I'll let you have it for fifteen dollars."

"I'll give you eight," my mother said.

Out there on the sidewalk, a few feet away from the store, it was settled. Nine dollars and fifty cents. I went home elated with a brown double-breasted suit in a cardboard box under my arm. I couldn't wait to put it on, but I'd have to wait. The wedding was still a month off, toward the end of May. Phil had wanted it earlier, as soon as possible, but sometimes my grandfather came home for Passover, which took place in April, and they were taking no chances that he might come in time for the wedding, so Lily had persuaded Phil to wait another month after Passover, just to make sure the old man was not coming. She was still in deadly fear of Phil and his parents finding out about him.

And so I too had to curb my impatience and wait to put on my new suit.

It was much too large for me. The sleeves of the jacket came below my wrists and the shoulders hung loosely. The trousers were too wide round the waist and too long. The cuffs hung down onto my shoes and the bottoms folded like an accordion. I had tried the suit on in the store, and all this must have been perceptible to my mother. But it had not bothered her. She preferred it that way, figuring with her usual prudence that eventually I would grow into it and I would not have to buy another suit for several years. In the meantime, she made several alterations and made it look fairly presentable on me.

The wedding day came at last, and I could put my suit on. Surveying myself in the long mirror that hung at the back of the bathroom door, I was well pleased with what I saw. My mother was too. They were all gathered around watching, even my sister Rose, who usually remained aloof from family affairs. However, there was a contemptuous sneer on her thin, pointed face as she looked, and then without a word she turned and walked away.

Joe was more voluble. He was downright angry at my mother for having chosen a suit that looked exactly like his, brown and double-breasted and with a vest. Except that mine might have been a comic version of his. He was smart-looking and handsome in his brown double-breasted suit, everything fitting his slim body well, whereas mine hung baggily.

"He looks like a scarecrow all dressed up to frighten the birds away," my brother Saul said, and laughed.

"Couldn't you have picked another color at least?" Joe said to my mother.

"It was such a good bargain I couldn't let it go," she said. "But don't worry. They won't mistake him for you."

Then she was sorry she had said that, for next moment Saul quipped, "Not with his face."

He might have said the same thing about himself. He and I resembled each other with our hooked noses and the glasses both of us wore. Joe was the handsome one of the three of us, with a straight nose and dark eyes with long lashes.

At any other time I might have felt incensed over Saul's remark and given him a punch in the ribs and said something about the way he looked—like a rabbi. He had chosen a black suit because that was what Orthodox Jews wore and a rabbi especially. His prayer shawl fringes stuck out of the waist as prominently as ever, and lately he had taken to wearing a yarmulke that was perched on top of his head like a bird's nest.

But I was in no mood for fighting. Looking into the long mirror that hung on the back of the bathroom door, I was quite pleased with the way I looked. I thought I looked quite spiffy, a regular swank. To go with the suit, I wore a striped shirt that Uncle Saul had once worn, and one of his ties also, a bright yellowish color. The pants were still too long in spite of all my mother's cutting and sewing, and the bottoms still folded like an accordion onto my shoes, but as far as I was concerned I had never looked better, and I was looking forward to the wedding.

Well, they were all in a good mood and looking forward to the big celebration, for that was all it could be with the passionate love Phil had shown Aunt Lily all these months. Even my father seemed to be in a rare good mood, and he certainly had a lot to look forward to. There would be plenty of booze. Aside from the bottles Abe was bringing from his bootlegger's cache, others in the family had announced they were bringing bottles.

My mother had been up almost the entire night baking cakes for the occasion. We were loaded with these and the wedding present, a milk jug that my mother thought the newly married couple should have, when Sam drew up in front of our house with the big, secondhand Maxwell for which he had traded in his much smaller Ford. We hurried down the steps with our packages when we heard the horn blow.

There it was at the curb, a bright yellow color, with Sophie and the two girls perched on the high backseat. It was a convertible and the top was down. The weather was warm and sunny. We piled in, scrambling for the best seats, trying to avoid a lap, squeezing in tightly. My father, looking up from his seat and seeing the sky, said, "What the bloody 'ell kind of car is this? Where's the other 'alf?"

It was explained to him that this was a convertible, with a top that folded. Sam offered to put up the top if it would make him feel more comfortable. My father chose to ignore this and said, "So long as you were getting a new car, couldn't you afford to buy a whole one instead of an 'alf?"

Sam's reply was to step on the pedal and send the car forward with such speed that wind gusted over our heads and Saul's yarmulke flew off. He gave a yell of dismay, and Sam halted the car with a screech of brakes. Saul jumped out and raced after his yarmulke, which was still rolling in the wind. He caught it finally and plastered it back on his head, and Sam lurched forward again, with all of us laughing so hard we were doubled over. There was even a sort of grin on my father's face that I had never seen before.

So it was in this extraordinarily gay mood that we drove to the West Side and my grandmother's house on Fourteenth Street. A small crowd of mostly young kids had collected around the stoop, as often happens at places where celebrations are happening, in the hope that some of the refreshments would be sent down and passed around among them. In the meantime their attention had been drawn to the large black limousine parked at the curb. A uniformed chauffeur was leaning protectively at its side, smoking a cigarette, eyes warning the crowd to keep its distance.

We couldn't help noticing it as Sam parked his secondhand Maxwell behind the limousine, and Sam, gazing at it admiringly, said, "That must be Phil's parents' car. Some beauty, eh?"

Yes, it was a beauty, and awesome, and the chauffeur immaculate in the dark uniform with peaked cap and shiny leather leggings was awesome too, and Sam was right, it was Phil's parents' car.

They were here already, and they looked lost and uncomfortable in the packed, noisy room filled with tobacco smoke and relatives and kids running wildly about. We saw the couple from a distance as we entered, the man as short and stubby as Phil and wearing a tuxedo, the woman in a dark evening gown, rich-looking to match the limousine downstairs.

Phil led us over to meet them. He had been the first to greet us. He too wore a tuxedo and he was in a high mood, as indeed he always was, but this time simply intoxicated with joy, as he himself said when he greeted us at the door. "I've never been drunk in my life," he said. "But tonight I am. Only I haven't touched a drop. I never do. But I feel as if I've drunk a gallon of what's in the bottles. . . . Come meet my parents."

He led us to them through the crowd and introduced us one by one. "Father, Mother, I want you to meet the people who've just come from England. . . ." He rattled off our names and we shook hands, and I couldn't help noticing the lack of warmth on their part, the woman especially. She was taller than her husband and she wore a lot of glittering jewelry. Barney said later that she out-jeweled my grandmother.

I noticed too that Phil repeated, "They just came from England," as if that might be some special attribute that would impress them.

I doubt if it did. I doubt if they were pleased at all with anything going on here. They looked very much as if they would rather have been elsewhere. The noise was growing. The bottles had been opened. The men were talking loudly and laughing, and quite clearly the drinking was having its effect. I heard my father's voice shouting at Eli, telling him to put the bloody bottle down and drink like a human being. The noise was tremendous. Children were chasing one another and screaming. Mothers were yelling at them. Now and then came the sound of slapping and a different kind of screaming. In the midst of all this bedlam the rabbi arrived and there was general relief. Now that he was here there would be less time to wait for the eating.

Things quieted down a bit after his arrival. He was a bearded man and fairly young, and apparently as anxious as everyone else to get this thing done with as little delay as possible. He shook hands briskly with those he had to and gave a few instructions for mounting a chuppah made of four tall poles and a piece of velvet over the top of the poles, under which the couple would be married.

Uncle Saul took his place at the piano, and Eli was pulled away from the liquor table to play the harmonica with him for the wedding march. Eli could barely walk, and he seemed to have forgotten where his harmonica was and was fumbling for it in various pockets as they led him into the front room, with his face flushed and grinning.

The rabbi continued to give instructions. The wedding march would start at the back of the apartment, in the kitchen. The groom would come first, accompanied by his father and mother. The bride would follow with her mother.

"Where's the father?" the rabbi asked.

I saw Phil's father and mother exchange a glance and I heard the father say, "Yes, where is he?"

"He's in New York," one of the uncles said.

"New York?" the rabbi said, slightly incredulous. "He can't be here for his daughter's wedding?"

It was Barney who spoke then, the big White Owl cigar wagging up and down in his mouth, his eyes twinkling. "He has an important board of directors meeting and couldn't get away."

The rabbi shook his head, taking the excuse seriously but deploring it. "Then let one of the brothers take his place," he said.

The choice fell on my father, who was the oldest, but he was already too drunk to stand up, so Uncle Morris took his place and the wedding march began, with Uncle Saul thumping out the opening bars of "Here Comes the Bride" and Eli, obviously very drunk, making a weird assortment of sounds with his harmonica.

Phil walked slowly and in time to the music with his father on one side of him and his mother on the other, Phil's face wreathed in one huge happy smile, but theirs quite noticeably grim.

And now the bride followed from the kitchen, wearing the long white bridal gown she had rented from a store, the back trailing on the floor behind her, my grandmother on one side, Uncle Morris on the other. They went through the dining room and into the front room, and there the couple came together, and judging from the look that came over Phil's face all of us expected him to seize her and give her one of his long, passionate kisses.

However, he remained calm, though you could almost hear the fast beating of his heart under the stiff white front of his tuxedo, and he remained still throughout the ceremony until he had stamped on the wineglass that signaled the marriage had taken place. Cries of "Mazel tov!" broke out.

Only then did Phil give vent to the powerful emotion that he had been resisting until now. He took Aunt Lily into his arms and bent her backward with her long veil sweeping the floor, and kissed her long and passionately, as he had always done, except that this was with a hunger that could not be appeased in the usual length of time but went on and on, while everybody yelled approval and applauded as though it were a performance on a stage.

And then, as soon as he had released her gasping for breath, her lipstick smeared on her face, there were congratulations from the crowd, everybody struggling to get to the couple, to kiss, to shake a hand, and then Uncle Saul began pounding away on the piano. It was a dance tune. Eli did not participate. He had gone back to the table where the bottles were—the bar, they called it. It was just as well. Uncle Saul did even better without his screeching harmonica. The rollicking piece he thumped out was easily recognizable as the hora, the Jewish dance of celebration.

A circle was formed. There were to be no exceptions. Everybody was dragged into it, kids and all. My sister Rose did manage to escape, shutting herself into a bedroom. Phil's parents tried to escape also, but hands forced them into the ring and everybody danced, with much laughter.

My mother and other women brought the food out from the kitchen, with my grandmother supervising. There were heaping plates of corned beef, steaming flanken, salami, bologna, potatoes, pickles, heaps of rye bread, and the cakes my mother had baked last night, filling the house all night long with their delicious smells. Soon a wild horde of kids swarmed down on everything, grabbing handfuls of meats and bread and cake and pickles, and devouring them in various parts of the house with my grandmother casting black looks at them and the pickle juice that was running down onto her floors, even onto the carpet in the front room, but she was unable to do anything about it—at least not yet.

The house was bedlam, with all the noise, all the eating and drinking, and it was very warm, and it was at this juncture that Phil's parents tried to make their escape. Phil pleaded with them to stay longer; Aunt Lily—still in her white rented bridal gown and flushed with the warmth of the room and the excitement of the event—implored them at least to have a corned beef sandwich before they left. It was the best, she said, bought at Levinsky's famous delicatessen on the East Side.

At this juncture someone in the room cried out, "Open a window, for God's sake, I'm dying from the heat." Phil was standing near one and immediately responded, opening it wide, and in that moment the sound of a voice singing below became audible. It was a man's voice—an old man's, obviously, because it was cracked and hoarse and not in good tune—and it was an old, sentimental love song, "I Love You Always," one sung often at weddings.

Phil became excited. Turning to his parents, he cried, "Look, there's an old blind beggar downstairs serenading us. Let me bring him up here for a glass of wine, besides what I'll give him in his tin cup. I'll have him sing for us right here. Now you must stay, you absolutely must. It would be a sin not to do this for him. Am I right, darling?"

He had said this last to Lily, and in his excitement he did not see the horror on her face. She was too stunned to reply to his question, because she had recognized that voice, as I had, as my grandmother and all the others had. They all had heard him, and guessed that he had come home unexpectedly to find a wedding in progress in his apartment. He would have learned that from the crowd gathered outside and the long black limousine with the smartly uniformed chauffeur leaning up against it. Now he was putting on an act that everyone imagined could only be vengeful.

But Phil did not know anything of this and undoubtedly did not notice the stunned silence that had fallen over those who did know, the family. He was bent on bringing the old man up here and would have gone himself in his impulsive fashion, rushing down the three flights of stairs, except that he knew if he left his parents' side they would escape in a moment.

I was standing near him, and he turned to me and said, "Harry, go down and tell that old blind beggar to come up here. He probably can't see his way up the stairs, so you'll have to guide him. Go on now, before he leaves."

I hesitated. From a distance I saw the stricken look on my mother's face. I thought she was going to tell me not to go. But she didn't, and I went down the stairs, wondering what I was going to say to my grandfather. Perhaps, though, we'd all been mistaken. Perhaps it was some other beggar.

He was there singing when I got outside, and there was no mistaking him. He wore the same ragged clothes that were his uniform, and he had the cane and the tin cup. Behind the blue glasses were, I was sure, the twinkling eyes, and when he saw me there was the chuckle. The crowd of mostly young kids gathered around him glanced quickly over toward me as I came out, hoping for the plate of goodies that usually came; seeing me empty-handed, they turned back disappointed.

I went up to him, afraid to call him "Grandpa" lest everybody hear and know. And he too kept up the pretense of not having any connection with me, being careful not to use my name.

"They'd like you to come upstairs and sing for them," I said. "And to have a glass of wine."

He had stopped singing and was looking directly at me. He pointed to himself and said, as if he could not believe the invitation, "Me?"

"Yes," I said. I was very nervous. Some in the crowd started to yell, "How about me? I'll come up and have a glass of wine." There was laughter.

"Well," the old man said, "how can I refuse?" He then addressed his audience, saying, "You'll have to excuse me. I've been invited to the wedding." He spoke to the chauffeur, who was grinning as he smoked a cigarette. "I'm going to join your master. Do you have any message for him? I'll be glad to give it to him. Shall I perhaps tell him you're tired of waiting for him?"

"No, don't do that," the chauffeur said, and laughed.

Those in the crowd started yelling, "Tell 'em we're tired of waiting for some food."

"I'll tell them," the old man promised, and then to me, "All right, young man, lead the way. I'm blind, you know, so you'll have to guide me."

I kept up the farce. I took hold of his arm and led him up the stoop and into the house, but once inside I let go of it and said, "You know the way yourself, Grandpa."

He chuckled. "I can't fool you, can I?"

"No."

"So who's getting married up there?"

"Aunt Lily and Phil."

"Phil? Who's Phil? Is that his car down there, the big black one with the chauffeur?"

"No, that's Phil's parents'."

"So he must be rich too. She landed a good one. But it's about time she landed someone. Why didn't they tell me she was getting married?"

I didn't answer.

"That's all right, Harry," he said. "I know. I know everything." He chuckled, then said, "But I won't spoil it for them."

I wasn't sure I knew what he meant, so I said nothing again.

We went up the three flights of stairs together, and he labored quite a bit as we got to the top and I had to slow down for him. But he would not let me help him, shaking my hand off his arm. We entered the apartment together.

They had been waiting for us, the family tense, and hoping as I had done that it was a mistake and the beggar was someone else. But at first sight of him all their hope vanished. I looked at them. My grandmother stood rigid, her face tight. My mother looked as stricken as she had before. The others—well, there was a variety of expressions, none pleasant. There was dead silence among them.

Even the children were hushed, all gaping at the blind beggar I had brought in.

But Phil launched into an effusive welcome, throwing an arm round the old man's shoulders, crying, "Welcome, old man! I'm so glad you came. I heard you singing down below. I want you to sing for us up here. But first you must have a glass of wine with us and join us in a toast to my beautiful bride. I know you can't see, but you must take my word for it—she is the most beautiful bride there ever was in this world. I wish you could see her." He swept a hand toward Lily, who was hovering a little behind him. He had no idea how close she was to fainting.

The old man gave a little chuckle. He probably knew how she felt and was obviously enjoying himself tremendously. "I don't have to see her," he said. "I am so well trained without my sight, which I lost in the war, in the battle of Mons, that I can sense beauty without seeing it. And I know your bride is what you say she is, and I congratulate you. Would it be possible perhaps for me to kiss the bride?"

"Why not?" Phil cried, but then, seeing Lily's pale face, he changed his mind quickly and said, "But first let's drink. Fill the glasses. Everybody drink! Come on, fill up the glasses."

They complied readily. All the members of the family, who knew what was going on, needed the drink. Even the men at the bar, who had drunk enough already, poured still more from the bottles. Eli had his head on the table and was out. He was the only one who didn't participate in the toast. Phil himself had placed a glass in the hand of my grandfather, one in Lily's trembling hand, and one in each of his parents', and was now going around with a bottle of sweet wine filling glasses, making sure that everyone was joining in the toast, and growing more and more excited, his face flushed, his eyes sparkling.

I had a glass in my hand too and was holding it steadily so that the wine would not spill out. I raised it, as did all the others theirs,

as Phil cried dramatically, "And now, ladies and gentlemen, to the
woman who has given me the greatest happiness of my life, to my
beautiful and lovely and sweet and delicious bride."

"Excuse me." It was my grandfather interrupting. "I have heard
all the voices here. I know the parents of the groom are here, the
mother of the bride, and all the brothers and sisters and relatives,
but where is the father of the bride? I have not heard his voice. Surely
on such a sacred occasion the father should be here to see his daughter get married . . . and to join in the toast with us."

Once again an uneasy hush settled over them. I heard my
grandmother make a strange sound and start toward the kitchen
with the glass of wine in her hand, Phil's eyes followed her with a
puzzled look in them. He looked questioningly at Lily, but she was
no help to him. The question had been asked before, and Barney
had answered it in his comical way. I wondered if he would give the
same answer now. But he was silent like the rest of them and did not
seem to be in a humorous mood.

Phil, however, remembered what Barney had said before and
gave the same answer to his guest, although I could tell from the way
he spoke that he had not quite believed Barney. But he said it, awk-
wardly: "He's in New York on a business matter. I believe he has a
board of directors meeting. Is that correct, Barney?"

"Yes, absolutely," said Barney, but it was in a sober fashion and
without the twinkle in his eyes, and the cigar he was holding in his
mouth had gone out and he was simply sucking it.

And then Phil's father spoke. He was a rather short man, much
as Phil was, and somewhat on the heavy side with a bulldog kind of
face. If you had read the financial pages in those days that face would
have been familiar to you. In fact, he was known as "the Bulldog,"
and it was easy to guess that this man was no fool. He had been eyeing the gathering with skeptical eyes throughout the evening, and if
not for his son both he and his wife would have gone long ago. Now
he spoke up loudly and for almost the first time, and in the forth-

right fashion that had earned him his nickname. "Listen," he said, "I don't know what's going on here with this phony blind beggar, but I don't like whatever it is. And I don't like this whole crowd here, and if you'll take my advice, son, you'll haul yourself out of this mess as soon as you can."

My grandmother had heard and now she came back, still holding the glass of wine in her hand. She approached Phil's father closely and said, "You don't like it here? Is that what you said?"

"Yes," he replied, looking her straight in the eye.

"Then you can get the hell out of here and take your whore of a wife with you. And take this, too."

She threw the glass of wine into his face. He wiped his face with a handkerchief and lost no time leaving together with his wife, with the stricken Phil running after them begging them not to take it seriously and asking them to stay longer, assuring them that though the family had certain peculiarities they were a nice, lively bunch of people and lots of fun to be with, and once they got to know them they'd love them as he did.

He followed them down the stairs, pleading, but neither one was moved. His father took Phil's hand off his arm and said, "Son, I'll give you the same advice as before. Get yourself out of this mess as soon as you can. I can get you a good lawyer."

Phil, crestfallen, went back upstairs. My grandmother was not done yet. She turned to my grandfather and said grimly, "Next time you decide to come, be sure you give me a month's notice or you'll find the door locked in your face."

"Maybe," said my grandfather, "next time one of my children gets married you'll give me a month's notice."

"Maybe," said my grandmother, "it would be still better if you didn't come at all."

"That suits me," said my grandfather. "I'll save myself a lot of money with the fare. I'm sure you'll be able to use it."

She said nothing more, but then, being in a vicious mood, did what she might have been expected to do. Sweeping her arms about, she turned to the others and shouted, "And the rest of you can go. I've had enough wedding. It's over. Go on, go, get out."

There was instant movement for departure. This included my grandfather as well. My mother came over to me and whispered in my ear, "Go and help your grandfather down the stairs. He might fall."

I went without hesitation. I felt terribly sorry for him. I took his arm as we were going down the stairs and he was grateful. He descended much more slowly than he had come up, evidently not steady on his feet. When we came downstairs he gave me a hug and said, "Well, at least I can say I attended my daughter's wedding." And he gave a chuckle and added, "Goodbye and good luck, and tell your mother she must not worry about paying me back. Tell her I still owe her."

"Goodbye, Grandpa," I said. "I'll tell her."

I watched him go down the street, limping and tapping his cane, from habit I suppose, and gradually he disappeared in the darkness. It would be years before I saw him again.

Chapter Twelve

THESE WERE TURBULENT TIMES IN THE LIFE OF THE CITY OF Chicago. It was the era of Prohibition, the day of the speakeasy and of Al Capone and rival gangs battling it out on the streets while corrupt police stood by and watched, or in some cases even fought on the side of one gang or another. On St. Valentine's Day, one gang marched into the headquarters of another, lined them all up against a wall, and mowed them down with machine guns. The newspaper headlines blazed daily with new killings or bombings of buildings.

In a small way, we were caught up in the drama of those days. It began for us with a loud, frantic knocking on the door. It was late. We were preparing for bed and could not possibly imagine a visitor at this time of night. I answered the door and fell back as Abe burst in gasping, "Shut the door. Shut it quick!" I obeyed and stared at him. His face was pale, his eyes wild and swinging around as if in search of someone. He asked us to look through the window and see if there was anyone down below. We did that. There was no one. My father was home that night. He poured Abe a drink and had him gulp it down, and asked what the bloody 'ell was going on.

Abe told his story in between gasps and shiverings. It had been one of those rare times when he had a job in a tailoring sweatshop. He had worked late and had come home tired and hungry, only to learn from a frightened wife that the bootlegger who stored his barrels in their closet had been there not too long before to ask for him.

He'd told her that he had been getting a lot of complaints from customers that the liquor he had sold them was heavily watered. He never drank his own liquor. He knew better. But he did that time and found it to be true. There could be no doubt as to who was responsible for adding water to the barrels he stored in the closet in order to cover up what he had been taking out of them, and he wanted to talk to that person. His tone was grim. He'd be back later, he said.

When Abe heard all this he didn't wait. He knew the penalty for crossing a bootlegger. Bodies had been found in the Chicago River, weighted down with cement blocks, bullet holes in heads. It was the usual method of punishment and disposal. Abe knew all that, and he'd run. His wife, Lizzie, hadn't waited much longer before she packed a few things, took the two children, and ran also. Abe never saw her again. It was something she had been planning to do for a long time anyway. None of us ever heard from her again.

In the meantime, Abe was safe with us—although he was never too sure of that and had me constantly looking through the window. Then one day I noticed a black car draw up at the curb and a man I had never seen before get out and look up at our floor. I withdrew from the window quickly and whispered to Abe, "There's a tall, skinny man downstairs looking up at us."

"That's him," said Abe, and his face turned white. He got up and looked around the room, as if seeking an escape.

We were sitting in the kitchen, and my mother was at the sink preparing our next meal. She seemed to know what to do. "Come with me," she said. "Hurry." She led him into the bedroom that she shared with my father, and I followed, listening. She told him to get undressed and into bed, and turn to one side with the covers pulled up to his head and pretend he was asleep. Then she closed the door.

We waited. A few minutes later we heard footsteps coming up the stairs, slowly, heavily. Then a knock at the door. I answered it. A tall, skinny man with an acne-scarred face, somewhere in his thirties, stood there and said, "Is Abe in?"

"Who?" It was my mother answering. She had followed me to the door.

"You know who," the man growled. "I know he's here."

"Well, he isn't," my mother said. "He doesn't live here and he hasn't been here for a long time."

"We'll see," the man said, and before I could shut the door he had stepped in and was looking around. My mother and I watched him fearfully. He was looking everywhere, the dining room, the living room, the bedrooms, opening doors and not bothering to close them.

"You've got no right to do that," my mother protested.

"Lady, I've got plenty of right," he said. "I've got a lot of right."

He seemed to have overlooked my parents' bedroom, which opened off the kitchen, and my mother was beginning to hope that he'd forget it altogether and leave. But that wasn't the case. He started to go toward the door, and my mother sprang forward to stop him. "You can't go in there," she said. "My husband's there in bed and he's sick. He just dropped off to sleep and I don't want to disturb him. He's very ill."

"Oh, yeah?" the man said, and opened the door and looked in.

I managed to look in also. Abe was doing exactly what my mother had told him to do. He was lying on one side with the covers pulled up to his head, apparently in a deep sleep. The tall, skinny man stood there looking at him, evidently not too sure. I think my

mother's heart was in her mouth at that moment. It seemed almost
certain that he was going to walk over to the bed and yank the covers off. But he didn't. He turned away, finally, and walked out.

At the door he stopped and said just a few more words: "Tell
Abe I'll find him and he'd better learn to say his prayers now."

We smuggled Abe out of the house at night. Uncle Louis drove
him in his cab to my grandmother's house, where he found refuge
for a week or two, but the fear hung over them there too, and Abe
was smuggled out once more under cover of darkness and finally
found sanctuary in the one place his hunter would never think of
following him: with my aunt Sophie and her husband, Sam the barber. Scarcely anyone at that time knew that Elmwood Park existed,
and even if they had gone there, they never would have been able to
find the solitary house near the railroad tracks.

Abe never recovered from what had happened. Perhaps the
worst part of it all was the loss of his wife and children. They could
not be found anywhere, though the family worked diligently to find
out for him, asking people who had known Lizzie, hunting down
clues, but never finding a trace of her.

Abe meanwhile declined both mentally and physically, a permanent guest, apparently, at Sophie's house. When we came to visit we
usually found him lying in bed, no matter what the hour of day, and
as time went on senility crept over him even though he was a relatively young man, not much into his forties. After a while he failed
to recognize any of us and called us by the wrong names. The one
thing that stuck in his feeble mind was his wife, Lizzie. He seemed to
think she was still around, and he asked for her constantly—the
beautiful wife with the electric lights and bathtub, who never answered his call.

ABE'S DOWNFALL HAD BEEN AS much a catastrophe for my father,
Eli, and the other drinking brothers as it had been for Abe himself.

It had meant the drying up of the well that had kept them in free moonshine for many months, and now they had to seek out their own source of supply. This was not too difficult if you had the money, and my father had that. He was doing well at Hart Schaffner & Marx. He was making more money in a week than he had made in a month in England. How much of that he gave to my mother I don't know, but it wasn't as important to her now as it had once been.

There were others in the family to give her money. Joe, Saul, and Rose were all working and earning, and they gave her a portion of their wages every week, so she was well supplied with money and was even putting a little aside to pay off the debt she felt she owed to my grandfather. Every week I went with her to the bank and helped her make out the deposit slip, which she handed to the teller together with the dollar or sometimes two dollars that she deposited. Then, happily, she tucked away her bank book into her handbag.

Yes, she was happy, and in those days it must have seemed to her that everything she had dreamed about America had come true. She had enough money not only to cover the expenses of the household but to have a bank account, something she had never had in her life before and which she mentioned proudly in her letters to England. "Oh, yes," she would say, dictating to me, "in case I haven't told you before"—she had, several times before—"I now have an account in a bank too. . . . Life has decided to be good to us for a change."

Life was indeed being good for a change, with a nice apartment only a block from a park, where you could hear band concerts in the summer, go rowing on the lake, or sit on a bench and feel a cool breeze and see green grass and trees and flowers all around you. It was like living in the swanky houses up the park, Hollywood Park, for instance.

We had a parlor and the furniture was almost paid off; we had a piano, on which my sister Rose played every night after she came home from work, with great thumping sounds that had no melody but were simply a lot of noise. But what difference did that make? We had a piano. I was going to high school. I was already in my third year and in another year I would graduate and go on to college. Yes, there was another step up in store for us. I had decided on that myself. College was too big a thing for even my mother's imagination to embrace. But I was getting older and able to make my own decisions. I would go to the University of Illinois in Urbana and study to become something that wasn't quite yet clear in my mind. Perhaps I'd become a writer. I was writing stories for the school monthly magazine, and the English teacher in charge had a better opinion of me than the drawing teacher who'd criticized my work in front of the whole class my first year.

But all that was only part of the shining glory of those days, when it seemed that we were so close to the fulfillment of our dream. There was a contentment in the household that had never been there before. My mother bought herself a new hat. It had a wide brim and a bunch of cherries on one side. She looked at herself in the mirror and smiled. I had never seen her do that before. I smiled with her. I told her it was very beautiful. She was a little surprised and grateful. Who had ever said that to her before? She looked again in the mirror, adjusted the hat a bit, and smiled again.

In addition to all the luxuries we already had, we bought a Victrola. We bought it from Phil, of course, and he and Lily came over to our house one evening to have dinner with us and show us how to use it, how to wind it up and put the needle in, and how to put the record on and take it off without scratching it. He had brought a record for us as a gift. It was a popular song called "Yes, We Have No Bananas," and we played it over and over, listening delightedly to it without ever tiring of the repetition.

These were good times for a lot of other people as well. There were more cars than ever out on the streets. New roads were being built to accommodate them, and in the Loop there was already congestion. Lots of folks were buying radios too, and you could hardly go past a doorway without hearing the squawking sounds coming from them. And people were packing the movie theaters to hear the new talking pictures that so amazed and fascinated everyone.

My brother Joe and Uncle Saul were having no difficulty selling their magazine subscriptions, and Uncle Saul seemed to have forgotten completely his plan to study law, while Joe no longer spoke of becoming a journalist. The two went from door to door, knocking and telling whoever opened it that they were working their way through college, and—as Uncle Saul put it—their hands grew tired writing subscription orders.

Joe bought another suit. He had one already, but he could afford a second one, and my mother did not object, although my father grumbled and wanted to know what the bloody 'ell anybody needed two suits for. Joe paid no attention to him; he'd soon be twenty, and he was smoking a pipe and going out with girls. Then, oddly, he began to take weekend trips to Davenport, Iowa. We soon found out that it was a girl he went out there to see. He had met her through some friends when she was visiting them, and he was in love with her—and what was more, he was going to marry her.

It came as a shock to my mother. I recall it was an evening after we'd had dinner, and he was preparing to go out when he told her this. I don't think my mother had ever recovered fully from the marriage of my sister to the Christian boy across the street when we were in England, so the first thing that entered her mind should not have been a surprise. "Is she Jewish?" she asked.

"Yes," answered Joe.

I saw the relief cross my mother's face. But, this hurdle overcome, there were other questions to ask. How old was she? What kind of family did she have? What did her father do? Were they rich, poor, or what? Why did they live in Davenport, Iowa, of all places? And what kind of place did they live in? Did they have a parlor? Was there a piano in the parlor? How many were there in the family? Oh, there were a million questions and Joe, growing more and more impatient, anxious to get to his friends, tried to answer them all.

Finally, my mother asked, "Why don't you bring her here to dinner?"

Joe hesitated. I know what he was thinking: my father. How would he behave? You never could tell. But reluctantly he said, "All right. Next time she comes here to visit her friend I'll bring her."

We waited four weeks before that happened and he brought Rose to the house. Yes, Rose. Another Rose in the family. It would make three Roses: my sister, my aunt—married to Uncle Barney—and the new one.

She was shy and rather pretty, with large dark eyes and dark hair, and she was wearing a blue dress with short, flouncy sleeves that showed slender white arms. She sat next to Joe at the table and seemed a little afraid of us. My father had barely acknowledged the introduction when she first arrived, and he sat at his usual place at the end of the table, as far away from us as he could get, with his head bent over his plate and silent throughout the early part of the conversation. He soon broke that silence, saying roughly, "Pass those pickles."

His words were addressed to our visitor. The jar of pickles was in front of her. She was startled by the command and the roughness of the voice, and fumbled as she reached for the jar, causing it to tip over and spill juice and pickles over the tablecloth.

Then my father barked, "What's the matter, don't you know how to pass some pickles?"

Joe became angry and said, "You don't have to speak to her like that."

"Who the bloody 'ell asked you?" my father said, equally angry.

Joe, who was usually in deadly fear of my father, found the courage to speak up. "You've got no right to talk to her like that," he said.

My mother, who had jumped up at once to clear the mess off the table, tried to quiet things down, waving a warning to Joe, but the damage had been done. Joe had answered back, and there was no stopping my father now. He sprang up and lashed out with the back of his hand, whacking Joe across the face. Joe let out a yell of pain, jumped up with a hand to his face, and ran out. Rose, looking bewildered for a moment, got up and followed him.

My mother was furious and turned on my father immediately, something she never did in front of us. "You animal," she said. "Did you have to do that? Couldn't you keep your temper in for once? The girl's your visitor. She's going to be your daughter-in-law. Did you have to carry on like that in front of her?"

"Who gives a goddamn who she is?" he shouted back. "And who needs her for a daughter-in-law? If she can't pass a jar of pickles without spilling them on the table, she shouldn't be anybody's daughter-in-law. Let her stay home. And watch out I don't give you a crack in the face."

I gave a lot of thought to that episode and wondered if my father hadn't brought it about deliberately in the hope of breaking up the romance before it reached marriage. I had seen his face tighten when my mother first broke the news to him that Joe was planning to get married, for it would mean a loss of income to the house and he would have to make up for it. I am sure this was in his mind that afternoon and the pickles were a secondary consideration.

It did nothing, however, to break up the romance between my brother and the girl from Davenport, Iowa. But Joe had not told us everything. There was something he had been keeping from us, for my mother's sake, knowing how it would hurt her. It came out at last.

Rose and her entire family were moving to New York. The father was a self-taught auto mechanic and had seen great prospects in New York, a city where there were more of these newfangled cars than anywhere else in the world. Henry Ford was turning them out by the thousands every day, and the rich were buying big limousines, which broke down often, and men who knew how to fix them were in great demand.

There was no time for a wedding now. Joe would go to New York with them and the wedding would take place there.

Yes, indeed, it was a blow to my mother. Once more she was being deprived of a wedding for one of her children. The first time had been in England, when my sister had married Arthur Forshaw in secrecy. And now it was Joe. It would be too expensive for her to go to New York. She would have to be satisfied with photos of the wedding. But going to New York would be a good thing for Joe, she thought, so she got over her disappointment.

My father, however, cursed. He was thinking mostly of the ten dollars a week that Joe had contributed to the family. That money would be lost. He called Joe a bastard, a thief, a dog, a piece of dung.

My mother plugged her ears with her fingers and ran out of the room. We had been eating dinner and were at the table. I remained sitting there with my eyes fixed on him and hatred in them. His eyes met mine and the hatred was returned. Neither of us said anything, and I got up and left the table.

But my father's bitterness was not over. There remained still more to deal with, and this time he did not curse and his actions were strange to me.

WE WOKE UP ONE MORNING on a Sunday and Saul was not in the house. His bed had not been slept in. It was not unusual for him to come home late on a night after we had all gone to sleep. He worked overtime at the mail order house often, sometimes late into the night. But he was always there in the morning, saying prayers as soon as he awoke.

"Where is he?" my mother asked, perturbed. She had gone from room to room looking.

Even my father and Rose were looking, going from room to room futilely, as if he might be hiding under a bed or a sofa.

Clearly, he had not come home last night. He had not eaten any of the food my mother always left for him on those overtime nights. Where, then, was he? She was thrown at once into a frenzy of fear. Nothing could have been more terrible to her than the loss of one of her children. She became distraught, and it was then that my father's actions surprised me. Ordinarily, he would have been totally indifferent to the welfare of any one of us. If it had been a sickness, a mishap of some sort, he would have shown no compassion and would have distanced himself immediately from the situation. But now he was clearly concerned, and after our search was over he announced grimly, "I'm going to the police."

It was a logical thing to do and showed some caring within him. Chicago was a city full of crime, and for those who were out at night it was especially dangerous. Saul easily could have met with foul play on his way home late at night. My mother took to weeping. She rarely broke down like that.

Sooner than we had expected, my father came hurrying back from the police station. His face was dark and angry. He had to go back to the police station, but he needed something. "Give me one of Saul's tzitzit," he said.

My mother stared at him through her tears. "What for?" she asked.

His anger became directed at her. "Don't ask so many questions," he said. "Just give it to me, the tzitzit." Then he explained. "The goddam police," he said, "they asked me all sorts of questions. How big he was, how old he was, what size shoes he wore, what kind of clothes. And when I told them he wore tzitzit, a prayer shawl, they'd never heard of them—they're Irish, so how should they know anything? They wanted to see one and put it in the report they're making out. So give me the damned thing and let me get this over with. I don't want to spend the rest of my life on this business."

Clearly, he had lost much of his concern, and my mother lost no time taking out a fresh tzitzit from the drawer where she kept several of them, all freshly cleaned, folded, and put away carefully.

My father needn't have hurried and my mother needn't have been so upset. Saul was quite safe, and in these moments while the police were making out their missing persons report—and calling

My mother, pictured here in England around 1915. Ma invented dreams for us to make up for all the things we lacked and to give us hope for the future.

An early family portrait in Stockport: Rose, Ma, and Lily are in the back row, I am on Ma's lap, Saul is on the left, and Joe on the right.

My parents in 1908. Shortly after their marriage, my father's family left for America. Grandmother Bernstein wasted no time in putting as much distance as she could between her and her oldest son.

Grandmother Bernstein, heavy and double-chinned with a massive bosom and the glower on her face that was always there.

My sister Lily in Stockport in 1922. A secret romance between Lily and Arthur Forshaw, a Christian boy from across the street, had carried on for years.

Rose, "the Duchess", in Chicago in the 1920s.

My high school graduation photo, taken in 1927. Ma was very proud.

At the Chicago Post Office, a grim,
dark, hulking building that looked
like a prison, where I worked in 1927.

At City Hospital on Welfare Island
in 1932; I had been caught in some
kind of gang warfare, and the best
thing for me was to keep out of it
and say as little as possible.

My mother and I in the early 1930s in the Bronx, New York.

With Ruby, the love of my life, in the spring of 1935, on the day after we got married.

Our first apartment on Bleeker Street. Here I am in 1936, with Ruby and my Corona typewriter.

Joe, Saul, and myself (left to right), *shortly after we moved to Chicago with the family in 1922.*

Here I am with Ruby in Mexico, in 1997, photographed by our daughter, Adraenne. The real embodiment of "the Dream."

up a rabbi to find out how you spelled *tzitzit*—Saul was sitting in the boxcar of a railroad freight train heading west, although it wasn't until we received a card from him that was postmarked Provo, Utah, telling us that he was safe and sound, that we knew what had happened to him.

We didn't know everything. I learned about it from him many years later, when we were both fully grown men and were talking one day and going back over the past with the amused tolerance that age gives you.

He had been thinking of running away from home for a long time, he told me. I did recall that he was generally very silent among us and said little about himself. Joe was always communicative about his life, telling us of his experiences when he knocked on a door or rang a bell, never knowing who would come to answer it. Once a bulldog leaped at him and would have torn him to bits if the owner hadn't been right behind to call off the dog. Once a young housewife in a negligee invited him in to have coffee with her. That was all Joe told us, but it was enough to indicate what happened after the coffee.

Saul, on the other hand, never spoke about his work or the people he worked with. It was something that he kept inside himself, tormenting him, the jeers that he got from his fellow workers over the yarmulke he wore and the tzitzit, and how practical jokers would sneak up behind him and pull at the fringes. But worse than all that was the sin he was committing by working on Saturday, the day he was supposed to be in the synagogue praying.

It had been plaguing him the whole time he had been working at Sears, and he kept it to himself until it was no longer possible to do so. He knew as he entered the big gray building of the mail order house that he could not keep this up much longer. The sin of working on a Saturday was in itself becoming too heavy to bear. On these mornings he always entered the plant with a prayer on his lips, asking God's forgiveness for working on the holy day, but there was more than that troubling him, a premonition almost of something going to happen.

The day began as all the other days did, with the mail clerk dumping his portion of the orders that had passed through various other hands before reaching his, then filling these orders by going from bin to bin and shelf to shelf where the various products were kept, and the wrapping and packing of these goods.

The work was monotonous and tiresome, and he had developed a strong dislike for it. The hours seemed to drag, it seemed as if the lunch bell would never ring. He brought his own lunch from home, a sandwich my mother had prepared for him that was strictly kosher—he never would have eaten the food in the plant cafeteria, as so many of his coworkers did—and that morning around eleven, that sandwich was very much on his mind, and the hunger he felt could very well have contributed to what was soon going to take place.

It was about this time that he picked up his next order. As a rule, customers sent in their orders on the form that was in the catalogue, but occasionally they came in the form of letters. This one came on a postcard. It was for BVDs, the popular men's underwear in those days, and Saul was about to fill it when he glanced at the other side. The card was from Colorado and showed a scene of the Rocky Mountains.

It was a fascinating and awesome sight, and Saul gazed at it spellbound. He had heard of the West and its beauty, and here it was with all its majesty and strength. It carried him away momentarily from the prison of his surroundings and gave him a yearning that he'd never had before, to be in a place like that with all its freedom and beauty.

Suddenly he felt a tap on the shoulder. It was one of the foremen who went around checking on the order fillers. "What are you supposed to be doing," he asked, "working or looking at pictures?" He was a thin fellow with quick, sharp eyes, and he carried a notepad and pencil around with him and jotted down the names of those he found doing something wrong.

Saul had never been questioned before and was in no mood for it now. He snapped back his answer: "What's wrong with looking at a picture?"

It got him extra punishment. "I'm giving you five extra demerits beside the two you got for loafing on the job," the foreman said, and wrote in his notebook.

Ten demerits total got you fired. Saul went back to work, boiling with anger, and five minutes later he felt his yarmulke being snatched off his head. This was not the first time it had happened, and most of those times it had been Callaghan, a tall Irish fellow with a constant grin on his face, who was the tormentor. That day it was Callaghan again, with the same grin on his face, holding the yarmulke in one hand and about to throw it to someone else, who'd keep on passing it round until Saul was able to rescue it.

This time, however, he did not go on the chase, but struck out with a fist and caught a surprised Callaghan on the nose. However, Callaghan was quick to recover, and the fight was on. They were both swinging fists and there was yelling among the order pickers around them, and foremen were making their way quickly over to the scene with notebooks and pencils poised for action.

The same one who had caught Saul reading the postcard was the first to arrive on the scene. He wasted little time and didn't bother to write anything in his notebook. "Report to the office," he said.

Saul knew what that meant. He knew also that of the two, he was being singled out for extreme punishment. It meant being fired. Callaghan was being let off with five demerits.

Saul didn't go to the office. He was burning with resentment and sick of the whole place, and that picture postcard was haunting him. It was still early, but he didn't go home. He wandered about a bit, trying to pluck up the courage to do what he knew he really wanted to do. Then, finally, he headed for the freight railroad yard, which was not far from where he was. There he was able to find a train that was headed west, and he had no problem boarding an empty boxcar. Soon he was on a journey that would take him all over the United States and would last several years, during which time, among common hoboes and vagrants of all sorts, he never gave up wearing his yarmulke and tzitzit, and the fight with Callaghan was only one of many that took place in his wanderings.

Chapter Thirteen

SO NOW THERE WERE JUST THREE OF US LEFT: MY SISTER, MY BABY brother, who was no longer a baby but a growing kid of seven in the second grade at school, and myself, seventeen, soon to graduate from Lane Tech and go on to college. Of the three of us, Rose was the only one working and bringing money into the house.

She did this regularly without fail, every Saturday, handing a ten-dollar bill to my mother silently, never talking to her, still the embittered girl from England who had been cheated out of her parlor, still filled with hatred. She must have been around twenty-three then, a strange girl whom we hardly knew. She locked herself in her room as soon as she had finished her dinner after coming home from work. Only occasionally did she come out and bang away on the piano for a few minutes, then go back into her room. She had no friends. She knew no one.

I think my mother felt a great deal of pity for her. She tried hard to break down that wall between them, speak to her, bring her into the life of the family, but always to no avail. Her feelings toward Rose were also mixed with a great deal of gratitude, for she knew that the ten dollars came out of a meager salary and left her with very little for herself. Without it my mother would have had a hard time making ends meet. My father, true to his old self, gave her only a small portion of what he earned; he cursed both Joe and Saul for what he called abandoning us—"those rotten, ungrateful bastards"—but did not attempt to make up the loss of income my mother had suffered.

She didn't say anything. She managed with what she had. She knew how to manage. She would walk for miles to find a street market where food was sold at bargain prices, and she would come home walking slowly with a heavily loaded bag in each hand.

The days of relative wealth were over, apparently. But she did not give up. There was still me. And after me there would be Sidney. But Sidney's working days were far off. Here I was about to graduate from high school, then go to college and become something. My father didn't share that feeling. He saw no reason why I shouldn't go to work right now, when money was needed. Never mind graduation. Never mind college. He glowered darkly at me. But I was no longer afraid of him. I glowered back and, I must say, there was something brewing between the two of us.

My mother saw it and was fearful. "You mustn't look at him like that," she whispered when he was not in the house, having clumped out to go drinking.

"I don't care," I said to her. "If he looks at me that way, I can do the same to him."

"He's your father," she said.

"He's no father," I said bitterly. I had friends. I visited their homes. I knew what a father was. I added, "He's no husband either."

"You shouldn't say that."

"I should," I said. "It's time somebody said that. You know I'm right. Ma, why do you stay with him? I don't know how you've stood it all these years."

"What could I have done?" she asked.

"You could have thrown him out," I said. "Or you could have left him, like I say you should do now."

"It's not that easy. I had six children to take care of. Where could I have gone? How could I have lived? Believe me," she added sadly, "I thought of that many times, but I knew it couldn't be done."

"Well, it can be done now," I said. "You don't have six children to worry about anymore."

"I don't think it's any use," she said.

"Why not?"

She was silent for a moment, then: "I gave him a promise."

"What promise?"

"Before we got married he told me all about himself, when they were in Poland, how they'd gone off to England and left him alone by himself. He cried when he told it to me, and I felt so sorry for him, and I promised him he would never be left alone again."

"Oh, that," I said irritably and with contempt. "I've heard that one before. You told us already. After the way he's treated you, you shouldn't feel bound to a promise you made when you hardly knew him and what he was. Besides, remember what Grandpa told us. He said it wasn't true and they wanted to take him but he wouldn't go. That's more likely the truth."

She was silent again for several moments, brooding, with her head bent a little, then she asked, "Where could I go?"

"We can go anywhere we want," I said, and thought eagerly, *If only I could persuade her to do it. Oh, God, how wonderful it would be to get rid of him, to live without him.* "You won't be alone. I'll be with you, and I'll bet any money Rose will go too. If she has to choose between you and him, she'll choose you, no matter how she is toward you. And you'll have Sidney. So what is there to be afraid of? I'll get a job, and you'll be better off than the way you are now with the stinking bit that he gives you every week."

"What about your school?" she said.

"I'll get a job after school. Anyway, I'll be graduating soon, and then I can get a full-time job. I'll bet I can make more money for you than what he gives you."

"What about college?"

"I can put off going to college until I've made enough money to pay for it and leave some for you."

"No!" She said this with such emphasis that the plan I'd just conceived was crushed immediately. "Your uncle Saul said that, and he's still a door-to-door salesman. Joe was going to be a journalist, and he too is selling magazines door-to-door. You're not going to be like them."

I was silenced for a moment, then I said bitterly, "What are you going to do, then, go on letting him treat you like so much garbage? Listen to his shouting and cursing and watch him come home drunk almost every night and throw up in the bathroom and know that what he's spilling into the toilet is paid for with the money that belongs to you? Is that what you're going to do?"

She shook her head slowly several times, brooding all the while. "No, no," she murmured. "It always made me sick."

"Then why do you put up with it?" I wanted to know. "I can understand how it was when we were all kids. But we're not kids any longer and we can help you. Why, why do you have to stay with him?"

But she still had no answer, and perhaps she could no more fully understand it than I did.

She did say something finally: "Let me think about it."

BUT THERE WERE OTHER THINGS for her to think about and to worry over. There was Rose. Suddenly, inexplicably, her habits seemed to have changed. She no longer came home from work, had her dinner in silence, then locked herself in her room. Nor did she bang away on the piano as often as she had before. Now there were days when she did not come home for dinner at all, without telling my mother, so that the dinner was left uneaten and wasted. She came home very late, often after we had all gone to bed. She seemed very busy. But with what? We were puzzled, and I think my mother was a bit alarmed. What could all this mean? Was she going out with somebody? A man? Impossible.

One good thing came out of it for my mother. Now that Rose was away so much it gave her an opportunity to go into Rose's room and clean up the place. From the glimpses she'd been able to have of it in the past she knew it was in a horrible mess, with things lying about on the floor, the room dusty, the curtains long since needing to be washed and ironed.

There might have been an opportunity to go in there and clean it up while Rose was away at work, but she had always kept the door locked even then and had taken the key with her. But now with her new busy life and mysterious absences, she evidently had forgotten to lock the door, so my mother went in one day with a broom and dustpan.

She was appalled at the condition she found it in. Everything seemed turned upside down: dresser drawers half opened and with clothes sticking out, things lying about on the floor everywhere, as if Rose had been in a great hurry.

I was in the kitchen doing my homework when I heard my mother call my name. I ran in. She was in the midst of straightening out the mess and had gathered together a pile of books, pamphlets, and what looked like leaflets of some sort, and she seemed baffled by them. "They were all over the place," she said, "and I don't know what to do with them. She needs a bookcase or something. Since when has she started reading books?"

It was a good question to ask. Yes, indeed, when had she been reading books? I could not remember a time when she had sat with one in her hand. If she'd ever looked at anything, it had been the weekly magazines we had read in England, the *Magnet* or the *Gem*, and it was clear then she had no taste for books.

I looked at them curiously. One was a large, fat book with worn covers and had evidently come from a secondhand bookshop. It was called *Das Kapital* and the author's name was Karl Marx. I knew very little about this kind of book myself, but I had heard vaguely this name being connected with Russia and the revolution there. There were some thinner pamphlets bound in paper covers, the word *revolution* in nearly all the titles. Then I came to a leaflet and I stared at it for a long time, feeling a shock go through me. It announced a talk to be given on the subject "Why I Became a Communist." The talk had been delivered about two weeks earlier at a well-known radical meeting hall on the West Side. It was sponsored by the Communist Party of America and the speaker was Rose Bernstein.

For several moments I was unable to speak. I showed it to my mother, then read it to her, and she was as horrified as I was. Perhaps we should not have been so shocked. My sister Lily had belonged to some radical organization back in England, and so had her husband. But not a Communist. Nothing could be worse than that: a Bolshevik, a Russian revolutionist.

It explained certain things to us, however: her mysterious comings and goings, her change of habits. But how had this come about?

"I don't understand it," my mother said, worried and perplexed. "How could she have got mixed up in such a thing?"

Yes, how was it possible for someone who had once pretended to be a duchess, who had lived in a dream world of being aristocratic, who had refused to work in a dress shop that catered to the lower classes, suddenly to become a member of a party that wanted to do away with the entire upper class?

We would not know the answer to that for a little while longer, but in the meantime my mother had the satisfaction of cleaning up Rose's room. She even did a little decorating, putting a new fancy bedspread over the bed, adding a vase with artificial flowers on the dresser, and straightening out the books that had so puzzled her, and me too.

She gave it a last look of pleasure as she left the room and said, "I hope she'll notice the difference when she comes home tonight. I hope she'll like it."

Rose didn't come home that night, though. This had never happened before. In view of all the strange things that had been surrounding Rose lately, however, it did not frighten my mother so much as when Saul had disappeared. But she did not tell my father for fear he would run to the police station, as he had done that other time. If the police got involved, they might discover that Rose was a Communist, and then what?

To her great relief, however, Rose came home in the evening at dinnertime and seemed much like her old self, giving no greeting, going right to her room and slamming the door shut, then emerging soon afterward to go into the kitchen for her dinner. I had already finished eating and was doing my homework, and cast a look at her as she came in. There seemed to be nothing different about her, the same stiff face that ignored me as well as my mother and Sidney who was playing some game on the floor. The same drab clothes that were out of style a long time ago. Skirts had been growing shorter and shorter, and for most women were up to the knees. Hers were close to the ankles.

She sat down at the table and did what she often did when the chair was a short distance away from the table. Instead of pushing the chair up to the table, she pulled the table up to the chair. She would do that even if other people were sitting at the table, causing much consternation and spilled glasses. This time she was alone at the table.

My mother served the food to her, then dared enquire, "How do you like your room?"

For a moment it seemed as if she was not going to answer at all, then she asked abruptly, "What room?"

"Yours," my mother said, and I was sure she felt nervous talking with Rose, something she rarely attempted, knowing whatever she said would be ignored with silence. "Yours," she repeated. "I cleaned it up for you and made a few changes."

"Who asked you to?" Rose said.

"I thought it needed it and I'd save you the trouble of doing it yourself."

"I hope you like it," Rose said.

"Me?" My mother was surprised. "Why should I like it? It's your room."

"Not anymore," Rose said, starting to eat with her head bent low over the plate, much more like my father than like a duchess.

"What do you mean?" my mother asked, startled.

There was a brief pause as Rose ate. Then, "I'll be leaving the house tomorrow."

This time genuinely shocked, my mother said, "You mean you're not going to live here anymore?"

"That's what I mean."

"Where are you going?"

I had felt the shock too. I was waiting for the reply to this last question. Rose took her time answering. When she did I was not sure I'd heard her correctly. It was spoken in her half-choked, haughty, upper-class English accent. It sounded like "I got married yesterday."

My mother may have had some doubts also that she'd heard correctly. She was too stunned and bewildered to say anything for a moment, then she said, "You got married? Who did you marry?"

"A man."

It was a cryptic answer and did not supply much information, but it would have to do for the time being, for she made it plain that was all the talking she was going to do for one day. As soon as she had finished her meal she retreated to her room once more and shut the door with a bang.

It only served to disturb my mother still further. For the third time she had been cheated out of a wedding for one of her children.

But that was not the uppermost thought in her mind, and I have no doubt she spent a sleepless night thinking of the major concern, which was whether this man was a Jew or not.

She did not have to wait long to find out, for the very next day Rose brought the man home with her to help carry out her things, which she had packed in two of the much-worn suitcases we had brought from England. And the minute he walked through the door you could see the Irish on his long, ruddy face. His name was Jim Morse.

It was the oddest thing about Jim, the way we took to him right away and the way he was accepted into the family, so different from the time my older sister had married the Christian boy across the street when we lived in England. That had been a calamity. Lily was considered dead, in accordance with Jewish law, and we'd sat shiva for seven days.

But with Jim it was an altogether different matter. I don't know if this was because times had changed or because we were in America, where there was so much mixture of all kinds of people. Or was it because of Jim himself and his warm, friendly nature? However, once the introductions were over, made stiffly by Rose—who was on the defensive and prepared for the worst, it was clear to see—we found ourselves chatting with him with perfect ease, laughing with him and liking him.

He was a tall, lanky fellow, not very handsome, but healthy-looking with ruddy cheeks and large, honest gray eyes. His laugh showed big, strong, white teeth, and he laughed often. He seemed comfortable with us, even my father, who was silent most of the time but would have a good deal to say about this later. Jim stretched his long legs out before him, clasped his hands over a lean stomach, and seemed to be enjoying himself among us, while Rose sat silently a short distance away from him, probably nervous and perhaps still fearful of some critical remark one of us might make.

He came from Arkansas and, although he did not seem to want

to talk about it, told us enough to let us know that he was from a
large, poor family there. What his father did for a living we never did
learn, but Jim, the youngest in the family, had broken away from
them only recently and been in Chicago for just a few months. What
he did for a living was something else that he seemed hesitant to talk
about, and this time it was coupled with a warning glance from
Rose.

We did find out later, however, that he was a sandwich man in a
cafeteria. It was not, to be sure, anything to be ashamed of, but neither was it anything to brag about, and it was no wonder that Rose
wanted it to be kept hidden from us. Certainly Jim was a far cry
from the kind of husband she had pictured for herself in the days
when she lived in her imagination in the world of high society.

But these were different days for her. She had been proud of her
job in Madame LaFarge's exclusive dress shop, but that pride began
to wear off after several months of working under a woman who
could never be pleased and who demanded long hours and gave so
little pay that Rose often did not have enough to carry her through
the week for lunches and carfare after giving my mother ten dollars
out of her fifteen-dollar-a-week salary. The pride turned into resentment, then rebellion, and she was ripe for the recruiters of the
then burgeoning Communist Party. It was at one of their meetings
that she met the tall, skinny fellow from Arkansas, Jim, who had
been recruited by the salad man in the cafeteria where he worked.

Jim was ripe for it too, but more for social reasons than anything
else. He was lonely, he knew nobody in Chicago, and he was tired of
going to burlesque shows and movie theaters; when the salad man
suggested he come and meet some nice people and learn something
about the world at the same time, he went readily. He found himself
sitting next to a haughty-looking girl who gave him a sense of inferi-
ority and discouraged the looks he cast at her sideways. Still, during
the intermission they got to know each other, and Jim felt happy
about having come. He was, however, even more awed by the British

accent that she affected strongly at these meetings in order to let them know that she was very different from them.

Rose's feelings toward Jim at this first meeting were somewhat uncertain. The discovery that he was a sandwich man in a cafeteria had given her a bit of a shock. She wasn't at all sure that she wanted to continue with the acquaintance. A sandwich man! Really, now! But the sad truth was that Jim was the only man who had ever paid any attention to her in her whole life. And she was getting on in years. She was edging close to twenty-four. This thought too must have gone through her head, and together with that was the matter of her newfound ideals and the fact that she could no longer believe in class distinctions.

There was something else. The cafeteria where Jim worked was not far from Madame LaFarge's establishment, and Rose could go there for lunch. Jim—making sure first that the boss was not looking—would carve a roast beef sandwich for her so thick that she had difficulty opening her jaws wide enough to bite into it.

And then someone gave Madame LaFarge the leaflet announcing Rose's talk, "Why I Became a Communist"—the chief reason being her exploitation in the exclusive dressmaking shop. Rose was fired that day, and the following day she and Jim got married at city hall, with the salad man and a Communist organizer as witnesses. That was the day she failed to come home.

After my mother had talked with Jim for a while, I think, most of her fears vanished. When she told my father that Jim was "better than nothing," I don't think she meant it in a derogatory sense. I think she liked Jim from the start, and the fact that he was not a Jew didn't seem to bother her much.

There was just one difficult part to overcome that day, and that was when the time came for departure. The two of them stood near the doorway, with Jim holding the two torn suitcases in his hands. We'd had a lot to say before this, but now an awkward silence fell over us.

Quite likely my mother wanted to take Rose in her arms and hold her for a while, as she'd so often wanted to do. But even now the stiffness was there in Rose, and my mother could not breach the distance between them. Mind you, even in that moment the business of the parlor in England could not be forgotten.

My mother must have been choking back her tears. She managed to say, "Well, I hope we'll be seeing you again soon."

"Not very soon," Rose said in her haughty accent, looking away from my mother.

"You can't come any sooner?" my mother asked, with an attempt at humor.

Jim broke in quickly. "Don't worry, Ma"—he was already calling her Ma—"we'll see you again very soon."

I saw Rose give him a dirty look, the kind she often gave my mother or any one of us, and I thought, *Poor Jim*. We did quite often in the future feel sorry for Jim.

They left, and my mother broke down then and went off to be by herself and weep. My father had not said goodbye to them. He was sitting with his back to the door, glowering darkly at the floor. I am sure he was thinking of the money Rose's departure was going to cost him.

Chapter Fourteen

THE MAIN CHICAGO POST OFFICE WAS A GRIM, DARK, HULKING building on Dearborn Street, with a tall flight of steps leading up to the entrance. From the outside it looked like a prison, and for many of those working inside that's what it was, as I would soon find out. On a cold February night, bundled in a heavy overcoat with ear-muffs covering my ears under my cap, I mounted those steps and entered the building to begin my job as a substitute clerk.

A week earlier I had graduated from Lane. A few months before that, I'd taken a civil service exam for the post office, realizing that I'd have to work for a few months to make enough money to start college. My mother and I had argued about this before. She had wanted me to go straight to college, and she still wanted it, but with less vigor than before. The fact was, the loss of Rose's income had made things difficult for her. As she might have expected, my father gave her no more to make it up than the little he had before, and history could have repeated itself, with her waiting and shivering every Saturday to see what he would dole out to her. But it never reached that point. There were just two of us now for her to worry about, Sidney and myself, and I had a job and would soon be earning money that I could give her.

It was to be a night job, and I had prepared beforehand by sleeping late that day. A guard directed me to the superintendent's office. I had to climb two flights of narrow iron stairs to get there. Three other new men were there already, waiting for the superintendent to come in. We all stood silent, eyeing each other covertly out of the corners of our eyes.

One of them was wearing a raccoon coat, and I would learn later that this was Dave, a former student at Northwestern University, who like myself was here temporarily until he'd earned enough money to go back to college. The other two were Joe, a worried-looking fellow with a bad case of acne, and Shorty, a potbellied little man with a swarthy complexion, an Italian whose real name we quickly abandoned to call him by his well-earned nickname.

It wasn't long before a large, burly man swung through the door and into the room calling out a jovial "Good evening, boys."

Yes, he'd called us "boys," and we might have taken offense except that there was a friendliness about him that made up for it. He checked out our names and the letters of acceptance we'd brought with us, and gave us a bit of a pep talk about working for the government and the great future we could find working in the post office. He added a few other things, such as the importance of the job, the service we would be performing for the good of the country, and how we represented the cream of the crop, having passed an exam that hundreds of others had failed. Finally he said, "Now, you boys just follow me. I'll take you on a tour and show you how a post office operates and the part you're going to play in it."

Dave and I exchanged glances and smiled. We had already sized each other up as kindred souls, a cut above the other two and perhaps everyone else in the post office, one a college man already and the other soon to be, both of us tolerating our surroundings through necessity. Dave was about a year older than I, and it would turn out that we had much in common, particularly in our thinking.

The four of us tramped along, with the burly superintendent leading us, and it came as a bit of a surprise to us when he opened a heavy door and led us into the mailing room. We had not been prepared for the din: the whirring of belts overhead, the rattling of metal cans, the voices shouting. We saw rows of men standing in front of stacks of wooden cases that were divided into pigeonholes, each one marked with the name of a state. The men were holding bundles of letters in one hand and with the other hand were thrusting letters into the various pigeonholes, their arms going back and forth swiftly like machines.

Shouting over the din in a voice that grew slightly hoarse, the superintendent announced that this was the mail sorting room, where we would be working most of the time.

Once again Dave and I glanced at each other, but this time without smiling. We were both thinking the same thing: the exam we'd taken to get in here had specified a clerk's job, which meant working at a desk. I had dressed accordingly for it, putting on my brown double-breasted suit, which had served me well over the years, with occasional alterations by my mother to accommodate my growing figure, and which I put on only for special occasions. Dave had done the same thing with his blue serge suit. We both wore starched white shirts and ties that matched the suits. Yet, looking around, we saw rows of men working in their shirtsleeves, a few just in their undershirts. Was this a clerk's job?

I decided to reserve judgment and give myself a little more time. Perhaps I had been mistaken. I paid little attention to the rest of the tour. It was a blur through which I saw vaguely other parts of the post office workrooms, the second-class and third-class rooms, the parcel post room, the weighing machines, the stamp windows. I was too preoccupied battling my disappointment.

Finally the superintendent brought us back to the mail sorting room, with its factory-like atmosphere. "Here you are again, boys," he said. "This is where you'll be every night from now on. It'll soon feel like home. I hope next time I see any one of you it'll be twenty years from now, when you come to my office to apply for your retirement. Good luck."

Then he was off, and a thin, spidery man with a pallid complexion and head cocked to one side, as if he might be seeking something, suddenly appeared with a small notebook and pencil in one hand, and in a squeaky voice began assigning each of us to one of the cases. I discovered later that he was one of the foremen who went around to ensure that all the men kept working. All the foremen carried the same kind of notebook and pencil, and just as was done in the mail order house where my brother had worked, demerits were given to those who broke a rule.

One good thing happened that pleased Dave and myself: We were assigned to side-by-side cases, and we soon got to know each other. Aware of the spidery foreman hovering nearby, we talked out of the corners of our mouths while keeping our eyes on the pigeonholes and tossing mail into them from the piles that had been dumped onto the ledge in front of each of us. The pile never lessened. It was replenished continuously by a man wheeling a wagon loaded with the mail that had been collected from the mailboxes by carriers. There was no end to it. The arms in front of the cases flashed back and forth. It went on and on through the night.

But for Dave and myself there was some relief in our talk. He'd had one year at Northwestern. He lived in Evanston still, not far from the university, in a small furnished flat with a sister, who was also a student at the university and still there. They came from a small town in southern Illinois where their father was a minister. There hadn't been enough money for both of them. Dave had to take time off from college to work in order to finance another year.

I was in the same boat, practically. I told him about myself, how I'd just graduated from Lane Tech, where I'd initially thought about becoming an architect, but now I thought I wanted to be a writer. Talking helped pass the time and break the dull monotony of the work. But without realizing it we had grown careless and forgot to lower our voices, especially when Dave began to tell jokes, of which he had an inexhaustible stock, most of them dirty, and he soon had me convulsed with laughter and the mail tumbled out of my hand.

Suddenly, I felt a tap on the shoulder and a thin, squeaky voice was saying, "What's your name?"

I turned round. It was the spidery foreman. He had his notebook and pencil poised ready for writing. I gave him my name. He wrote it down. He wrote something else. "You get ten demerits," he said, then turned to Dave. "What's your name?"

So Dave and I started our careers in the post office inauspiciously, with ten demerits each.

The shift began at eight. Somewhere around midnight the foremen went round the rows of cases bawling out through cupped hands, "Everybody to lunch!"

There was no time lost. We all dropped our letters onto the ledges, and the rush commenced for the narrow iron stairs. Dave and I kept together. We followed the others down two flights of stairs to the basement and into the din of the cafeteria, with its rattle of crockery and metal trays, chatter of voices, and laughter. A haze of cigarette smoke half covered the scene, and men sat at tables eating or playing cards or simply lounging. Dave and I trailed after the others alongside the steam tables with trays in our hands, selecting our food, and we were able to find an empty table. Joe and Shorty soon joined us.

Shorty was probably the oldest among us, but he was vague about his life. Maybe he'd had so many different kinds of jobs he could no longer remember them. He was certain of one thing: he was going to be rich someday. The post office was only a stopgap for him too. Right now he was working on an invention for a new kind of wine press that would bring him a fortune. He was also writing a play about a girl who went wrong and was driven out of her home by an intolerant father.

Dave and I winked at each other. It was obvious to us that Shorty was a nut. Joe didn't say anything. It was hard to say how he felt about Shorty. Joe was inclined to be silent. He gave us little information about himself or the kind of jobs he'd had. Then one thing came out that astonished us: he was married and had four kids. Four! We let out gasps. He couldn't have been much older than Dave. But Joe was grinning—he'd been holding something back. "You can call it practically five," he said.

"What!" Dave and I yelled it simultaneously. Shorty just sat looking blank.

Joe nodded. He was still grinning. "That's right," he said. "In about another month."

"Holy smothering Moses," Dave said. "Then you'll probably be working in this dump for the rest of your life."

Joe shrugged. It didn't seem to bother him. Then he said, "I've had worse jobs."

"You have?" Dave said, and I shared the incredulity that he felt. "Such as what?" he asked.

Joe didn't answer. He simply shrugged. "Working for the government isn't so bad," he said. "After twenty years you can retire and they give you a good pension."

"Twenty years in this place would drive me up the wall. I'd never make it. They'd be carrying me out in a straitjacket after one year," Dave said.

I agreed with him, absolutely, but there wasn't time to say much more then. We only got half an hour for lunch, then a bell rang and we went back up the narrow iron stairs to the mail sorting room.

Chapter Fifteen

WE WERE SO SURE OF OURSELVES, DAVE AND I, CONFIDENT OF OUR future, as so many people were in those heady times. Prosperity filled the air. People were becoming millionaires in the stock market. There seemed to be no end to it all. Dave and I felt part of it, and we were filled with pity for people such as Joe and Shorty, who'd never get anywhere in life and who'd probably be working in the post office for the rest of their lives. We weren't like them. We were going places.

In the meantime, we had to put up with this grind as the nights of dull, monotonous work went on. It never varied, and the piles of mail dumped on us never lessened. The hours dragged with interminable slowness. We stood in one place hour after hour, with only our arms in motion. One night, though, something else was sprung on us suddenly.

"What's this?" Dave asked, looking at the stack of small white cards fastened with a rubber band that the spidery foreman had tossed onto his ledge. The foreman was carrying a basket filled with them, and he tossed a bundle over my shoulder onto my ledge. I looked at it. There were street names with postal areas on the cards. There were about two hundred of them in the package.

"Yeah, what is it?" I asked.

An older man standing at the other side of Dave said, "That's your scheme."

"What's it for?" Dave asked.

The older man answered, keeping his eyes on the case in front of him, tossing mail into it, speaking out of the corner of his mouth. He was an ex-newspaper man who'd been working here ten years and was quite expert at sideways conversation. His name was Tomlinson.

"It's a present from the postmaster general. You'll soon be getting a letter from him telling you all about it. And it'll tell you that you've got to memorize every single one of those fucking names— or you get kicked out."

He was right. The letter came the following day and informed us that we would be tested on the scheme and if we failed to pass the test the post office would regretfully ask for our resignation. The letter also congratulated us on having entered the postal service. Other new men had received the letter and their little bundle of cards, and most of them lost no time memorizing the names on the cards. It occupied every moment of their spare time. You could see them in the cafeteria, sitting at the tables, turning the cards over and mumbling to themselves. Joe and Shorty were among them, and they shunned our company at the table so that they could be by themselves to study their scheme. I had no doubt that this went on at home and when they were riding on streetcars to and from work.

I made a feeble attempt myself at studying the cards, but gave it up almost immediately. Dave did the same thing. We scoffed at the others. They weren't fit for anything else.

"It's just a lot of shit," Dave stated.

I agreed with him. We were both inclined to quit right then, but we didn't. I loathed the place and the job, and couldn't wait to get out of there at night. The shift varied in the length of time you worked. We were being paid by the hour and it could end late or early, depending on how much mail had been brought in. Often Dave tried to get me to go with him to one of the all-night entertainment spots he knew so well and visited so frequently. He spent his money freely—a good deal of it on clothes, as he was always buying a new tie or some fancy shirt, and much on these nightspots. He knew of a speakeasy not far from the post office that attracted a lot of men from there on payday, since it doubled as a whorehouse. Dave tried hard to get me to go there with him, but I refused. I was afraid of clap and syphilis, and besides, I was saving my money. I knew that I was going to need it, both for college and to give to my mother while I was away.

I always hurried quickly out of the post office when the shift ended, and raced to the corner to catch the Division Street streetcar home. Often I missed it and had to stand there shivering for fifteen minutes until another one came along. Usually, there was a bunch of charwomen waiting for it also, with their buckets and brushes and mops in their hands, dancing from side to side to keep warm and jabbering away in some foreign language, their breath showing in white puffs against the darkness.

At last, at last, the streetcar came lumbering along. I would let the charwomen go in first, and I would follow into the stale but welcome warmth, and would sit near a window and watch the dark streets roll past and the harsh grinding of the streetcar wheels would often lull me to sleep.

I usually got home around three in the morning and immediately went to bed. At first, when I had just started working at the post office, I had difficulty falling asleep, and when I did it was with nightmares of tons of mail flashing before my eyes, and addresses with names like Robinson and Melrose and Teitelbaum and Richards and street numbers and states like Iowa, Nebraska, California, Florida, and letters and more letters, and more states, Washington, Oregon, Ohio . . .

Gradually, however, after I had grown accustomed to working there, these nightmares vanished and I slept soundly, not awakening until it was almost noon. My mother was alone in the house. Sidney was at school and of course my father was at work, and it was pleasant being with her and seeing her smile.

"So how was it?" she would ask.

"Oh, fine," I would say.

I told her nothing about my discontent—the intolerable dullness and monotony of the job, and the scheme that had to be learned. I told her nothing about Dave, either. I didn't want to spoil the pleasure she was having at the way things seemed to have worked out. I was making good money, in her opinion—"enough," she boasted to the relatives, "to get married on." It was her measure of any man's worth. I was getting paid fifty cents an hour, which was considered quite good in those days. It came to about twenty-five dollars a week, which was far more than my brothers or sister had earned, and I gave my mother a good portion of it, enough so that she didn't have to beg my father for more money every week. I still went with her to the bank, where she deposited her two or three dollars proudly into an account that by now had reached a little over fifty dollars.

"I just hope," she said to me once, "that your grandfather lives long enough for me to be able to pay him back."

It was still there on her mind, that consuming desire to give back to my grandfather the money he had spent on our tickets to America. She told me she would never rest until that debt was paid off, no matter how often I repeated to her what my grandfather had said to me: that she owed him nothing, that he in fact owed her.

Then one payday, when I got up in the late morning and gave

her the money that I always gave her and offered to go with her to the bank after I'd had my breakfast, she seemed embarrassed and said, "I don't have to go to the bank."

"What do you mean?" I asked, puzzled.

"I took the money out of the bank," she confessed, and went on to explain. One day recently, on her way to do her shopping, walking to a distant street market in one of the poorer neighborhoods, she had come across a man giving a speech from a small stepladder to a crowd of people gathered around him.

His voice was hoarse from speaking, but it was powerful enough to hold their attention and what he was saying gripped them all with fear. She, too. She listened with a rapidly beating heart. The man was telling them that the present days of so-called prosperity would soon be over. So-called because the wealth was an illusion. It belonged to those who already had money. They simply had more wealth. But for the poor nothing had changed. The poor remained poor. Soon, however, there would be drastic changes brought on, not by revolution but by capitalism itself.

"Capitalism," said this man, "is like some strange beast that devours itself. This so-called wealth of today, which exists mostly on paper and is paper, will disappear overnight as if it had been a mirage. Folks, you will see an America that you have never seen before in all its history. There will be few jobs. Factories, shops, businesses of all kinds will close. Even banks will be closed and the precious money you have saved will be gone with them. People will be hungry. You will see long lines of people waiting for someone to give them bread. . . ."

On and on he went, painting such a dark picture that the listeners shrank with fear, and my mother was one of them. But she had her wits about her. She turned away before he had gone much further and ran to the bank. She withdrew it all and carried the money home, clutching the purse in which it was contained. Then she hid the money under the mattress of her bed.

I listened to her story, appalled. "Ma," I said, "you shouldn't pay any attention to those street-corner speakers. They don't know what they're talking about. The country's never been in such good shape as it is now, so how can everything break down like that man said? He's crazy. The banks will never go broke. Let's go there and put your money back into it."

But she was still under the hypnotic spell of the speaker. She couldn't, she said. She was afraid. And what was wrong with keeping it under the mattress? I shrugged. I gave in to her. Perhaps she was right. There was nothing wrong with it, and if it made her feel better, then fine.

We had no more arguments about the matter, and maybe I was amused more than anything else when I gave her the money each week and saw her go into the bedroom and stuff the dollar or two in with the little bundle under the mattress.

Meanwhile, the good times in the country continued without a sign of any collapse, and if the mail coming into the post office, much of it business mail, was any sign of it, times couldn't have been better—and safer—than now, because the mail seemed to be getting heavier and heavier. This worked to the advantage of Dave and myself, for help was needed more than ever, and when we applied for extensions on our scheme tests they gave them to us readily. Joe and Shorty had already taken theirs and had passed with flying colors, and both seemed more at ease and in jollier moods than they had been before. So were others. Now, having passed their scheme tests, they were in line for becoming permanent staff instead of substitutes, with regular hours and weekly pay with vacations.

But for Dave and me the shadow of uncertainty still hung over us. We didn't care. I was eighteen. Dave was nineteen. We were cocky about the future, about ourselves, and contemptuous of a job that we felt was beneath us and of the people around us who would be sorting mail for the rest of their humdrum lives.

The weather was growing warmer, and the steam heat in the

mailing room was becoming superfluous and made us sweat, and the smell of the sweat was everywhere. Dave and I broke away from the place as soon as the call was sounded for the lunch break, and instead of eating down in the basement cafeteria with what we called the herd, we walked some distance to a chain cafeteria, Pixley and Ehlers, famous for their bowl of soup that was a meal in itself. It was good, though, to get out into the fresh air, to breathe it in, and to be away from the noise and stuffiness and sweat smells of the post office, and especially from the grind.

Dave and I walked rapidly and laughed and joked and talked. As the warmer weather came on, Dave had dispensed with his raccoon coat and was wearing a slicker, a bright yellow raincoat with pictures of half-naked women painted all over it, popular outerwear for college students in those days. I wished I had one too, but I was not a college student yet, and besides, I would not have spent the money. I was saving my money, hoarding every cent I could. I had a bank account and took pleasure in increasing it every week.

I was careful to keep any knowledge of it from my father. It was the same with the little hoard my mother had hidden under the mattress. If he had known of its existence, he would have stopped giving my mother any money at all. As it was, he gave her a bare minimum, aware that I was working and providing her with the bulk of the money for household expenses. Whatever he kept of his pay he spent on his drinking and gambling. It was a lot like the old days. He ate his dinner and left, and his leaving was much the same as it had been before: in such a hurry that he had not fully put his coat on and one sleeve dangled behind as he groped for it while striding to the door. Then the door banged shut. He was gone for the night. Where to? There were no pubs. There was no Jewish gentlemen's club where he could play cards and drink. But he had found new haunts on the West Side. We had learned that from Uncle Saul, who was about the only one of the brothers on speaking terms with him. He had quarreled with the others, but he had soon made friends elsewhere—including in the Romanian restaurant that he frequented most often. There they served liquor in teacups and—Uncle Saul told me this privately when my mother was not with us, saying it with a little wicked grin on his face—they also served women upon request. I did not want to hear any more, and I felt sick. More than ever I wished I could get my mother to leave him.

I made doubly sure that my father would not know of my bank account, keeping the bankbook with me wherever I went, and from time to time I had my mother look under the mattress to make certain her money was still there. But I made one mistake. Uncle Saul was my mentor, my advisor. I trusted him and confided in him. He gave me a lot of advice on how to apply for college and what courses to take. He knew all about such matters, and he thought I should become a lawyer. He himself was going to become one as soon as he found the time. But he was very busy with other things. In the meantime, he wanted me to start studying law as soon as I entered college in the fall. It was good to be able to talk to someone like that, to have someone interested in you. He took the place of a father, so I confided everything to him: how I was saving my money carefully, the bankbook I always kept with me, my mother's money under the mattress. And he patted me on the shoulder and said I was wise for my age and I'd make a damn good lawyer.

My father usually came home from work about the same time I was getting ready to leave for my shift at the post office. We never spoke to each other, didn't even glance at each other. But this time he did glance at me. He did more than that. He halted right in front of me and held out a hand. "Let me have your bankbook," he said.

I could not believe what I was hearing. I stared at him. Nor could my mother. She too was staring.

"Why are you asking him for that?" she said.

"You keep out of this," he answered roughly. He kept his eyes on me. He was drunk. I knew that. I could smell the liquor on him. This was something unusual. He had never before stopped off after work for a drink. He did all his drinking at night after dinner.

The anger was building up inside me, but I kept it in check. "Why should I give you my bankbook?" I asked.

"Because I'm your father, and you're under twenty-one, and you do what I tell you."

"You're no father," I said. "You're just a dirty rotten bum."

Then he swung with his fist. I stepped back in time and put up my own fists. I heard my mother shout at me. Out of the corner of one eye I saw Sidney shrinking back into a corner, frightened. He was about eight years old, still just a child.

I thought, *This is no place for this to happen, with my mother here and Sidney.* But I had very little time to think. He was advancing on me with a murderous look on his face, and I had to defend myself. I clenched my fists and moved a little, like a boxer.

He swung again and missed. No question, he was quite drunk. But this time I did not move back. I had to defend myself or I was going to get hurt. I swung my own fist and caught him a blow on the mouth. It was a good one too. I saw the incredulous look on his face. The last thing in the world he expected was that one of his children, who lived in mortal fear of him, would strike back at him.

I did not give him time to reflect on it. With that single punch, all the rage that had been pent up in me for years broke loose, and I gave vent to a torrent of blows on his face, sending blood streaming from his nose and his lips, blackening his eyes. I hit blindly and I could not stop even though I heard my mother screaming at me to do so, and I could also hear Sidney's whimpering. My father staggered backward and made no further attempt to strike at me, but suddenly broke away and ran, shouting at the top of his voice for the whole house, the whole street to hear, "Look what he's done to me! Look, look, my own son! He's tried to kill me. Call the police! I want the police!"

He ran down the stairs and out into the street yelling it. The entire street came alive: People rushed to the scene, heads popped out of windows, and our Polish landlord came rushing into our house wanting to know what was going on. The police came, and I thought for a while they were going to arrest me.

They didn't. I was lucky. They were sympathetic. My father was drunk. That was enough for them. One of them said, "I had a father like that. I know what it's like."

They decided to take him off, first to the hospital to get his wounds tended. I'd done quite a job on him, they said with some satisfaction. He'd have to be cleaned up and then they'd take him to jail to dry out and answer my charges.

But there weren't going to be any charges. I had decided that even before they left. I knew what had to be done, and I said so to my mother, who was not yet fully recovered from the shock of what had happened. I said, "Ma, we've got to get out of here. You've got to leave him, and now's the time to do it."

She looked at me bewildered. "But how," she asked, "how can we go off just like that? Where would we go to?"

"We'll go to New York," I said. "Joe's there, and he'll help us find a place to live, and you'll never have to see him again."

"But what about your job?" she said.

"Never mind my job. I'll get another in New York."

"But what about college?"

"Ma," I said, "I'll put it off a bit longer. I can always go to college. There's other, more important things to do right now. We've got to get away from him. He'll be back in a day or two and it'll start all over again. I can't stand any more of it. You can't either. We've got to get away from him, and now's our chance. He won't know where we've gone. We'll not tell any of the relatives. We'll just go and disappear."

I saw her still hesitating, and a thought came to me suddenly. If Uncle Saul had told him about my bank account, then he also could have told him about Ma's money under the mattress. "Ma," I said, "is your money still under the mattress?"

"Yes. Why do you ask?"

"When's the last time you looked?"

"Two days ago, when I was changing the bedsheets."

"Go and look again." The more I thought of it the more likely it seemed. His coming home drunk right from work meant he'd had money to stop off somewhere. I started toward the bedroom myself. My mother ran ahead of me. I came in to see her lifting up the end of the mattress at the head and to hear her despairing cry: "It's gone! It's gone!"

Yes, it was gone; my hunch had been right. There was no question that he'd taken it, and in me there was bitterness at Uncle Saul's betrayal. I told her all about my confiding in Uncle Saul, and fury came on her face along with the despair. Now there was no longer any hesitation about leaving. "All right, we'll go," she said. "If he can do this to me, then I can leave him."

We packed that evening, and Sidney helped us willingly. I don't think he felt as strong about my father as I did, but I know that Ma meant everything to him, as she did to me, and leaving suddenly like this to go to New York was fun in addition to everything else. He got his own things together and we got ours. We were only able to take relatively few of our possessions, leaving much behind that we would have liked to take but couldn't.

We filled two suitcases, which I carried, and I think my mother took the brass candlesticks that she had smuggled out of Poland, now wrapping them in newspaper and stuffing them in a shopping bag along with a few other household treasures. I noticed that as we were leaving and about to close the door behind us for the last time she paused and gave a look back at the living room, the parlor, the big ugly piano that she thought was so beautiful, the couch and matching chairs that were paid off, the carpet—the dream that had almost come true. How close she had been to achieving it, and now she was forced to leave it all behind.

I could feel the sadness inside her, and the regret, and the uncertainty at what lay ahead. I felt some of it myself, but mingled with that was a sense of relief and almost joy at the prospect of living without my father and all the misery that he had caused us.

We went down the steps and out into the street. It was dark, and not many people were about. I was glad of that. I didn't want anyone to see us or to know where we were going.

Chapter Sixteen

WE WENT TO NEW YORK BY BUS. IT WAS THE CHEAPEST WAY TO GO, and the buses ran often. In fact, there was one about to leave when we reached the bus station, and we rushed to buy our tickets and check our luggage. There were ample seats in the bus; I sat in one with my mother because I wanted to talk to her, and Sidney had a seat alone behind us.

I knew how my mother was feeling, and I wanted to comfort and reassure her. As soon as the bus started off I put my arm round her and said, "Ma, everything is going to be all right. I've got money in the bank and I'll send for it as soon as we reach New York, and in the meantime I've got a few dollars in my pocket that'll tide us over, and Joe will be there to help us. As soon as we reach a stop I'll send him a telegram to meet us in New York."

"I'm not worried," she said. "I've got a few dollars in my pocket-book too. The only thing that worries me is your job. You'll lose that. It was such a good job, and you were able to save money for college."

"Ma," I said, "it wasn't such a good job." I told her of all the things I had been keeping from her, the dullness, the monotony, having to stand on my feet for hours at a time, and the scheme I had to learn. "I'm not sorry I lost it, Ma," I added. "I don't think I could have stood it much longer anyway. And I think they would have fired me before I quit."

She listened and sighed. "I was always thinking it was such a good job and you liked it."

"No, I didn't," I said. "But that's not the important thing. I'll get another job in New York. There are plenty of jobs. And eventually I'll be able to go to college, too. The important thing is we've got rid of him. It's something you should have done a long time ago."

"I know," she said slowly, brooding a little. "I thought of doing it so many times, but I couldn't. You know why."

"Yes, I know why. We talked about that before. That's all past history. You don't have to worry about taking care of your children anymore. It's time your children took care of you."

"There's only you," she said.

"And Sidney."

"He's only eight."

I gave a glance behind. Sidney was absorbed in a puzzle I had bought for him some time ago and that he had chosen to take along as one of his most treasured objects. "He'll grow up," I said.

"Yes, I know. But in the meantime there's just you." She seemed still to be brooding, thinking of something that troubled her.

"What's wrong with just me?" I asked.

"You might meet some girl and you'll want to get married and have a family of your own."

"Oh, come on, Ma," I protested. "That's a long way off—if it ever happens. You're not worried about that, are you?"

"I'm not worried," she said. "Why shouldn't you meet some nice girl and get married? But it might happen, and I wouldn't want you to feel tied down to me."

I understood now what all the brooding had been about. She had been looking ahead, far ahead, and seeing nothing but uncertainty lying in front of her. All her life it had been that way, from the very day she had been born. With both her parents dying while she was still an infant, with poor relatives haggling over her disposition, not wanting to add to their own already crushing poverty, how else could it have been?

My heart ached for her. I drew her closer to me and said, "Ma, I'm going to make you a promise. No matter what happens, I'll never leave you alone. I'm going to look out for you as long as I live."

She started to cry but stopped herself, trying to smile. "It's good of you to say that," she said. "But I don't want you ever to spoil your life on account of me. Just remember that."

"All right, Ma," I said. "I'll remember it. But right now stop worrying. You've done something that should have been done a long time ago, and we're all going to be happier for it. Oh, what a relief it's going to be to wake up in the morning and find he's no longer in the house. How wonderful it's going to be not to awaken in the middle of the night and hear him coming home drunk, never to have to see that dark, glowering face and hear his snarling voice."

She gave a little laugh and wiped her eyes with a handkerchief at the same time. "I feel that way too. I should have done this a long time ago." Then after a brief pause, she added, "It'll be a big shock to him when he comes home and finds us gone."

Was she, in spite of everything, worrying about that? "Let it," I said. "He's given us plenty of shocks."

She said nothing, and as the bus rolled on and the landscape flashed past us, I wondered if somewhere inside her there wasn't pity for him and a touch of regret about the whole thing.

THE FIRST THING I NOTICED about Joe when he met us at the bus station in New York was that he looked much older than when I had seen him last time. His hair had thinned, so he was partly bald, and there seemed to be a worried look etched on his face, with several deep lines on his forehead.

My mother must have noticed it, too, because as he embraced her and she kissed him, she looked up at him anxiously and asked, "Are you all right, Joe?"

"Yes, I'm all right," he said.

But he wasn't, clearly. We would not find out until later that there was every reason for the changed look in him. Things were not going well with him. He was having trouble making a living. He had tried various things, even working for his wife's father, who had bought a gas station in Brooklyn, and he had suffered badly in the attempt to become an auto mechanic. He was clumsy with tools and he wasn't accustomed to hard physical work. He'd been forced finally to go back to selling magazine subscriptions door-to-door, but it was not the same as it had been in Chicago. Or was it that times had changed and people did not have the money they used to? He did not know, but it was getting harder and harder to sell, and on top of all that Rose was now pregnant, in her sixth month in fact, and soon there'd be a child to take care of.

At the moment they were living with his in-laws in an apartment in the Brownsville section of Brooklyn, and he was going to take us there first before taking us to the room he had rented for us in a nearby apartment that belonged to his wife's aunt.

But there was something else, something behind that worried look on his face that he could not tell us at that first moment. It was not until the two of us were alone and we had gone to get our suitcases from the checkroom that I found out what it was, and it left me stunned. He whispered it to me even though the one he did not want to hear it, my mother, was not there.

"Lily's dead."

I simply stared at him, an eruption of emotions inside me. I could not believe what he had said to me. But it was a cold, hard fact.

He had received a letter from Arthur that morning. We had probably received one too in Chicago. Lily had died suddenly of a heart attack.

It must have been very difficult for Arthur to write those letters.
Joe showed his to me afterward. The pain and grief showed in the
unsteady handwriting, and there were spots here and there where
the ink was blurred. He must have been crying as he wrote it. He
told us something that we knew already, that Lily had had rheumatic
fever as a child and that had weakened her heart. She had been ill for
some time before the fatal attack came, but they had not wanted to
tell us about that, knowing how it would affect my mother. We
would learn later that the Forshaws were taking care of the baby.

"You mustn't tell Ma yet," Joe said.

How could I, even if I had wanted to? What would she have
done? Gone out of her mind? Somehow, I couldn't help thinking
that she would instantly connect it with her having left my father.
Would she think of it as a sort of punishment? God's punishment?

We got the two suitcases, and with Joe carrying one and me carrying the other we went back to where Ma and Sidney were waiting
for us. We took the subway to Brooklyn. It was our first ride in one
of these underground trains, and we sat in a packed car, having been
fortunate to find seats for all of us. It did not, however, take my mind
off what Joe had told me, and I was in a daze the entire time.

I was not in a much better state of mind when we arrived at the
place where Joe now lived with his in-laws, the Alters. I do remember feeling some surprise, similar to the time when we had first
come to my grandmother's flat in Chicago. The Alters were busi-
nesspeople, they owned a gas station, they had to be well-off. The
name Brownsville itself suggested quiet, pleasant, rural surroundings. But the place was one vast city slum, with block after block of
tall, grimy tenements. They lived in one of these tenements, and Joe
led us through a dark, odorous hall and up well-worn stairs to a flat
on the fourth floor, just one floor below the top.

The moment we entered there were smells and noise and seemingly swarms of children of different ages, from a toddler still in diapers up to Rose herself, the oldest in this huge family, with her smiling face and swollen belly. Mrs. Alter was frying lamb chops, and she lifted a harassed face from the stove and came forward to greet us, holding a frying pan in one hand, welcoming us as best she could.

There seemed to be numerous rooms in the place also, and one of them was Joe's and Rose's. He did not offer to take us in there and show it to us, but it had to be small and dark and cramped, and soon there would be another one to occupy it with them. I think my mother was appalled at everything she saw, at knowing this was where her son lived, but she did not give her feelings away and smiled through everything. Watching her, I thought, *Oh, God, I have to tell her, and she will not be smiling then.*

Despite the noise, the crowding, the surroundings, we were glad to accept Mrs. Alter's invitation to stay for dinner. We had not eaten a good meal in the two days it had taken us to come from Chicago, and the lamb chops she was frying smelled good to us, despite the smokiness that came from them and filled the house. I don't know how many sat at the table, but our shoulders touched, so close were we sitting to one another. Mr. Alter had also arrived, together with the two sons who worked with him in the gas station, all three in grease-stained denims, with smudged faces and blackened hands. We had to wait until they had washed and changed into clean clothes, and then the meal began, and by that time we were starved for it.

We left almost as soon as it was over, thanking our host and hostess for their hospitality, they in turn expressing regrets at not being able to put us up. The regret was genuine—they were nice, kindhearted people, and it gave my mother some reassurance as to Joe's welfare. There were many things that left much to be desired, but there was no question that he was being well cared for. And on the whole we were glad that there had not been room to put us up. The noise, the crowding, would have been too much for us. We were very tired.

Joe led us over to where we were to stay, only a block or two from his own building and in a similar kind of tenement, this one with two wide steps leading to the entrance. Then up two flights of dark, worn stairs to a door that was opened by a short, squat woman who resembled Mrs. Alter very closely. She was her sister, a widow who lived alone in a dark, poorly ventilated, narrow flat that had two bedrooms, one in which she slept, the other rented out to us.

Joe left us almost immediately, but in doing so exchanged a look with me that asked if I had told our mother about Lily. I shook my head. I was putting it off until what I considered the proper time, and I did not quite know when that would be, although I knew for certain this was not it. We were all worn out and couldn't wait to get to bed. We had been traveling on the bus for two days and nights and had hardly slept. Our room had two beds, one a single, the other a double, so the arrangement was simple. Ma would sleep in the single, Sidney and I in the double.

We lost no time getting undressed and into bed, and I think all of us must have fallen asleep immediately. I think, too, all of us must have awakened at about the same time. It was around the middle of the night. Half in my sleep still, I had felt the itching. I scratched and tried to go back to sleep, but then I felt the crawling on my body and sat up quickly to find Sidney doing the same thing, scratching himself vigorously and complaining, "There must be bedbugs here."

My mother was awake also and scratching herself. She got out of bed and turned on the light. We looked at our beds and gasped. They were bedbugs, all right, and they were swarming all over the two beds. Sidney and I got out of ours too and we all stood helpless not knowing what to do.

"We can't sleep here," my mother said.

"Shall I wake up the landlady and tell her?" I asked.

She hesitated. "What can she do?" she asked. Bedbugs were no strangers to her. We'd had them in England, but my mother had fought them vigorously, using a candle flame to burn their nests in the springs, finally getting rid of them. But it took time and effort, and here we were in the middle of the night. What, indeed, could the landlady do? And yet there was no one else to turn to. "Go and tell her," she said finally.

I went to the door of the other bedroom and knocked. It took several knocks to rouse her, and she finally opened the door and stood blinking sleepily at me in a bathrobe. I told her.

She seemed surprised. "Bedbugs?" she said. "I never had bedbugs in my house. What bedbugs are you talking about?"

"Come and see," I said.

She followed me to our room and looked at the bugs crawling about on both beds. She was shaking her head. "I never had them before," she repeated. "You must have brought them with you."

My mother became angry. "In my house in Chicago there were no bedbugs," she said.

The woman became angry too. "So go back to Chicago," she said. "And take the bedbugs with you, because they're not mine." Then, without further argument, she shuffled off in her slippers to her bedroom and slammed the door shut after her.

Certainly, she had none of the goodness and hospitality of her sister. But what could we do? Go back to bed and try to sleep? We shuddered at the idea. What else was there to do? Go back to the Alters' apartment and wake up Joe and tell him? But what could he do in the middle of the night? Only one thing seemed certain: we had to get out of there before our own luggage became contaminated.

We packed up. I grabbed the suitcases and we left. We went down the stairs and out into the street. It was still dark. The sky was clear and stars showed. It had been a warm day, but the air was cool now, and we shivered a little as we stood there uncertainly, not knowing how to proceed further.

My mother decided. "We'll wait here," she said, "until it's morning and then we'll go to see Joe. There's no use waking him up now. He couldn't do anything. We'll just have to wait."

It seemed the wisest course. We sat on the stone step and huddled close together for warmth. Sidney and my mother soon began to nod and then were asleep with their heads on my shoulders at either side of me. I remained awake, troubled. What had I done? I'd pulled her away from a good home that was as close to her dream as she would ever get and brought her into this misery more because of my hatred for my father than anything else. I'd had no right to do it. And Sidney too—he would have to start all over again in a new school, make new friends, get adjusted to new surroundings.

And on top of all that I had to tell her that her daughter had died, and that alone was enough to destroy her. She would have to go through sitting shiva, the Jewish ritual of mourning for the dead. It would be the second time for the same daughter.

I remembered the first time vividly, all of us sitting in our stocking feet in the darkened room saying prayers for the dead. And I remembered how Lily had come bursting in, protesting that she was not dead but very much alive, and how my mother had pretended she did not hear her. I remembered all that, and wondered how she could go through the ritual again, this time with Lily not here to protest. If at least she had remained in the comfortable surroundings of her home in Chicago it would have been more bearable for her.

So I sat there all through the night with their heads on my shoulders, shivering in the cold and dreading the morning that would soon come.

It came with a gradual fading of the darkness, the stars disappearing as pale light spread across the sky. The street began to awaken slowly, with a few people coming out of houses, a few cars starting up their motors, a truck going by and lights appearing in windows. Once the door behind us opened and a man came out. He made a grumbling noise at the obstruction we formed sitting on the step, and my mother and Sidney awakened and we all three stood up to let him pass.

We remained standing there, shivering, afraid the door would open again to let somebody else out, and we looked at one another, wondering what we were going to do, since it was still too early to go and see Joe. In my desperation I thought we should go anyway, even if we had to wake him up, and I was about to say that when a car drew up suddenly at the curb in front of us. We looked at it, not thinking it had anything to do with us. The driver, a young man, got out and came toward us, and even though the early morning light was still dim, my mother recognized him immediately and let out a cry that was a mixture of surprise and joy: "It's Saul!"

Chapter Seventeen

BROWNSVILLE, BROOKLYN, IN THOSE DAYS WAS A HUGE GHETTO composed largely of Jewish immigrants who had fled the anti-Semitism of Poland and Russia and other parts of Europe to find refuge in America. It had once been farmland, but with the extension of the subway to that distant region development quickly took place to accommodate the influx of immigrants, and block after block of big, ugly tenements went up and were soon packed with families.

Pitkin Avenue was the main thoroughfare that ran through the area, swarming with people at all hours and brilliantly lit at night. Its stores, many of them displaying kosher signs, were constantly busy; its theaters, with glittering marquees offering movies, vaudeville, and Yiddish plays, added still more to the crowds. There were shuls, big ornate ones and small, cramped ones, everywhere. And it was toward one of these Saul was heading that morning when he accidentally stumbled on us.

He saw us from a distance, he told me later, the three of us huddled there on the steps, and could not believe his eyes. He thought
for a minute he was back in the hot desert out West where he had
once trekked in his wanderings, seeing a mirage, as had actually
happened to him. But as he drew closer it became real, and then he
stopped and jumped out.

How long had it been since we had seen him last? We too might
have thought we were seeing a mirage. It had been years since he had
run away from home, and this was the last place on earth we might
have expected to see him again.

So much had happened to Saul since that day when he walked
away from his job at Sears, Roebuck and Co. and slipped into a boxcar at the freight yard. He had traveled all over the United States, in
boxcars, hitching rides on highways, walking. He had seen the beautiful Rocky Mountains, which had first caught his attention on a
postcard when he was working in the mail order house. He had
feasted his eyes on them for days and could hardly tear himself away
from their beauty. He had met hunters and had learned to eat the
animals they killed—deer, elk, rabbit—despite the fact that they
weren't kosher and forbidden by Jewish law. But he would have
starved if he hadn't eaten them. He drew the line at wild boar, however. He could not bring himself to eat pig. Not even when he was in
jail.

I was shocked when I heard that he had been arrested once for
vagrancy. It was in a small Virginia town, when he had come back
east. He was sentenced to two months in jail, but it was a strange
sort of incarceration. He was the only prisoner there, and he was
well treated by the chief constable and his wife. They liked him and
he liked them, and he was almost sorry when the time came for him
to leave.

Gradually, he made his way to New York. He had thought of
coming home to us in Chicago, but had decided that he would
rather make something of himself first. Through all those three

years of tramping about he had lost none of his religious beliefs, and he still wanted to become a rabbi. But he was now twenty years old and it was late for him to start the studying that was required. Besides, a seminary cost money that he did not have.

He found that out when he arrived in New York. He had gone immediately to the Jewish quarter on the East Side and made enquiries at a seminary there. They must have felt sorry for him. They saw a skinny, not too well nourished young man, wearing a tallith and a yarmulke, obviously an Orthodox Jew, who wanted to become a rabbi. It was a highly commendable ambition, but one they could not assist. He was poor and homeless, and he had little education, judging from what he told them about his background. In England he'd attended a Christian school called St. Peter's, and he'd gone there as far as the seventh grade. It was no recommendation, but they'd have been willing to overlook that if he'd had money at least to pay for seminary costs. But he had nothing. He was penniless. His family, he said, was in Chicago, but he hadn't seen them in two years. What had he been doing during that time? He was vague about that; he didn't seem to want to talk about it.

So they sent him away. But they didn't forget him. One of the people who had interviewed him, a woman who was active in synagogue affairs, thought about him constantly, and one day she heard of an opening for a young man of strict Orthodox upbringing in the Union of Orthodox Rabbis. It was just perfect for him. If he couldn't be a rabbi himself, he would be among them—the next best thing.

He had left her the address of the place where he was living, a cheap hotel in the Bowery where you rented a bed, not a room, the bed costing fifty cents a night. Fortunately, he had been able to find a job as a stock boy at Gimbels department store. It was a dull, poorly paid job, much like the one he'd had at Sears, Roebuck, so when the offer of a job with rabbis came, he jumped at it. He was elated. No job could have suited him better.

The office of the Union was located then in Brownsville, and he

moved to Brooklyn immediately, finding a room in the apartment
of a Jewish family. He liked his job more and more each day, and
they liked him. A good deal of it was clerical work, but it also involved soliciting funds to help build up the organization, and he was
especially good at that. He joined one of the small shuls that prolif-
erated around Pitkin Avenue, and he was quite content and beginning to think of getting in touch with us in Chicago and perhaps
even going there to visit us.

He knew nothing of Joe's presence in New York, even though
they lived only a few blocks away from each other and must have
passed each other in the crowds on Pitkin Avenue often without
noticing. Then there came that morning. Part of his job was driving
visiting rabbis to various places in the city. He had been taught to
drive the organization's beat-up old car, and that morning, after services at shul were over, he was to meet a rabbi from Cleveland at
Grand Central Station and drive him to Brownsville. It was while he
was on his way to the little shul for early morning services that he
saw us.

There was something fantastic about it. I remember thinking I
must still be asleep and this was all a dream. I heard my mother dis-
tinctly cry out his name. The shock must have been great for her.
She ran toward him, and he met her halfway to the steps and they
embraced. When he broke away from her he went up to me and then
to Sidney and took hold of our hands. He seemed bewildered himself. He kept looking from one to the other of us, as if he could not
believe our presence. Then he said, "I don't understand. What are
you all doing here?"

Well, there was a lot to tell him. I blurted out as much of it as I
could. My mother added some, Sidney chimed in with a little more,
and eventually, still standing there on the sidewalk in front of the
house, we were able to fill him in with everything that had happened. And I had been able to take him aside and whisper to him the
news of Lily's death. He had listened attentively to all the other
things without much expression on his pale, ascetic face, and it was

hard to judge if he thought we had done the right thing in leaving my father. But this about Lily clearly shocked him, and then there was something else flashing across him, and I knew what it was: the realization that we were late for sitting shiva, which was supposed to begin the day after the death, immediately following the burial.

He swung into action immediately, and there couldn't have been a better person to help us. He knew all the social workers, the Jewish benevolent associations, the people whose business it was to help those in need.

It did not take him long to find us a place to live, an apartment on the top floor of a two-family house on a quiet street, to assemble enough furniture to make the place habitable, and to stock a refrigerator with food.

Nor could there have been a better person to break the news of Lily's death to our mother. It was a blow to her, a terrible blow that halted everything else with her grief. But Saul managed to soothe her and to guide her mind toward the ancient ritual of mourning for her dead daughter.

Last night, when we were sitting huddled together on the step, it had occurred to me that I was no longer the young boy I had been the first time we sat shiva for Lily, and my feelings about religion had changed: I no longer believed in all this or its meaning and would not want to go through the ritual a second time.

But I did, for the sake of my mother. It was enough for her to have to bear with the loss of a daughter whom she had adored without having this thrust at her too. I would conform, but just this once, I told myself, and never again. Yet there were limits even now.

Saul had sent for Joe to join us and had arranged for several members of his congregation to sit with us. And now, he told me privately, taking me aside and keeping his voice low, he would send for Rose. Not Jim. He did not want Jim here. Jim was Christian. Rose would have to come by herself. Then he shocked me, saying he would also send for our father.

"No," I said, and I spoke loudly enough for everybody to hear, and he looked around quickly and shushed me. I lowered my voice, but I spoke fiercely: "Not that bastard. We're done with him. That's why we're here instead of in Chicago."

"I must," Saul said quietly.

"Why must you?" I demanded. "What law says you must?"

"The highest law," he replied.

"Just what does that mean?" I asked.

"It means the Ten Commandments. I believe in them, and one of them says 'Honor thy father and thy mother.' I must honor him, no matter what he's done. He belongs here to sit shiva for his daughter."

"Well, I can tell you this," I said, "Ten Commandments or no commandments, if you bring him here, then I'm not going to be here."

He was shocked. "You have to," he said.

"No, I don't have to." I was furious, and I said what I hadn't intended to say, no more to him than to my mother. "I don't believe in this anyway and I'm only doing it for Ma's sake, because I don't want to hurt her feelings. But if he comes I won't stay, and I don't care whose feelings I hurt."

Saul was silent for a while, then he said, "All right, I'll just send for Rose."

"You can save yourself the trouble," I told him. "Rose won't come."

"Why not?"

"Because she's a Communist and Communists don't believe in religion."

"Is that what you are?"

"No," I said, "I'm not a Communist, but I don't believe in religion."

He said nothing more. He swung round, his face tight, and he did not speak to me again for some time.

Rose did come, and although Jim had traveled with her to New

York, he did not come to the house to sit shiva. Rose sat with us and held the prayer book in her hand but did not read any of the words.

My father did not come. I don't know if Saul had sent for him, but even if he had, my father could not have come. He was sitting in a jail and was being held for trial on charges of being drunk and disorderly and assaulting a police officer.

But someone else came whom we had never met before. In all the excitement of our strange meeting with Saul and the rush to get us settled in new quarters, the sad news that had to be broken to my mother, and then the ritual of the mourning that followed, Saul had forgotten to tell us of the important development that had taken place in his life. Or had he really forgotten? I have never been sure about that. I think perhaps there was a certain reluctance on his part to tell us, a touch of embarrassment that he would be fighting against for the rest of his life. You see, Saul was married.

Saul had never been at ease with girls. He had never gone out with one. He did not know how to talk to them, and he always hung his head when he was in the presence of one. He was still like that when he got through with his wanderings and settled in New York to live and work, and it was during the time he worked as a stock boy at Gimbels that he met Estelle and fell madly in love with her, but from a distance and without even having spoken to her.

She was a salesgirl in the bargain basement and very different from the kind of girl you'd have expected Saul to be attracted to, much less fall head over heels in love with. At least she was Jewish— that part was all right, a saving grace in my mother's eyes when she got to meet her after the mourning period was over, but it was the only favorable thing my mother saw in her. The rest she viewed with skepticism, as we all did.

To begin with, she was about ten years older than Saul. And then she chewed gum constantly, and she wore high heels and very short skirts, and her long face was smothered in cosmetics—rouge, powder, thick red lipstick, mascara—and she wore tight dresses that showed her large, pointed breasts. Her voice was high-pitched and came out in shrieks. What was all the more remarkable, considering the suitor, was that she knew nothing about religion or keeping a kosher home. She came from a broken family. Her mother had run off with another man, leaving Estelle and her two brothers to be raised by their father.

After her first visit to us, when they had left, my mother summed her up with just one word: "Trash." She was bitter and sad. This coming on top of what she had just gone through was too harsh a blow. "Saul was either blind or mad," she said.

All her children's marriages thus far had been disappointments to her. Even Joe's marriage, after seeing the crowded hovel in which he lived and the difficulties he faced with a coming child, had hurt her badly. But Saul's was the worst.

I think Saul knew how we felt about his wife. But it didn't alter his own feelings. The hardest obstacle had been approaching her the first time and asking her for a date. It had been agony for him, and Estelle had gaped at him in astonishment, seeing this very, very Jewish fellow with the yarmulke on his head and tzitzit fringes sticking out of his trousers, stammering out what she had wished other men would say to her but least expecting it from him.

She'd laughed. She herself told us that, on one of their visits, showing no consideration for Saul, who was sitting next to her on the sofa, looking embarrassed. She told us how he'd barely gotten the words out and how it seemed so funny to her. She said no at first. But then she thought it over. She was getting on for thirty. No men were tearing down the door to get to her. She was spending boring nights with her father, and occasionally she went to visit her mother and her mother's fat little paramour.

So she changed her mind about Saul and let him take her to a movie and afterward into the hallway of her apartment house, where she let him kiss her and squeeze her pointed breasts, and was amused at his breathlessness. As soon as he got his job with the

Union of Orthodox Rabbis, at a much better salary than at Gimbels, they were married in a simple little ceremony at her house by a rabbi from Saul's congregation.

My mother had known nothing of this until now, and perhaps she wished she hadn't known even then, because it was quite clearly not a happy marriage, with Saul constantly battling to turn Estelle into an Orthodox Jewish wife and Estelle resisting, and the two of them fighting and arguing over it. Once, Saul came to us with his face scratched and bleeding, his shirt torn. Her mother had arrived to side with her in the argument they were having over her refusal to buy meat from a kosher butcher, and the two of them had attacked him with their nails and driven him out of the house.

He went back. Despite my mother's attempts to keep him from returning to her he went back to fight and argue again, and in the end, after their son had been born, he won the battle and she became an obedient Jewish housewife, attending the synagogue with him, maintaining a kosher home and doing all the right things, except that when she spoke of him she couldn't stop laughing.

Chapter Eighteen

Sixth Avenue in 1930 could well have served as an economic barometer of the times. From as far uptown as Fiftieth Street all the way down to Twenty-third Street, the ancient red-brick buildings that were stained black with soot housed nothing but employment agencies. They stood side by side in block after block, and in front of each one there were boards with crudely lettered signs on sheets of white paper advertising jobs, and in front of each one there were knots of men and women with anxious faces pressing forward to read these signs.

The El structure in those days ran overhead, darkening the street, and El trains rumbled by constantly, showering dust on the heads of the job seekers. It went unnoticed by them, for their attention was riveted on the signs, and sometimes they fought for better vision, shouldering other people out of the way, or if it was some luckless short person standing on tiptoe to see past the heads of the luckier, taller people in front of him or her.

In good times the knots of job seekers gathered in front of these agencies were relatively small, but in bad times they were large and the jobs posted grew infinitely less desirable. The vacancies were mostly for porters, dishwashers, busboys, janitors, laborers, menial jobs with low pay, yet the crowds grew and in the summer of 1930, about a year after we had come to New York, they were so thick that they blocked passage along the street and passersby had to step off the curb to get past.

It was hot, and the faces of the people studying the jobs posted on the boards were perspiring, and sweat trickling into their eyes blurred their vision. The El trains overhead ground and screeched incessantly, and the dust showered down on heads. I was in those knots of people and because I could read quickly, I was able to move from one to the other faster than most of them. I was expert at this. I had been doing it for over a year.

On each corner, at the end of a block, there were men with little pushcarts, some improvised from baby carriages, selling apples. They had once worn white collars and shirts and well-pressed suits to jobs in offices. An apple made a good enough lunch, and I bought one for five cents, a big, shiny red one, and I ate it as I went slowly along the street, pausing to read, while the sun beat down on my head and perspiration rolled down my back along the prickly dust showered down from above.

The Great Depression was in full swing. Everything my mother heard that man say in Chicago had come true. Millions were unemployed. Banks had closed, taking with them the life savings of many people. My own savings had been transferred in time to a bank in Brooklyn that remained solvent, and we had been living off them for the past year. They were almost gone now. I'd have to get a job of some sort and Sixth Avenue was the only place to find it.

So I had joined the legion of job seekers and went there daily, starting at Twenty-third Street and working my way gradually uptown, my neck growing stiff from arching forward over the heads of others to see the signs, my eyes watering with the perspiration that gathered as the sun's heat increased. And as I went along I wished so often that I had my job back in the post office and wished, too, that I had not been so cocky and superior about my future and so contemptuous of working there.

I am sure I was not the only one with similar regrets about the past. I met people as I was job hunting—you stopped and smiled and talked. There was a man with five college degrees, a heavy, middle-aged man with a paunch, wearing a tweed suit that must have added considerably to the heat he was feeling and evidenced by the sweat on his tired face. He had been a college professor. He had taught ancient Greek philosophy. We strolled along together for a while, talking. I was shocked when I heard what he'd been, and I began to wonder if I had lost much by not having gone to college.

There was also the chemical engineer. He was a few years older than I and married, with five children, another college graduate, and he was in a worse fix than I was. There were others like these two now looking for jobs on Sixth Avenue, willing to take anything, even a porter's job if they could get it.

Well, they couldn't. I couldn't either. I had tried it. I had gone up the stairs to the office and asked for a job washing dishes in a restaurant. The man seated behind a desk with a cigarette in his mouth looked at me skeptically and said, "Let me see your hands."

I stretched them out toward him, and he looked and shook his head. "You're no dishwasher," he said.

It was the same with all of them. Hands were the giveaway. If they were soft and white, you were not qualified for any kind of menial job, and there was no use lying.

So what kind of a job was there for the men who used to be professors, chemical engineers, architects, or even post office clerks? I was getting desperate. My little money was almost gone. Joe and Saul could not help us. They were barely making enough for themselves. Rose and Jim had gone back to Chicago. They couldn't do anything for us. Sidney was not even in high school yet. He had earned a little money after school selling ice cream in the parks, trundling a wagon and finding that most of his ice cream melted in the heat before he could sell it.

What were we to do? What was anybody to do? But there was little comfort in knowing that others were in the same boat. It was every man for himself, as I found out one day when my eye was caught by a sign that said Clerk Wanted. Clerk! My heart skipped several beats. Unfortunately, I was at the back of the crowd gathered before this agency. But that didn't stop me. I pushed. So did several others. We all scrambled for the stairs. They were dirty, well-worn stairs, dented in the middle from legions of feet tramping up and down. They were littered with cigarette butts and dead matches. I raced up them, elbowing aside those who got in my way. I burst into an office that was so crowded it didn't seem as if there was enough room for another person. A thick cloud of cigarette smoke hung over the mob.

And yet, frantic, I managed to bludgeon my way through to where there was a railing separating everyone else from a fat, unshaven man in shirtsleeves sitting at a desk. He was smoking a cigarette and surveying the mob in front of him calmly. There was a clamor of voices all asking for the clerk's job. Mine, too. He didn't seem to hear them. His eyes roved, then they fell on me and my heart jumped.

He pointed a finger. "You," he said.

It was me all right. Delighted, pushing others aside, I went through the gate to the desk. There was a chair.

"You a clerk?" he asked.

"Yes, sir," I said.

"Where'd you do your clerking?"

"The Chicago post office."

"The what post office?"

"The Chicago post office. In Chicago."

"You mean you was in Chicago?"

"Yes, sir."

"Whatcha do there?"

"I worked in the post office. I was a clerk there."

"Oh, yeah? Well, I got a job being clerk. It pays twenty a week. You wannit?"

"Yes, sir," I said.

He scribbled something on a slip of paper, asked my name and wrote that on it too, then handed it to me. Breathless, triumphant with my luck, I hurried out, pushing my way past disappointed faces and ugly looks from other applicants. The address that was on the slip of paper he had given me was not far away, on West Fifty-second Street, an old building with a creaky elevator operated by an elderly man who wheezed and coughed along with the sound the elevator made as it crawled up to the tenth floor. I walked along a narrow corridor, checking numbers on doors for 1012. I came to it at last, and the name on the door was West Side Garage Owners Association. It sounded big and impressive, and my nervousness grew. I didn't have the job yet; they might not want me.

I turned the knob and went in. There was nothing big and impressive about it. There was just an office, most of it empty. There was no receptionist or anything like that, only a desk at the far end of the room and a man sitting there. On the wall behind him were two dirty windows that let in little light. He wore a suit with a tie that didn't match the color of the suit and was poorly knotted, and he was smoking a cigar and typing.

He looked round at me and said, "What d'ya want?"

"The agency sent me," I said, showing the slip of paper the agency man had given me.

At first he didn't seem to remember, and my heart sank. Maybe it was too good to be true after all. But then he shifted the cigar from one side of his mouth to the other and said, "Oh, yeah, come on over here."

I walked across the room to him and handed him the slip of

paper. He scarcely glanced at it before he threw it on the desk in front of him.

"What kind of work you do?" he asked.

I told him about the post office. There wasn't much to tell, but he seemed satisfied and nodded a few times, then asked a peculiar question: "You a regular sleeper?"

I was puzzled. "Sir," I said, "I don't know what you mean."

"You don't have to call me sir," he said. "I'm Jeffrey, Jeffrey Sugarman. You can call me Jeff. What I'm trying to get at is this. Do you go to bed about the same time every night and get up at the same time in the morning?"

"Just about," I said, still puzzled.

"Would it bother you if you had to break that up? I mean, if you had to go to bed later and get up later, break things up so that you sometimes might have to sleep part of the time days and part nights?"

"No," I said, willing to say or do anything to get the job.

He nodded and shifted the cigar again, once more seeming satisfied. "You see," he said, "I've got a job that calls for doing that. What I mean is, you might have to work four hours days and four nights, or three hours days and five nights. And no telling what it's gonna be. I tell you and you just do it. No complaints. No nothing."

"Sure," I said.

"OK," he said. "I think you might be the right man for the job. When can you start?"

Elated, I said, "Right now, if you want."

"I want," he said. "I think you've got the right spirit. We're going to get along, you and me, Harry. How old did you say you are?"

"Twenty."

"You live with your parents?"

"With my mother."

"No father?"

"No."

"Too bad. What happened? He die?"

I hesitated, then said, "Yes."

"And you're the breadwinner." He shook his head. "It's tough. Well, you'll be all right here. I pay eighteen dollars a week."

"The agency said twenty."

"The sonofabitch lied to you. Eighteen's all I can do."

"That's all right," I said, disappointed but still glad that I had the job.

"OK," he said, "then let's get to work. Here's what I want you to do."

Coming home that day, I had the pleasure of giving my mother the joyful news that I had a job. But it was a bit difficult telling her that I would have to get up at two o'clock that night, take the subway back into New York, go to a garage located on West Forty-ninth Street, and jot down the license plate numbers of every car going in and out of the garage. I was to do that for two hours, then go to another garage nearby and do the same thing. Then I would go home, get some sleep, and go back to New York about two in the afternoon and repeat the same process for four hours. I would stop off at the office on my way home and leave my lists of numbers there with Jeff, who was the only one I ever saw in that office.

Such was the nature of my work, a puzzle to my mother and to me. To this day, I have not been able to figure out the purpose of what I was doing, though I suspect that it was part of some underhanded scheme for getting automobile owners to patronize garages that belonged to the association. Whatever it was, I know that my presence outside the various garages jotting down license plate numbers did not go unnoticed by the garage owners or their managers and employees, and seeing the dark looks they cast at me and hearing the mutterings going on among them, I became conscious of a sense of danger and grew worried for my safety.

I told Jeff about it, and he laughed, waved the cigar in his hand back and forth a few times, and said, "You got nothing to be scared of. You're doing nothing wrong. You ever heard of a law says you can't write a license plate number down? There ain't no such law, so stop worrying. Nobody's gonna hurt you, and if they do, we'll sue the pants off of 'em."

I was only partly reassured, and for another month or so I continued with the job, but in a sort of haze caused by the odd hours and lack of sleep, together with the fear that haunted me constantly. Under normal circumstances I would have quit the job long ago, but these were times when any kind of job was a precious thing to have, and it was all that stood between us and the dreaded prospect of having to go on home relief, the fancy name given to welfare that so many people were on.

"I'll never do that," my mother had said when we talked about it once. "I'd rather starve."

"You won't starve," I assured her. I felt pretty much the same way she did about going on home relief.

It seemed impossible then that I could not find some sort of job, and indeed, I had gotten one, albeit after weeks of searching on Sixth Avenue. I could not forget either that I had been singled out from perhaps a dozen others who had rushed up those stairs when the magic word *clerk* was posted among the job lists. I'd been picked out of all the others, and that could have been another source of satisfaction if not for what took place one hot summer night while I was busy jotting down the license plate number of a big black Packard that had just rolled into the garage I had been watching.

Suddenly, without warning, the pencil and pad were snatched out of my hands. Four men had surrounded me and clutched me by the arms and the collar. The one who had grabbed the pad and pencil was scanning the lists of numbers I had written down, and another was saying, "What the hell you doing?"

I was frozen with fear. The nightmare I had always been afraid of had come true. "I'm writing down license plate numbers like I was told to do," I said.

"Who told you?"

"Jeff."

"Sugarman?"

"Yes."

"What he tell you to do?"

"Write down the license plate numbers of every car that comes in or out."

"Well, you wrote your last one, and here's something to remember it with." He smashed a fist into my nose. Blood streamed out, and I gave a yell. But that was only the start. Now the other three men pitched in with fists, punching hard at every part of my body. When I doubled up and finally fell to the ground, they continued kicking with their feet until I lost consciousness.

I woke up in the hospital. They told me afterward that I had been found in the doorway of an abandoned warehouse on Tenth Avenue. A passing motorist had seen me and notified the police. An ambulance had taken me to the City Hospital on what was then called Welfare Island. A detective tried talking to me, asking if I knew who'd beaten me, but I was in no shape to answer his questions.

They'd done quite a job on me: broken nose, broken jaw, one eye almost knocked out, broken ribs, and a leg fractured from their kicking. I was in the hospital for several months, in a ward that had about twenty-five beds all close to one another. My neighbors on either side of me changed constantly, so I never got to know any of them. But I was in too much pain for socializing anyway, and I used that as an excuse for not wanting to talk when the same detective came again. I'd had time to think back on what had happened and to realize that I had been caught in some kind of gang warfare over control of garages, and the best thing for me was to keep out of it and to say as little as possible.

The police left me alone after a while. I mended slowly. I was able to talk to my mother and Sidney when they came to visit me.

My mother had suffered a terrible shock when the police first notified her I was in the hospital. She had rushed down with Sidney, but
I could not speak to her then. Afterward, as I began to recover, I told
her everything, and she cried and said I could have been killed.

Well, I could have been. I thought of that later, when I was
alone. I thought of a great many things lying there, listening to the
groans of the other patients around me, the cries of pain, the shouts
for a nurse or orderly. This was the accident ward. There were all
sorts of accident cases thrown together in the ward, some not so ac-
cidental—beatings like mine, shootings that were intended murder,
stabbings resulting from fights. Quite a few were homeless men who
had been picked up in gutters or doorways after being struck by hit-
and-run automobiles. These last were a problem to the doctors and
nurses. Not having anywhere to go, they clung to the hospital long
after their injuries had healed, putting on such a good act of pretending to be lame or still in such pain that they confused the doctors and nurses. The result was that the ward was perpetually
overcrowded.

Every so often the staff held what was called a roundup. Without any warning, patients would be yanked out of their beds and
one by one marched before a panel of doctors, whose sharp eyes fer-
reted out the fake limps and groans and sent those men back onto
the street—perhaps soon to be hit again by some speeding auto and
returned to the hospital.

I often watched these roundups with a great deal of amusement,
betting with my other legitimate bed neighbors which ones would
be caught. I did not know then that the day would come when I
would be one of them.

In the meantime, after a month or two in bed, my greatest desire was to get out of there and go home. I was bored with my surroundings, and I worried a great deal how my mother and Sidney
were getting along without me. I was sure that by now the money I
had hoarded in Chicago had been exhausted. How then were they

getting along? I did not dare ask. I knew that Sidney was still in the ice-cream business, with greater skill than before, having learned how to protect his stock against melting. But what he earned could not possibly pay all the household expenses. What then?

I lay there worrying and wanting to go home, wanting to pitch in and do what I could to make some money. I had a lot of gloomy thoughts then. I was seeing a side of life that I had never known existed. The homeless men were only part of it. There were others around me who, like the men I had met on Sixth Avenue, had known better days and were suffering severe economic problems. Their stay in the hospital from whatever accident had brought them there only added to the suffering. They were all worrying about the same thing I was.

It was then that I began writing the short stories and sketches that were later published in the "little magazines" of that day—*The Anvil, Story, Literary America, The Hub, Manuscript,* and many others that came and went and whose contents portrayed the Depression years with grim, harsh realism—and with a truthfulness that the bigger commercial magazines did not possess.

There was a lot of good in this for me. I had at least discovered what I wanted to write and was capable of writing, and it pointed an arrow for me in the direction I wanted to go. But I was a long way yet from becoming a writer. I knew that and did not deceive myself. There was still the problem of making a living, and how that was to be done I hadn't the faintest idea. So I lay brooding a great deal of the time and worrying about the future.

Then Sidney came alone one day without my mother, bringing the fried fish cakes she had made for me and knew that I liked so well. I was glad to see him. There was a closeness between us that did not exist with my other two brothers. I had been his caregiver when he was an infant and young child, taking much of the burden off my mother's tired hands. I'd taken him for long walks in the parks, and I guess in a way I'd played father to him.

"Where's Ma today?" I asked him.

"She's busy with things in the house," he said, then added, "He keeps her busy, you know."

I was puzzled. "Who keeps her busy?" I asked.

And then he blurted out something he was not supposed to tell me. My mother had exacted a promise from him, but Sidney could not have kept any secrets from me. "He's back," he said.

I was still puzzled. "Who's back?" I asked.

"Our father."

I stared at him. He was smiling a little. "Are you trying to be funny?" I said.

"No." The smile disappeared. "He came back a few weeks ago."

I still couldn't believe this. But a sick feeling was beginning to take possession of me. "Who let him in?" I asked, thinking that the only way he could have come back was by forcing his way in.

"Ma did."

"She let him in?" This was even more incredible. After all we had gone through, after what he had done to her stealing that money, she had let him in? "She couldn't have done that."

"He was crying," Sidney said. "I was there when he came. He knocked on the door and I answered it, and he was standing there, and it gave me a shock. I didn't know what to do or say, so I called Ma and she came to the door, and when she saw who it was she tried to close the door but he wouldn't let her. Then he started to cry and beg her to let him in, so she did, and they went in the front room and I didn't hear any more until Ma came out and she was crying too. And she said she was going to give him another chance and he'd be staying with us, and I wasn't supposed to tell you while you were in the hospital."

Sidney told me all that and I listened, growing more and more sick. After all we had gone through, all the misery he had brought us, she had taken him back. She was giving him another chance. I couldn't wait to talk to her.

She came, finally, and no sooner had she sat down beside the bed than I launched into the subject. "Sidney tells me you've let him come back." I could never get myself to say "Father" or "Dad." It was always "him" or "he."

She nodded, looking sad and perhaps guilty too. "What could I do?"

"You could have kicked him right out," I said angrily. "We had enough trouble getting away from him. I wouldn't want to have to go through it again, but I'm afraid we will."

"No," she said, "I don't think so. I think he really means what he says, that he'll behave, he'll never act the same way again, he'll stop drinking."

"That's a lot of baloney," I said bitterly. "And you know it. You've made a big mistake."

"Harry," she said desperately, "what could I do? He cried. He cried and cried, and he reminded me of my promise."

"What promise?" I asked.

"When we'd first met. Back in England. I told you about it—how we walked up to the park and sat on one of the benches and he poured his heart out to me and told me how he'd been put to work when he was a child, and then how when he was still a young boy the family ran off to England and left him to be by himself. When he told me that my heart broke and I promised him then that I would never do that to him. I would never leave him alone."

"Oh, that," I said, remembering now. "He was just conning you, Ma. Grandpa told us it was something he made up and the real story was they'd wanted him to go but he didn't want to go, so they left without him."

But Ma was shaking her head and saying, "I don't know, I don't know," and she was looking very troubled, as if she really did not know who was telling the truth. But whether it mattered or not was something else. Her heart had been touched then, just as deeply as it had been the first time. And there was something else.

He had a job. He was working in a tailoring shop. He had told her that, knowing how hard pressed we were for money. I myself was in the hospital unable to work, and the little Sidney brought in selling ice cream did not help much. Perhaps this too had been in the back of her thoughts when she gave in to him.

There was nothing I could do, and the same misery that I had felt all my life came back and washed over me, driving me into a feeling of deep despair.

I no longer wanted to go home. I could not bear the thought of going back there and seeing him again, hearing his voice, listening to his roars and the sounds he made when he came home drunk late at night.

Why didn't he die? I wondered. I envied the other fellows I had known whose fathers had died, some from sickness, some in the war. He had escaped the war. I remember the time he went with a group of men from our street to the town of Chester to take his physical exam. The rest of them had all been drafted, but he came home smelling of the whiskey he'd drunk on the way back to celebrate his freedom. He'd been rejected because of something that he never talked about. He was smirking at his escape, and his eyes fell on me and he saw the unmistakable disappointment on my face, for I had been indulging in some wild dreams of his being taken off to war and killed by a German gun. I am sure he knew exactly what had been going on in my mind, for he laughed and sneered, "Better luck next time. Maybe the Germans will come over here and kill me."

I didn't say anything. I said very little more to my mother now. Perhaps I could not blame her. Perhaps if I had been well and working she would not have done what she did. I lay in my bed, plunged into the worst sort of gloom. And thereafter when the doctors made their rounds and asked how I felt I did not answer eagerly and tell them I felt fine and ask when I could go home. In fact, I said just the opposite, and when the time came to get off the bed and test my fractured leg to see how well I could walk, I limped badly and said it

was still very painful. I had become another of the faking malinger-
ers, the homeless men who clung to the hospital because it was so
much better than the doorways and gutters from which they'd
come.

And with most of my pain gone, I was able now to get around
on crutches, so staying there wasn't too bad for me either. Welfare Island was situated on the East River, and I could go down from the
ward and sit on a bench and read or watch the boats and barges go
by. I'd come up and have my lunch, then there might be some sort of
entertainment in the recreation room or a movie, and in the evening
there was the companionship of other patients who were my age,
and we could sit around the ward and tell dirty jokes and have a few
good laughs before we went to bed.

No, it wasn't bad at all, but they caught on to me finally and I
was discharged. Another patient leaving at the same time gave me a
lift in his car. I hobbled my way up the stairs to our apartment, was
greeted tearfully at the door by my mother, and went inside with
her.

He was home. The job he was supposed to have had had turned
out to be part time, three days a week, and this was one of the days
when he was not working. I saw him from the distance sitting in the
front room. His back was toward me and he was listening to the
radio. My heart sank immediately. It was as if a dark shadow had
fallen over me.

He turned his head round. We stared at each other. Neither one
of us said anything.

My mother had been watching us anxiously, perhaps fearful of
some outburst, and there was relief on her face when nothing happened.

"I'll get you something to eat," she said. "You must be hungry."

Chapter Nineteen

"On our block," I wrote, "there is this row of sad-looking old frame houses, half buried among the towering cliffs of Bronx apartment houses, a lost relic of a past when all this area was country, with rolling hills and fields and woodlands, with here and there a trickling brook shining in the sun. Somehow, as the change took place from country to city, this block of houses had been overlooked by the developers.

"The houses," I continued, pecking away at my tiny typewriter that I had bought in a secondhand shop for ten dollars, "were all alike and built close together with porches that slanted downward with the weight of their age. There were three apartments in each house, and ours was the one in the basement of the house in the middle of the block. The rooms were dark and had a musty smell. . . ."

I remember it was a Saturday when I wrote this story, which

would be published in *Manuscript,* and the reason I remember is because that Saturday, before it was over, would prove to be a momentous day in my life.

If I had known then how it would turn out, I would have felt less gloom than I did when I came to a halt halfway in my story, unable to continue writing about surroundings that only added to my depressed state. Besides, it was evening, and it was getting too dark for me to see well, and we were stinting on the use of our electricity and not at all sure how we were going to pay the electric bill this month—or the gas bill, or the rent.

The Depression was in its fifth year, and there seemed to be no end to it. There had been a surge of hope when Franklin Roosevelt had been elected president, but so far we had heard nothing but a lot of fireside chats and some fine speeches, one of which told us that the only thing we had to fear was fear itself.

But the apple peddlers on street corners had grown in number, and the crowds in front of the agencies on Sixth Avenue were thicker than ever, and the breadlines in front of the Salvation Army headquarters were longer, and I had virtually given up all hope of finding a job. I don't know how my mother managed with so little coming into the house—a little from my father, a little from Sidney, and now and then from me when I managed to sell an article to some magazine. In desperation I had even tried my hand at writing scripts for comic magazines and sold a few at ten dollars a script. The publisher finally went bankrupt, owing me fifty dollars.

In the meantime we had moved from one place to another, always seeking an apartment that was cheaper than the one before, until finally we landed up in the Bronx, in the block of old frame houses, where our rent was ten dollars a month. It was the cheapest so far, but we were soon behind on that and haunted by the fear of being evicted by our landlady, a fat, slovenly woman who shuffled about in carpet slippers and every day wore the same torn dress that had slits in the sides showing white underwear.

She had been pleasant and cordial at first. She lived in the apartment above us and would come down to knock on our door to ask if we needed anything. She lived alone, a widow, and was obviously quite taken with us. Her other tenants, who lived on the floor above her, a family of six people and very noisy, received much less attention. But it all disappeared when we fell behind with the rent; there were no more knocks on the door, and dark looks were cast at us when she saw us.

Evictions were common in those days. Often as you went by on a street you saw furniture piled on the pavement and stricken families huddled around not knowing what to do. We saw it coming to us.

It was about this time that I cooked up an article about the profession of bodyguarding, telling mostly from my imagination how bodyguards were trained to protect their gangster employers. I had sent it in to *Popular Mechanics* magazine and had heard nothing from them for about three or four weeks when one day there was a knock at the door. It was our landlady and she was holding an envelope in her hand. All her hostility had vanished, and in its place there was fear and abject apology. She handed the envelope to me saying in a trembling voice that although it was addressed to me she had opened it by mistake. By mistake! It wasn't likely, but I took it from her and opened it.

Inside was a check for thirty dollars, the stub stating that it was for "The Profession of Bodyguarding."

While I stared at it with the euphoric feeling that an author gets from an acceptance, the landlady was stammering, "I—I'm so sorry. I didn't know you were one of the boys. You must forgive me. I don't want trouble. My husband, he should rest in peace, he was a friend of Al Capone. . . ."

I realized then that she thought the check I had received was my salary for bodyguarding "one of the boys." I didn't clear it up for her. I let her go on thinking what was terrifying her. After that there was no longer any danger of eviction. Not for a while, anyway, not until we fell behind again and again, and some of her fear wore off.

Things only got worse for us and that basement apartment did not help. It was always so dark and airless there, and the musty smell never left the place no matter how hard my mother scrubbed and cleaned. For her, it could have meant the end of her dream. Even in England the house had been more tolerable: lighter and above ground, and with two floors. There was no sign of happiness in her any longer.

Perhaps, though, I am forgetting one thing. There was my father and the change that seemed to have come about in him. I don't mean that he had given up his drinking. He still drank, and seemed to have found a place downtown on the East Side where he had cronies who treated him to drinks—or so he claimed. He still went out, but not every night. Remarkably, he stayed home some nights, and there were fewer outbursts from him. I don't know if it was my presence or if he was somewhat afraid of me, but he seemed subdued, and once, astonishingly, I even saw him help my mother wash the dishes.

And he gave her money regularly every week, on a Friday, and he gave it to her mostly in small change. The boss at the place where he said he worked one day a week insisted on giving it to him that way, lots of change along with a few dollar bills.

A suspicion once came to my mind when I was thinking of all those coins he brought home. I did not speak to him, nor he to me, but I asked my mother, "Does he go to see his father?"

"I don't know," she said. "But why do you ask?"

I shrugged. I didn't want to tell her what I was suspecting; she had enough trouble, and I didn't want that planted in her mind. "I was just wondering," I said, "if the old man is in New York."

"Where else could he be?"

"He could have gone back to Chicago."

"I don't think he's been back since the wedding."

"How do you know that?" I asked.

"I just guessed," she said. "He was so mad at your grandmother for not having told him about the wedding that it wouldn't surprise me if he never went back."

"It wouldn't surprise me either," I said. "I think it was a damn shame."

It was odd that we should have been talking about my grandmother that day, for the following week news came that she had died. It was a bit of a shock to my mother, and I heard her asking my father if he was going to the funeral. Some of the roughness came into his tone when he answered no. Why should he go? What the hell for?

"She's your mother," my mother answered.

I heard him give a snorting sort of laugh, and a single word came out of him contemptuously: "Mother!"

There was some talk later of money she might have left. My father brought it up. He was suspicious. She'd always had money. My grandfather had seen to that. Even after the break with her at the wedding he had been sending her money. So what had happened to it? He wrote to Uncle Saul enquiring, and Saul's answer came back promptly, telling him there was no money left. Grandma had used it all up on doctors and hospitals before she died.

"The lying bastard," my father swore. He was like his old self, the voice roaring, his inflamed eyes bulging. Now he would go back to Chicago. He'd face them all, hold each one by the throat, make him tell the truth about the money. But he did no such thing, and it died down; he seemed to have forgotten all about it, and he sat home with my mother listening to Eddie Cantor sing "Happy Days Are Here Again."

As for me, I still continued to cook up fantastic articles—"What Men Won't Do for a Thrill"—and try to sell them to *Popular Mechanics* and the *American Weekly,* Hearst's Sunday supplement, where I had some luck from time to time at ten dollars an article.

But what I called my real writing, my short stories about myself, occupied most of my time. The little magazines paid no money, but that didn't matter to me, and I was gaining some attention. I received a letter from Clifton Fadiman, the editor of Simon & Schuster, telling me that he'd read one of my hospital stories and liked it, and inviting me to submit a novel if I had one. I didn't, but I would. Elated, I started writing one, but it was like so many others that I wrote afterward, never published. Nevertheless, there was enough encouragement in that letter to keep me writing chiefly about myself, and I have done that ever since.

But on this particular Saturday, in the midst of one story that I was writing about the block of old frame houses where I lived, I was suddenly assailed with such a feeling of gloom that I could not continue. I found myself taking stock of myself. I was twenty-four years old, I had no job and no prospects of getting one, I was still living with my parents, I was still trying unsuccessfully to become a writer, and the best I could do was get published in some insignificant little magazines that only a few people read. Never mind Clifton Fadiman. That was just a fluke.

I got up from the typewriter and knew that I wanted to get out of this dark, dank hole of an apartment and go out somewhere to meet people—talk with them, laugh with them. I thought of a girl. It was a long time since I had been out with one. But it took money to take a girl out. And I wasn't dressed properly for it anyway, and didn't feel like shaving and changing out of my unpressed, shabby trousers and not-too-clean shirt. Luckily, I had a few coins in my pocket that would be enough for subway fare to Manhattan and back.

I stepped outside and breathed in the fresh evening air. It was always like coming out of a cave when you left the basement apartment. It was early summer, and the air was soft and balmy. People were sitting on the porches or on the steps that led up to the porches. The sky was a pale color of twilight, and it reminded me a

bit of those summer evenings in England when the sun had set and
people sat outside on chairs smoking their pipes or cigarettes.

I saw my father and mother sitting outside on the two kitchen
chairs they had brought out, and it occurred to me how unusual it
was for my father to be home on a Saturday night and, what's more,
sitting there with my mother, the two of them side by side. Somehow, there was something reassuring in the sight. I marveled a bit at
the change that had come over my father, but wondered how long it
would last. We still didn't talk to each other.

He turned his head aside as I came out. But my mother smiled
and I saw a certain curiosity in her eyes, which were lifted up to
me. I rarely went out these days, and she was probably wondering
where I was going. She would not have asked, however, and merely
waved. I waved back and knew that her eyes were following me as I
walked on. I saw Sidney at the corner with some friends, and he
yelled, "Where you going?"

I didn't answer and simply waved at him. Truth was, I didn't
know where I was going other than Manhattan, but where in Manhattan I hadn't decided yet. I thought of the Village. It was always
lively there, and I might run into some people I knew who lived
there. But the Village cost money, and I was looking for free. It was
for that reason probably that I got off at Union Square, a stop before
the Village. It was lively there too, and there were always free lectures
at the Labor Temple or Cooper Union, or better yet, the soapbox orators in the square gave talks that you could listen to even if you
didn't agree with what they were saying.

Yes, it was lively all right, with surging crowds along Fourteenth
Street, shoppers streaming in and out of Klein's, the big bargain
store, others heading for the theaters, and the chestnut and popcorn
vendors trundling their carts among them with savory smells trailing after them. But most of the noise came from the square, in the
center of which a tall flagpole flying the American flag dominated
the scene. Around the flagpole were the orators of all different

brands of radical beliefs—Stalinists, Trotskyites, Lovestonites, So-
cialists, Social-Laborites—all mounted on short ladders, harangu-
ing the crowds in fierce, passionate tones. I shuffled from one to the
other for about an hour, then grew tired of it and wandered away
over toward the benches that were filled with people.

I was hot. I was perspiring and wanted to rest. I found a place at
the end of one bench and sat down. No sooner had I done that than
I heard the sound of someone singing. Singing? It could hardly be
called that. The voice was hoarse and cracked, and I recognized it at
once. Unmistakably, this was my grandfather's voice.

Yes, I saw him in the fading light, making his way along the
benches, tapping with a cane, shuffling slowly toward me with his
blue glasses shielding his supposed blindness, the tin cup held out
toward those seated on the benches, rattling the coins that were in it.

At last he came up to where I was sitting. He recognized me too
with a little start, halting and then, with the familiar chuckle, saying,
"So it's you, Harry."

"Yes, it's me, Grandpa," I said and noted at the same time out of
the corners of my eyes people on the bench looking at us. They'd
obviously heard me call him Grandpa. I couldn't help feeling a little
self-conscious, but I said, "Won't you sit down, Grandpa?"

"Yes, why not? I could use a little rest."

They made room for him on the bench, and I was sure they'd all
be listening to us with wide-open ears. But I didn't care any longer.
I didn't even bother to lower my voice. In fact, I was rather glad I'd
met him. I had thought of him often since I'd last seen him, several
years before, and he looked pretty much the same now as he had
then. His beard was scraggly, his face weatherbeaten and deeply
lined. He wore what I suppose was his beggar's uniform: shabby
clothes, torn shoes, an old felt hat with a ragged brim, and, though
it was a hot day, a long, much-worn overcoat that came down to his
ankles.

"So, Harry," he said, "how are you? How is everybody at home?
Your father, your mother, your brothers, your sister?"

"They're all well," I said. "About my sister I don't know. She's back in Chicago with her husband. We don't write very much. But the others are all right." They weren't. Both Joe and Saul were having trouble: Joe finding it hard to sell magazine subscriptions these days, and with a baby now, a little girl named Rita, having to borrow money from his wife's parents to make ends meet; Saul finding it difficult to live off the meager salary the Jewish organization gave him, and with his wife constantly dissatisfied and adding to his misery. As for us, how well could we be? But I didn't want to go into that with my grandfather. "How have you been?" I asked.

"I am still alive," he said. "At my age that is good enough."

"Do you hear from Chicago?" I asked.

"Chicago?" He chuckled. "Yes, of course I hear, now more than ever since your grandmother is gone. You know about that?"

"Yes, we heard. I was sorry to hear it."

He sighed. "Yes, I too was sorry. When you have a lot of children with a woman it means there must be some bond between you. I gave her a lot of work to do and I feel guilty about it. The children always depended on her, and when they needed something, even after they were married and supposed to be on their own, they went to her. And now that she's gone they come to me—to the direct source of supply." He gave another chuckle. "So long as I am not there in person to embarrass them, they don't mind talking to me in their letters. And what do their letters say? One says he needs a set of teeth, another must have a pair of glasses, or they're short for the rent. One good thing about the Depression, it's brought families closer together. Even your aunt Lily has been writing to me. Did you know that her rich husband died too?"

I was shocked. "No, they never told us. When did that happen?"

"Not too long after Grandma died. The poor man. I liked him. He was good to me at the wedding . . . the wedding that I was not invited to." He gave a chuckle that did not sound amused, and looking at him, I saw the bitterness in his eyes. He went on, "Yes, I liked Phil. He was worse off than any of us, being rich. It's harder to fall from the top than when you are at the bottom. He lost his business, the Victrolas, the fine office in the Loop. He could not get a job, not even selling Victrolas. His parents wouldn't help—they had disowned him for marrying into the family. You know where he landed? He became a milkman. Yes, he got up at dawn and delivered bottles of milk to houses.

"But it was too much for him, poor man. One day while he was climbing a flight of steps to deliver some milk he dropped dead from a heart attack. Now your aunt Lily writes to me. She is crushed by what has happened. She doesn't know what to do with herself, where to turn, and of course she has no money. Can it be that is why she writes to me now even though before this she never even invited me to her wedding?" He shook his head back and forth a few times. "No, I mustn't say that. But I have sent her some money and I have told her perhaps she would like to come to New York—and stay with me." He chuckled again, and this time he did sound amused.

I didn't laugh with him. I didn't say anything for a while. I was dazed by all I had heard. Vaguely, I was aware of the cacophony of sounds and voices around me: one of the speakers hoarsely denouncing capitalism, the worst evil ever inflicted on mankind . . . the rumble of trucks and distant honking of horns . . . and the smell of roasted chestnuts and popcorn in my nostrils. I began to think of something else.

"Have you seen my father?" I asked.

"Why should he be any different from all the others?" my grandfather asked. "Oh, he's become a very dutiful son. Yes, I see him. He comes to my room. Why do you ask?"

"Do you give him money?"

He shrugged. "If I have it, I give it to him. Business is not what it used to be. These days I have a lot of competition. Everybody is in the business."

My suspicion, however, had been confirmed. Now I was certain I knew where he got what was supposed to be his pay every Friday.

"I don't give it to him," my grandfather went on. "I give it to your mother. Only of course you must not tell her that. I told your father the same thing. She must not know. But it is more than money that I owe her."

"Why do you owe her?" I asked. He had said it before, and I had been curious then. But now was a good time to find out.

He patted my knee with his hand. "Harry," he said, "you don't have to know everything. Or perhaps you do. I hear that you are a famous writer and you are having stories published in magazines."

"Who told you that?" I asked.

"Your father."

I was a bit surprised. I couldn't picture him talking about me to someone in the first place, but to be boasting about me in such terms was a bit hard to believe. "He's exaggerating," I said. "I'm not a famous writer. I'm just a beginning writer."

"But you're a writer."

"I suppose." This was not a subject I cared to pursue, however. I was thinking of the one he had mentioned before and then seemed deliberately to change to something else. "You were saying before that you owed my mother more than money. What is it you owe her?"

He hesitated for a moment, then said, "You won't tell your mother that I told you?"

"No."

"She would not like you to know."

"I promise I won't tell her."

"All right, then. You already know about your mother, how in Poland her mother died and her father died when she was still a baby, and how nobody wanted to care for her and she was passed from one to another until when she was sixteen she was able to come to England. You know all that."

"Yes, I've heard about it."

"But what you don't know is about Samuel."

"Who?"

"Samuel—Shmuel, they called him."

"Who is he?"

"He was the man who should have been your father."

I looked at him, puzzled. "What are you trying to say, Grandpa?"

"Samuel was a young man who loved your mother. He too came from Poland. He worked in a hat factory in Manchester, and that's where your mother found work too when she came to England. They fell in love. There was talk of marrying between them. Samuel—Shmuel, I'll call him, like everybody did—was a wonderful fellow, a good, kind, honest young man, and handsome-looking, a bit of a dandy. He always dressed so well, and he had a mustache. . . ."

A thought was coming to me. I remembered a photograph in the assortment of photos my mother always kept in a cardboard box in a cupboard. I used to pore over them from time to time, and this one always puzzled me. He was not one of the family, as all the others were, and when I asked my mother who he was, she would answer vaguely that he was just an old friend she once knew, and then did not seem to want to talk about him. Yes, he was a handsome fellow, and he did have a mustache. . . .

"I think I know who you mean," I said. "I believe my mother had a picture of him."

My grandfather nodded. "Yes, she would. I too have one. He gave one to me. We had become quite good friends while I was doing the roof over in the hat factory. He liked my singing. And we both read the same kind of books—Tolstoy, Dostoyevsky, Gorky, of course. . . ."

I was startled and for a moment forgot the subject we had been talking about in this amazing discovery. "I didn't know you read books," I said, interrupting.

My grandfather smiled. "Why shouldn't I read books?" he asked.

I almost blurted out what promptly came to my mind, that he

was an old street beggar with whom you could not associate reading books of any kind, much less the great Russian masters. But I stopped myself in time and said instead, "I just didn't know, that's all. But go on, tell me more about Samuel—or Shmuel."

And I listened, with a new respect for my grandfather and a much better understanding that had never been there before, as he continued with what interested me still more.

"Yes, we got along quite well, the two of us, and we used to eat lunch together and I got to like him very much, and when he told me of how deeply in love he was with the little sixteen-year-old girl who had just come from Poland, I said to myself what a wonderful husband this girl was going to get and how well matched they were, for I had met her too and got to know her own sweetness and goodness, and I had learned of her unfortunate and tragic background. I thought this would make up for it, a marriage to this man, and what a wonderful life they could have together. . . ." He paused to pat my knee and say, "And what a wonderful father you could have had, Harry."

Yes, I thought, it could have been wonderful for me and for all of us in the family, and I felt a deep sense of regret inside me. But I said nothing and sat there thinking about it for a while, and finally said, "So why didn't he become my father?"

"Because I put a stop to it."

"You!" I looked at him in amazement. "But you just got through telling me you were close friends and you thought so highly of him."

"Yes." He gave one of his chuckles, but it was not the amused kind. "Only you can't trust an old devil like me, a common beggar. I took your mother aside one day when he was not around and told her that he was a scoundrel, a liar, a thief, and a fornicator. Worst of all, he was married already and had a wife in Poland with five children."

I listened to this, appalled. "But how could you say anything like that? After all the good things you told me about him?"

"How could I, eh?" He gave another chuckle. "Well, it was not easy, believe me. But I had been talking to my wife. I had been telling her all those good things. She knew your mother already. She knew all about her and she had already decided whom your mother would marry. There was our oldest son, a menace to all of us, a terror. She had thought we were rid of him when we left Poland without him. But he followed us, and now she saw another way to do it. This young girl from Poland was the answer. I objected. Yes, at first I objected very strongly. 'What are you talking about?' I said to her. 'What are you saying? This girl is already promised to Shmuel. They are in love. What has Yankel to do with all this?'

"But you must know what your grandmother was like. She was a very strong-minded person. And she could be as hard to deal with as Yankel himself. She told me, 'Never mind this Shmuel fellow. Who cares about him? Let him go to hell. You must go to her, the girl, and tell her he is no good, he is a scoundrel, he has a wife already. Yes, tell her that. He is married and has five children, and he has left them back in Poland.' "

"And she believed you?" I asked, incredulous.

He nodded. "She had never had a father. I was her father. So she believed me. I took her home to dinner and my wife did the rest. So now you know why I owe her. I have never forgiven myself. I do not hate my son. But I know what he has done to her. Do you understand what I mean?"

"Yes," I said, dazed by all I had heard. Vaguely, I was aware of the commotion of the square all around me; I felt far away from it all, and that is what I wanted to be. I had to get away from the old man and be alone. I felt a little sick. I got up.

"Grandpa," I said, "I have to go. I've got an appointment to meet someone." I looked at my wristwatch. "I'm late already."

"Ah," he said. "I'm sorry you must go. We don't meet very often. But perhaps you'll come to see me."

"Yes, I'll do that," I said. "Where do you live?"

"Not far from here. I have a room in a woman's house. I'll give you the address. You must write it down. Do you have pencil and paper?"

"No."

"You are some writer." He was feeling in his pocket. He came out with the stub of a pencil but no paper. Then he seemed to remember something. He gave a little chuckle and felt in his tin cup and came up with a white ticket. "A joker gave this to me. He said, 'Old man, I don't have any money, but I've got this, and maybe you can have yourself a good time or you can sell it to somebody. It's worth a quarter.' It's a ticket to a dance tonight. Maybe you can go. But you can also write the address on the back of it."

He handed it to me together with the pencil stub and I wrote down the address he gave me, which was on Second Avenue, a few blocks from where we were. And then I said, "Goodbye, Grandpa."

"Goodbye," he said. "But don't forget what I said to you. Don't tell your mother."

"No, I won't," I promised, and then I turned onto Fourteenth Street and joined the surging crowds there.

Chapter Twenty

FOURTEENTH STREET WAS ALIVE WITH CROWDS OF PEOPLE HEADING for the stores, the restaurants, and the theaters. The chestnut and popcorn vendors were busy, and knots of customers gathered around them, blocking passage on the street. I went past Klein's, the big bargain store with its endless streams of shoppers coming in and out. Then I came to Irving Place and my footsteps slowed down.

I was hesitating. I had been heading for the Labor Temple, but the thought of that dance ticket was in my mind. I took it out of my pocket and examined the printed side. The dance was being given by the League Against War and Fascism. It was a Communist front, I knew, but what difference did that make? It could be livelier, more fun than a lecture. And it was in Webster Hall, only a block away. I gave it one last thought and turned to my left. I had been there before. It was well known as a place where many prominent radical leaders gave talks and various left-wing functions were held. It only took a minute before I came up to its grimy, red-brick exterior, with a flight of wide stone steps leading up to the entrance. The doors were open and a man stood taking tickets.

I mounted these steps and gave him my ticket, then remembered the address written on the back and asked him if I could have it back for a moment so that I could copy the address—and could he lend me a pencil? Impatiently, he thrust the ticket back at me and told me to keep it.

I put it back into my pocket and began to climb another flight of steps that led to the dance hall, and as I did so the raucous sound of a jazz band and a voice singing came to me, growing louder as I went up the wooden steps, which were littered with cigarette butts and chewing gum wrappers.

Then I was at the entrance to the dance hall and stood there for a moment taking in the scene before me. The dance floor was crowded with swinging couples, and a thick veil of cigarette smoke hung over their heads. On the platform to my right the band blared and thumped, and a huge black woman in a low-cut sequined black dress strutted back and forth with a microphone held in her hand, bellowing out a song, her mountainous breasts jouncing with her movements.

I turned my eyes back to the dance floor, then to the side where some people were standing, and almost immediately I saw a girl in a two-piece orange-colored dress—later I would discover that she had made it herself—that caught my eye along with the rest of her. She was of medium height, with dark hair. Her back was turned toward me, so I could not see her face, but what struck me most in that moment was the erect posture of her slender body, and though she was standing still, there was something vibrant that seemed to emanate from her, and I thought of a bird poised on the branch of a tree, about to take off in flight.

I found myself walking toward her. I was not a dancer. I was clumsy and awkward at dancing, but I knew I was going to ask her to dance, and I did.

I tapped her lightly on the shoulder and said, "Would you care to dance?"

She swung round and I saw her face for the first time, and I liked what I saw. It was oval-shaped, the kind of shape I always liked in a girl's face, and she had a smooth complexion with little makeup, and I liked that too. Her large dark eyes were fixed on me with a look of mixed curiosity and interest. "Certainly," she said, and her voice was very pleasant.

So we danced, and I was my usual clumsy self, failing to keep in time with the foxtrot music, but she made me feel that I was doing fine—she leading, I suppose. She was a beautiful dancer and she loved to dance, and why she had been standing alone all that time, unasked, I'll never know. It doesn't matter.

The fact is, we spent the rest of the evening together, sometimes dancing, but most of the time sitting at a table in the canteen at the far end of the hall, talking, sipping beer—she very little of it, confessing afterward that she never drank beer and only did then to be social—talking and talking, and getting to know each other.

Her name was Ruby, and I don't know of anyone more aptly named. She was a precious jewel in all respects, and from that first moment of our meeting she brightened my whole life. All the gloom I had felt before this vanished, and I found myself laughing and talking as I'd never laughed and talked before. We had a lot in common. We were close to the same age, she a bit younger than I, and we had migrated to the United States around the same time, she from Poland with her widowed mother and younger brother. We both loved the same kind of music (classical, opera) and the same kind of books and authors (Steinbeck, Hemingway, Sinclair Lewis). In fact, she worked in a bookstore, Brentano's on Fifth Avenue. We had a lot to tell each other, I about my writing in the little magazines, which impressed her considerably.

It got close to twelve before we realized how late it was. People were beginning to leave, and she suddenly remembered the girlfriend who had brought her here. But the girlfriend had disappeared considerately after seeing her with a man, and she was now alone.

"Could I take you home?" I asked.

"I live in Brooklyn," she warned. "And far out in Brooklyn."

It didn't matter. The Bronx, where I lived, was at the opposite end of the world, but I didn't give it a thought. We rode out to Brooklyn on the subway, and it gave us a chance to talk some more and for me to be with her. But it was over finally, and we stood for a few moments at the entrance to the apartment house where she lived, both of us reluctant to part. I tried to kiss her goodnight, but she turned her head aside, smiling. However, I'd made a date to see her again—soon, the very next Monday, in fact, when I'd take her to a band concert in Central Park. I left her, treading on air. I was incredibly happy, only to arrive at the subway station to discover that I didn't have any money left for the fare. I'd spent my last few coins on the beer in the canteen.

It was one thirty, and there were still a few people coming and going at the station, but I couldn't bring myself to ask one of them for a nickel for the fare. Instead, after a few moments' indecision, I decided to walk. Why not? I was a good walker, I loved walking. And it was a beautiful night, the sky filled with stars and a thin crescent of a moon, the air soft and balmy. The distance from where I was in Brooklyn to the upper part of the Bronx was considerable, but that didn't faze me and I struck out.

It was a perfect thing to do for the way I felt, heady with love for a girl I had just met. I hardly noticed the dark streets I walked through, their emptiness, the buildings merged in shadow. I thought of her constantly, and walked swiftly with my feet treading on air. It was almost dawn when I reached the Bronx. The sky had grown lighter and the stars had disappeared. I came to my block and saw the old wooden houses still vague in the shadows that were left from the night. I walked down the short flight of steps to the door with my key ready, but found to my surprise that it was not locked. There was a light on in the kitchen at the far end of the apartment and I could see my mother sitting there at the table in her bathrobe.

I went in quietly just the same and walked up to the kitchen. She was smiling at me.

"What are you doing up at this time?" I asked.

"I couldn't sleep," she said.

"You've been waiting up for me," I accused.

"You've never been out so late before," she said. "I was worried."

"There's no need to be worried over me," I said. "I'm a big boy, Ma. I can take care of myself."

"Yes, I know. Did you have a good time?"

"Yes." I hesitated. I wanted to tell her about Ruby, but I realized it would not make her happy, and so I stopped myself in time. Instead I said, "I met some old friends in New York and time went by so fast I hardly noticed it. But you shouldn't have sat up for me."

"I'm glad you had a good time," she said. She seemed satisfied with my explanation, and relieved too, I think, and we said goodnight to each other and went off to our bedrooms, I careful not to disturb Sidney, who was fast asleep in the bed I shared with him. I couldn't sleep once I got into bed. I kept thinking of my mother. Finding her waiting up for me had dampened my spirits and had taken away all the joy I had felt on that long walk. I was not angry with my mother. I realized how dependent she was on me, how much all her hopes and what was left of her dreams were fastened on me, And—perhaps most important—how much protection I gave her against my father. And now there was Ruby.

I was tired from my long walk, but it took me a long time before I finally fell asleep.

RUBY AND I SAW MUCH of each other that summer. We had developed a routine that brought us together almost every day in the week and certainly on the weekends. I would go to Brentano's and browse among the books there until it was five thirty, then call at the office where Ruby worked. From there we would walk to the Automat on Sixth Avenue and Forty-second Street and have our supper of baked beans, a roll, and coffee, or perhaps macaroni and cheese and a slice of whole wheat bread. Then, holding hands, we'd walk to Central Park, and when we were there and safely concealed among trees and bushes, I would give vent to what I had been struggling against from the moment I had seen her. I would take her in my arms and give her a long, passionate kiss.

She no longer turned her head aside smiling when I attempted to kiss her, but responded with the same passion that I gave to her, arms tightly round my neck. And then, satisfied for the moment, we continued on our walk, hand in hand.

The park was our playground all summer long. There was outdoor dancing on certain nights and band concerts on others. It was all free. There was no money to be spent except on an occasional soda. We danced in the open air with a starlit sky above us, holding each other close, and I grew more proficient at it every day and more in love with her.

The band concerts were equally pleasant, sitting beside her on the packed mall, holding her hand, feeling her hair brush against my face, and listening to the music that came from the band shell. It was the Goldman Band that played, and, save for an occasional Sousa march, they played mostly the classical music we both loved. But there was one night when for some unaccountable reason our attention wandered from the music. There was nothing wrong with the performance. They were playing a Mozart symphony and playing it well, and the audience around us sat in deep silence, enthralled. But we were restless. Perhaps it was the kind of evening that had slowly descended on us. There had still been a bit of daylight when the concert started, but now it had grown dark, and a full moon had appeared in the sky. Surrounded by stars, it shone down on us with a brilliance that illuminated the entire sea of heads on the mall and made the lights of the bandstand seem dull in comparison. There was a touch of magic in the air, and Ruby and I sat close to each other, holding hands, the music becoming less and less audible in our ears and the fast beating of our hearts taking its place.

At last I whispered to her, "Would you like to take a walk?"

"Yes," she whispered back.

Fortunately, we were sitting at the end of a row of seats, so we did not have to squeeze past other people and disturb them. We made our way out easily and unnoticed, and began our walk along a path that runs round the lake. We walked slowly, with my arm round her waist and the moonlight shimmering in the water at our side. We said very little to each other, savoring our relief for a while at having escaped from sitting in the mall.

Then suddenly Ruby let out a cry. "Look!"

She was gazing straight ahead at a not-too-distant spot, and I looked there too and saw it. At first it seemed like a huge golden crown in the midst of a thick grove of trees. If there had been no full moon that night it would have been shrouded in the shadows of the other trees, but it was the moon that brought out the rich golden color of its branches and showed the shape that only a golden willow tree could have, a rounded domelike top that billowed outward and drooped down on all sides like an old-fashioned ballroom gown. Even from that distance we caught the fragrance that came from its slender leaves.

"Isn't it beautiful?" Ruby breathed.

I felt the same way she did about the tree. I have loved golden willow trees ever since that night, but never so much as then. We went toward it with our eyes glued on its beauty, fascinated.

We halted at last close up to it. Our wonder grew as we took it all in from top to bottom. It must have been very old. Its trunk was probably very thick, but most of it was obscured by the curtain of leaves that hung down, some of the branches trailing on the ground and into the lake. The fresh fragrance was even stronger. I went up to it, parted some of the branches that were thin and easy to move aside, and I peered into the darkness there.

After a few moments Ruby came up to my side, and I put an arm round her waist and let her peer in also. Then I said, "Want to go in?"

"Is it safe?" she asked timidly.

"It couldn't be safer," I assured her.

We both ventured inside, and I let the branches drop until we were completely enclosed and in the darkness. I put my arms round her and she put her head on my chest, and we stayed like that, close enough to hear our hearts beating. It was very still, and we could hear very faintly the band playing in the distance. Once, I looked up and got the feeling that there was a high, vaulted ceiling above us, and it made me think of a cathedral. Then all I thought of was her closeness, and finding her lips in the darkness and the long, breathless kiss that followed, and sinking slowly to the ground.

There was a thick carpet of dried leaves that must have formed at the base of the tree over the years, and it made a soft bed for us as we lay with our arms wrapped round each other. I could still hear the band playing off in the distance. The only other sounds came from our fast breathing and the thudding of our hearts, and then too there came that one little virginal cry of pain from Ruby, but I was very careful and gentle with her, knowing it was her first time, and after that there was the breathless joy of our lovemaking, and the magic of the night.

Later, when we were lying still and close to each other, I found I could see through the curtain of branches as far away as the lights of buildings on the rim of the park, and they were like a glittering necklace wrapped round the dark throat of the night.

WHEN I GOT HOME I found my mother waiting up for me. She had not done that since the night I walked back from Brooklyn. And like that time, she was sitting in the kitchen in her bathrobe. She looked up at me, silent, and I looked back at her.

Then I spoke. "Ma, why are you up?"

She didn't answer my question. Instead, her lips trembling slightly, she said, "Harry, you mustn't get married."

It was almost as if she knew what had happened that night and what I had been thinking: that I wanted to marry Ruby. But I said, "Who's talking of getting married?"

"You're going with a girl, aren't you?" she said.

There was no use trying to hide it any longer. I had been doing that all summer long, pretending that I was staying out late with friends. But it hadn't deceived her, and I saw that she was close to tears. "Yes," I said, "I am seeing a girl. She's a very nice girl. I'll bring her here sometime to meet you. I think you'll like her."

She said nothing for a moment, then asked, "What's her name?"

"Ruby."

"You have a cousin by the name of Ruby in Chicago."

"Yes, I know. I've met her."

"So there'll be two Rubys in the family."

"Ma," I said, "I didn't say I was getting married."

"You didn't say you weren't," she said, and managed to smile a little in spite of the threat of tears.

I went up to her and put an arm round her shoulders. "Ma," I said, "I'm never going to leave you. I don't want you to ever worry about that."

"I'm not worried," she said. "But marriage is not good for everybody. For your brothers it hasn't been good. For your sisters it wasn't the best. And look at me." She managed to smile again, as if this were a joke. "I've been married since I was sixteen, and look at the life I've had."

I thought of what my grandfather had told me about her. I wanted to broach it to her, ask her if it were true or something my grandfather had made up, but I couldn't. However, I did ask, "Ma, weren't you ever in love?"

She gave me a quick, sharp look, then said, "Love? What's that? Who knows what love is?"

"*I* know, Ma," I said gently. "I've always loved you."

She put a hand on mine and looked up at me with something like gratitude in her eyes. "I know," she said. "I shouldn't have said what I did. I know what love is. I've loved you and all my children, even Rose." She added this last with a touch of sadness in her tone and her head bent. Then she recovered and lifted her head up and looked at me. "But for you I've always had something special. You're going to be somebody. You're different from all the others. So you didn't go to college. But you're a writer. You're having things published in magazines. That's why I'm so afraid you'll get married and once you're married you'll be like all the others. Like me."

"I'm not getting married, Ma," I repeated. "So please stop worrying."

She seemed reassured and we both said goodnight—although it was day practically—and went to bed, I to my room and to the bed I shared with Sidney. I was unable to sleep, however, and lay for a long time thinking and worrying over the conversation with my mother. Evidently, one part of her dream remained intact: I was to become somebody. This had not changed, even though the rest of that dream seemed to have dwindled to virtually nothing.

I lay awake for a long time, not noting the thin gray light creeping into the room, nor the heavy breathing of my younger brother beside me, thinking only of the little likelihood there was of my achieving what she expected me to do. But mostly what I worried over was her fear of my getting married, when I knew that what I wanted more than anything else in my life was to get married to Ruby. I must have fallen asleep at last.

Chapter Twenty-one

Autumn came too soon. There was no more Central Park for us. The band concerts and the outdoor dancing were over. So long as the crisp, bright, sunny weather stayed we could take long walks as a substitute. We both loved walking. Sundays we'd take the Dobbs Ferry across to the Palisades and hike there, among trees that had changed color and were masses of brilliant reds and yellows and browns, with the Hudson River glittering below the cliffs.

We'd come back to Manhattan and have spaghetti and a glass of wine at a small Italian restaurant that was cheap and had good food. Then, glowing with health and filled with our dinner, we'd go to the free concert at Stuyvesant High School, and I'd take her home and kiss her for the last time and go back to the Bronx, and that was our Sunday.

But then the chill winds came and the rain, and there was no more walking. The trees began to shed their leaves and turned into bare skeletons. We went to see our beloved golden willow one day after a rain, and it too stood stripped of all its glory, with thin branches filled with dead leaves lying in a sodden mass around the base of its trunk. It was the final blow, the end of what we used to call our golden boudoir.

Now we had to rely for our lovemaking on some charitable friends' borrowed apartment, or Ruby's home when her mother and brother were not there, though we were always fearful that they might come in and interrupt us.

I had already been a visitor in Ruby's home for dinner several times and had met her mother, a shy, quiet little woman, and her brother, who was equally shy and quiet. I used to catch Ruby's mother glancing at me with obvious curiosity, and I don't think that curiosity was ever fully satisfied.

Ruby told me when we were alone that her mother liked me but she could not understand how I made my living. Ruby had told her that I was a writer, but she did not understand what a writer was. And there was something else she had asked—if we were going to get married.

I was silent for a moment. This was a subject I had been trying to avoid. But I asked, "And what did you tell her?"

Ruby didn't look at me as she answered. "I said perhaps."

"Is that what you wanted to say?" I asked, knowing that I should not have gone any further, but wanting to hear what she thought just the same.

"No," she said.

"What did you want to say?" I asked, persisting in that same direction still.

"I wanted to say yes."

Only then was I silent, and I have never forgiven myself for that because it was what I would have wanted her to say, and I should have said it myself. But there rose in my mind all the objections I had been thinking of long before this to getting married. I had no job. I had no way of earning money. I was a long way from being a writer. But mostly it was my mother I was thinking of and the conversation we'd had that night when I'd assured her I was not going to get married.

I had thought of that often, and there were nights when I had not slept thinking of it, nights when I wanted so desperately to be with Ruby, and other times when I was with her and so much in love with her and realized how much I wanted to marry her so that I could be with her all the time. Then the picture of my mother would come to me, with her sad eyes and her tears and her whole unhappy life, and there would be a picture of my father with his dark sullen face and coarse voice, and I would ask myself, how could I abandon her to his mercy?

I was torn between one thing and the other, and that ambivalence continued all through the fall and into the winter; and when the cold days came along with the snow there was less opportunity than ever for us to be together, and we were both miserable about it.

I remember one day we braved the bitter cold and a strong wind to meet at Brentano's after her day's work was over and to walk down Fifth Avenue to our favorite haunt, the Automat. Ruby was wearing her raccoon coat, which was quite fashionable in those days, and I had an overcoat that was about ten years old and so thin that it gave little warmth.

We walked huddled close together, buffeted every time a cold blast came. It was the rush hour. People were hurrying to get home. We did not notice them. We were busy with our talk. Its subject was marriage. Ruby had brought it up. Her mother was pressing her for an answer.

I saw it all only as hopeless. I didn't see how we could do it. I repeated what I had said already. I had no job and no prospects of getting one, and if by some miracle I could get one I would have to support my parents.

But Ruby brushed all that aside. "Listen, Mr. Gloom," she said, "I have a job and I have some money saved up in the bank and that would do for us, and I could help out your parents too. Believe it or not, I have two thousand dollars saved in the bank."

"Great," I said with a touch of bitterness. "You're a rich woman. Congratulations. Only I wouldn't make a very good kept man."

"You won't be a kept man. You'll be working too."

"At what?"

"Your writing."

I gave a short laugh. "The great American novel," I said with the same bitterness.

"It doesn't have to be the great American novel," she said, "just a plain ordinary novel, which wouldn't be that ordinary, I'm sure, judging from all the encouragement you've had from Clifton Fadiman and those letters he keeps writing to you, and the one you got from Edward J. O'Brien . . ."

This was true. Clifton Fadiman had written me a note reminding me of my novel almost once a month since that first letter had arrived. And the letter from Edward J. O'Brien had further swelled my head. It told me that he had selected one of my short stories for inclusion in the honor roll of his next volume of *Best Short Stories*, which he published in England.

But my head wasn't swollen that bitterly cold day, and I was in no mood for praise. I wanted a job, not pats on the back. I told her that.

She grew silent for a moment, then said, "I don't think you really want to marry me."

"Yes, I do," I protested.

"No, you don't," she said, and burst into tears.

I walked along at her side feeling uncomfortable, aware that pedestrians, hurrying past us, were glancing curiously at us. I put my arm round her shoulders, drew her closer to me, and said, "I just don't want you supporting me and my parents."

"That's a good excuse, isn't it?" she said brokenly, dabbing at her eyes with a handkerchief that fluttered in the wind.

"It's not an excuse," I said. "It's the truth." There was no more to

it than that, but I had never gone into it with her and I didn't want
to do that now.

WE WERE MARRIED IN THE spring of 1935, 3 May. It was not much
of an affair. If Ruby and I had had our way, there would not have
been any kind of ceremony. We would have gone to a justice of the
peace and had it done briefly that way. But Ruby's mother wanted a
religious ceremony performed by a rabbi, as did my mother, so for
their sake we agreed, and on a Friday morning in early May we were
in the living room of the rabbi's home in Brooklyn, with just a hand-
ful of people present: my mother and father, Ruby's mother and
brother and her aunt, and the rabbi's wife and a girlfriend of Ruby's.

It went swiftly. The rabbi cooperated fully with my request. I
had taken him aside before the ceremony and whispered to him that
I didn't want any religious frills and that Ruby and I wanted to get
away as quickly as possible. He was only too glad to oblige. It was
Friday, and the Sabbath eve loomed ahead. He had many things to
do at the synagogue. He was a short, brisk man, and he moved about
quickly improvising a chuppah—the canopy under which the ceremony was to be performed. He had four poles mounted on stands,
and he spread a large piece of purple velvet cloth over them. His wife
helped, and she also put a plate of sliced sponge cake and a bottle of
wine on a table for refreshments afterward.

I saw my father eyeing the bottle with something like disgust.
He did not drink wine. It was either whiskey or nothing for him. In
fact, I was surprised that he had come at all, and thought the
prospect of whiskey must have been the lure.

The preparations were soon completed, and Ruby and I stood
under the chuppah close together. She was wearing a yellow dress
along with a corsage of gardenias that I had bought for her with the
windfall that had come suddenly just before the wedding, a check
for twenty dollars from *American Weekly* for an article entitled "The

Exciting Life of a Fashion Model." I had given half the money to my mother, and the other half had paid for the corsage and a wedding ring that looked like gold but wasn't.

Ruby looked very beautiful in her yellow dress and the white corsage pinned to the dress. Her mother had placed a veil over her head, and we smiled at each other, she through the veil, as we stood there close to each other. The velvet canopy touched my head slightly, and I had to bend to avoid it. Obedient to my request, the rabbi raced through the ceremony so fast you could hardly make out the words. It was soon over, then I was crashing my foot down on a wineglass, the symbolic gesture that said we were married, and I was lifting the veil from Ruby's face and was kissing her, and everybody in the room was crying "Mazel tov!" and shaking my hand and kissing Ruby, and the rabbi's wife began serving the cake and wine, and I heard my father mutter, "Bloody cheapskates," and saw my mother nudge him in the side with her elbow.

Ruby and I broke away as quickly as we could, but not before I had said goodbye to my mother. All through the time we had been there I had avoided looking at her, but I knew she was not happy. She had sat there quietly at my father's side saying nothing to anyone. As I went up to her to say goodbye she tried to smile and she kissed me, but I know there were tears in her eyes, and it left me with a feeling of heaviness inside that dampened my spirits for a long time after we had left.

I hid it from Ruby, however. We took the subway into Manhattan to go to the furnished room we had rented, and soon forgot everything except that we were married. I kept my arm round Ruby and drew her close to me, and people looked at us and caught the fragrance from Ruby's gardenia and may have guessed that we'd just been married, and some of them smiled at us and we smiled back.

We were both very happy that day. The cold and blustery winter, the unbearable separations because of weather, the endless longing for each other, the uncertainties of the future when we were together—all were swept aside. We were married now, and on our way to our first home.

Our room was in a brownstone house in a row of similar brownstones on West Sixty-eighth Street not far from Central Park, a place we had always called our second home. We had rented it the day before, after the landlady had given us a sharp scrutiny and informed us in somewhat haughty tones that she took in only the best kind of people. Apparently we had made the grade. The rent was $7 a week, payable in advance. It was a lot to us; it would consume half of Ruby's weekly salary. But it was a pleasant room.

As we approached it eagerly that day of our wedding, mounting the tall flight of steps that led to the entrance, I carrying our two suitcases, I saw a face at the window of the ground-floor apartment. It was our landlady, Mrs. Janeski, whom we had already nicknamed Madame Janeski because of her haughty demeanor. I waved to her, but she did not wave back and I felt her eyes still on us while we climbed the rest of the steps to the big, heavy door.

Ruby and I went in, past the landlady's door, and up the carpeted steps. There was a fresh, clean smell about everything, and the banister shone with polish. Our room was on the top floor, another flight of stairs, then I put the suitcases down and felt for the key in my pocket. I opened it wide for Ruby to go in first, but she didn't budge. She stood there smiling at me. At first I was puzzled, then I understood. She wanted to be carried over the threshold.

"Somebody's grown conventional all at once," I said.

But I didn't mind. I stooped, picked her up in my arms, and entered with her into a bright, sunny room that was filled with the fragrance of the bouquet of flowers I had ordered delivered earlier. I put her down, and she went over to the flowers and sniffed them, drew in a deep breath, then came over to me and put her arms round my neck. We kissed for a long time, and it was all so very beautiful and wonderful.

Our honeymoon lasted three days, and it was spent mostly in Central Park. The weather was with us—it was warm and sunny, and we were able to take walks through the park. We visited our gold willow tree and stood for a long time admiring its spring beauty. The golden leaves were just beginning to open along its thin branches, which trailed gracefully along the ground.

Only we did not need it anymore for the purpose it had served before. We had our lovely room on the top floor of the brownstone. It served all our needs. It had a tiny alcove with a dressing table, something Ruby had never had before, and it had a makeshift sort of kitchen that was combined with the bathroom, and it had two windows looking out onto a garden below. And it was kept spotlessly clean by Madame Janeski's housemaid.

The three-day honeymoon was over all too soon, and on Monday morning I escorted Ruby to her job at Brentano's. I saw the landlady watching us from her window as we left. Apparently we were still under her scrutiny. I doubted if she kept the same watch over her other roomers. It was beginning to make me feel a bit uncomfortable. But I tried to ignore it as we went out.

It was another beautiful, sunny day, and we walked through Central Park toward Fifth Avenue, regretting as we walked hand in hand that we could not spend another day together. I left her at Brentano's with a last kiss and turned back to West Sixty-eighth Street feeling gloomy without her. As I came back up the high stoop I saw the face at the window once more, but this time as I entered into the hall the landlady's door opened and she came out.

"Is there something wrong?" she asked.

"No," I answered, surprised. "Why should there be?"

"I saw you and your wife leaving for your offices, and now you've come back. Are you ill?"

"No," I said, "I'm not ill. I'm quite all right. I don't go to an office. I work at home."

"Oh?" There was a touch of something else in her voice that might have expressed a certain skepticism. "And just what kind of work do you do?" she asked.

"I'm a writer."

Once again she said, "Oh," and this time there was quite clearly doubt. She said nothing more.

I went back upstairs feeling that we were no longer included in her "best kind of people" category and were in fact under suspicion from here on. The best kind worked in offices. They left every morning at the same time and came back in the evening at the same time, and that's what put them into the best class. The ones who worked at home were in a lower class, oddballs, suspicious characters.

I tried to put it out of my mind as I entered the room and got ready to buckle down to writing the novel that Clifton Fadiman wanted so badly. I took out my Corona typewriter from the cupboard and carried it over to the one table we had, which would have to serve also as a desk, and immediately saw the note stuck in the roller.

It was a message from Ruby, one that I would see every morning hereafter, and it was typed on one of the Western Union forms that she took from her office at Brentano's to use for writing notes. It was written as a telegram addressed to me, and it gave some instructions for the day:

DARLING, WE WILL HAVE MEATLOAF FOR DINNER STOP BUY ONE
HALF POUND OF CHOPPED BEEF STOP ALSO BUY ONE ONION AND
ONE CLOVE GARLIC AND ONE EGG STOP MIX ALL INGREDIENTS IN
YELLOW BOWL IN BATHROOM-KITCHEN AND PUT IN OVEN ABOUT
FOUR PM STOP I SHOULD BE HOME A LITTLE AFTER FIVE STOP BUY
CHEESE BUN AT CUSHMANS FOR DESSERT STOP FORGOT TO MEN-
TION WHEN MIXING INGREDIENTS FOR MEATLOAF BE SURE YOU
ADD ONE TON OF LOVE FROM ME STOP YOUR OWN DARLING STOP

I grinned as I read it. Ruby had a wonderful sense of humor. We'd had many good laughs. We would have many more in the future. Meanwhile, it drove thoughts of my novel out of my mind, and I began to think more of the household duties that were mine from here on.

I was about to tidy up the place when there was a knock at the door. It was the housemaid with her bucket and broom and cleaning cloths. She also dragged in a vacuum cleaner. She was a skinny young girl, with spectacles and buck teeth, and I soon discovered that she was Madame Janeski's daughter and a brisk, energetic worker. In no time the room was neat and shining again.

Before she left, her mother arrived, ostensibly to inspect the work she had done. She criticized things here and there, though it did not seem to bother the girl. But I think she was there more to look around the room to see if she might find some things that would bolster the doubts she had about her new tenants.

I saw her sharp eyes swivel from corner to corner. I watched her go into the bathroom and look there. But there was nothing she could have pinned on us—no empty beer and whiskey bottles, no signs of drugs or cigarette burns on the bedspread or tablecloth— and the best she could do was scold the girl for leaving specks of dust here and there.

I was no longer able to settle down to writing my novel. Once the room was tidied up I had my household duties to perform. I went out to do my shopping, carrying Ruby's instructions: the butcher shop for half a pound of chopped beef, the vegetable store for an onion and a clove of garlic, the grocery, the bakery. Both when I left and when I came back hugging my brown paper bag of food supplies, the landlady's face was at the window watching me, her suspicions deepened, I've no doubt.

I tried to ignore it, but I could never quite get over the uncomfortable feeling of being watched, not only by the landlady but by others, and having them know that I was the housekeeper while my wife went to work. Perhaps this was a common enough arrangement during the Depression, but it was still odd enough to attract attention. I felt particularly in the spotlight when it came to hanging out the washing.

The laundry had been a bit of a bone of contention between

Ruby and me at the outset of our upside-down marriage. Ruby had wanted to do the washing of our clothes, at least her own things, but I had insisted on doing all of it, pointing out that since she was the breadwinner it was only right that I should do everything that was needed in the house, and that included laundry—all of it. Ruby had given in reluctantly, perhaps with some apprehension.

I did all right with the washing, following her instructions, but when it came to hanging the clothes out on the line, which stretched from the side of one of my windows to a telegraph pole at the far end of the backyard garden, I was in trouble. I did fairly well at the start with my own shorts and undershirts and socks, but when it came to Ruby's underthings, her slips, her panties, her stockings, I messed up. I wasn't sure which way they were supposed to hang. But I did my best until I came to the bra, and then I tried various ways, the whole thing horizontally, then vertically, and I still wasn't sure when a woman's voice cried out: "Try hanging it from the straps!" With that came a burst of laughter from several other directions.

With a shock I realized that I'd had an audience all this time. There was a row of backyards stretching for the entire length of the block, and there were people in them sunning themselves on beach chairs. It was from one of these chairs in the yard next to ours that the voice had come, a woman in a sunsuit. The laughter came from other yards.

And to add to all this, I saw Madame Janeski standing below, shading her eyes from the sun, looking up at me.

It was Ruby who suffered more from my housekeeping—from my cooking especially. How often did she come home hungry, anxious to sit down to a good meal, only to be met by a smell of something burning and to find me cursing over the charred remains of what was intended to be a steak? More times than I can count. But the climax of all my efforts was a dish called red flannel hash.

I had found the recipe in a magazine and it sounded easy to make. Beets, potatoes, chopped beef—mix 'em and presto! a quick, tasty meal. Well, the very sight of it when I put it on Ruby's plate made her turn pale. It was red, very red, with streaks of gray and black and white. It is altogether possible that I slipped something else into it by mistake, but anyhow what she saw was enough and she ran choking to the bathroom.

After that, I agreed to give up cooking. I had already given up laundering, so Ruby had to rush home in order to do all the things that were now piled on her. I didn't like it. All that, combined with Madame Janeski's suspicious looks, now worse than ever since that clothesline affair, were beginning to take some of the joy out of our marriage. What saved us was my novel. I had finally struggled through the writing of it and had sent it in to Clifton Fadiman. We waited breathlessly for a reply and every time I heard the mailman's ring at the door downstairs I rushed down, taking two steps at a time, only to find nothing. I would go back upstairs moodily, perhaps to peel some potatoes to get them ready for Ruby, or to get my mind off everything by reading a book.

Finally, after a month of waiting, the letter came. My heart beat rapidly when I saw it on the hall table, the square envelope with the familiar Simon & Schuster return address in the upper left-hand corner. I tore it open as I ran up the stairs. I read it, and my heart almost burst: just a brief note asking me to come to his office with reference to my novel.

I wanted to yell. This was definitely it. Why else would he want to see me except to tell me that he was going to publish my novel? I felt like calling Ruby and telling her. But I waited to give her the big surprise that I'd always dreamed about. There was a bottle of wine on the table, with Clifton Fadiman's note propped up against it. There were two wineglasses ready. Ruby came at last. I watched her as she entered. She halted just inside the door and stared at the table, the bottle of wine that was an extravagance in our budget. I laughed, took her in my arms, and gave her a kiss that was much longer than the one I usually greeted her with.

Ruby was a bit taken aback, but she collected herself enough to say, her eyes still on the bottle of wine, "What's this all about?"

"Read the note," I said.

She took the note and read it, and I saw her eyes widen as she did so. Then she looked at me and whispered, "What does it mean?"

"Just what it says," I replied, smiling. "He wants to see me about my book. What else could it mean?"

Yes, what else could it mean? What else would he want to see me about except to tell me that he was going to publish my book? It seemed certain to us then. She flung her arms about my neck and congratulated me with a kiss. We filled the wineglasses and drank a toast to my success. We were drunk for the rest of the night, in such an ecstatic state that we could hardly sleep.

I DRESSED IN MY BEST suit the following day, put on a clean shirt with a carefully matched tie, and shined my shoes, and around ten in the morning I went to the offices of Simon & Schuster, then as still today in the midtown area. I was nervous and excited. I had never been in a publisher's office before. My only contact with publishers until then had been through rejection slips.

I sat for a while waiting before the receptionist told me to go in, and I was shown into an office where Fadiman sat at a desk, smiling, with a friendly greeting and a warm handshake that was encouraging to me. I had seen him before this. He lectured often at Cooper Union, so I was familiar with the rather short, spare figure and the cultured voice that suggested Harvard. It was an affectation. He was a City College graduate and he came from Brooklyn, where his father owned a drugstore. I learned that from some people who had lived near the Fadimans.

But there was no mistaking the warmth in his manner toward me, and he began with high praise of my writing and the promise he knew I had as a writer. The novel, which he said was quite interesting and had some of the talent that had attracted him to my work in the first place, had been well worth reading and had drawn favorable comments from members of his staff. I began to feel a glow inwardly at this point and was almost certain that in the next moment he was going to tell me it had been accepted for publication—but instead out came words that were so terribly familiar to me: "I just wish," he said, "we could publish it, but unfortunately it doesn't fit our list . . . it isn't quite the sort of thing we publish . . . although that doesn't mean to say you can't find a publisher elsewhere who'd take a different view of the book. . . ."

My whole world collapsed in that moment. I stared at him, stunned. Was that all his letter had meant? To call me in here to give me a pat on the back, and then to tell me that my novel was rejected? There flashed through my dazed mind the bottle of wine that had cost more than our daily allowance for food—four dollars, to be exact; the joy of my wife, and the bitter disappointment she would suffer now, although she would not show it; the year I had wasted struggling through my novel in between cooking and shopping and hanging out clothes, preferring cloudy days so that people would not be out in the backyards sunning themselves.

I thought of all these things as I sat there staring at the editor, who seemed to be looking back at me with a touch of sympathy in his eyes. I was wondering what I was going to do now, whether I could ever attempt to write another novel, what I could do to take its place, when that look I saw in the editor's eyes must have given me a burst of inspiration. I was going to tell him that it was perfectly all right, that I appreciated his interest in me and that he had called me into his office to tell me personally about it, but instead found myself blurting out, "Do you know where I could get a job?"

Anyone who had a job in those Depression days would have been asked that question a dozen times a day, yet he seemed startled. "Are you looking for a job?" he asked.

"Yes, very much," I said.

He thought for a moment, then shook his head. "I'm afraid I don't know of any right now," he said. "But if something comes along I'll let you know."

This was the stock answer I had been getting from people for the several years I had been looking for a job. I gave up. I shook his hand, thanked him for his interest in me, and said, "Goodbye, Mr. Fadiman."

Just as I reached the door, I heard him call out, "Just a minute." I halted and turned round.

"Do you read much?" he asked.

Did I read much? I stared at him. Did a duck swim much? "Yes," I said. "I read very much."

"Then hold on," he said. "I might have something for you."

He picked up the telephone, and a new era began in my life.

Chapter Twenty-two

To READ BOOKS AND GET PAID FOR IT SOUNDED LIKE A PIPE dream—too good to be true. I thought of that as I raced up to the story office of Metro-Goldwyn-Mayer on Broadway, where Clifton Fadiman's younger brother, Robert, was story editor. There was no time to be lost.

I got to the building in ten minutes, breathless, went up in an elevator to the twenty-fifth floor, and walked along a corridor lined on either side with doors marked with various departments of the movie studio until I came to the one that said "Story Office." Inside, I sat on a bench for a while with several other people until the receptionist told me to go in.

Robert Fadiman resembled his brother only slightly. He was a fidgety little man with none of the calm, urbane manner and cultured accent of Clifton. Seated at a large desk piled with books and manuscripts of various sorts, some in boxes, some bound in covers of different colors, among them several long, thick strips of galley proofs, he grinned at me and twisted about restlessly, crossing and uncrossing his legs, and speaking to me with a distinct Brooklyn accent. Once he got up as he spoke, to cross the room and pull the shade down a trifle to keep the sun out of his eyes, then going to the door and saying a few words to someone out in the corridor, then back to his desk to cross and uncross his legs.

But however disturbing his restless movements and grinning face were to me, his words soon reassured me. He spoke mostly of what a great firm MGM was and what great actors they had, but he didn't ask the questions that I had feared—what experience I'd had reading manuscripts, where I'd worked before this, what college I'd gone to, the sort of things a job applicant for a position of this sort might expect. There was nothing like that. Perhaps his brother's recommendation over the phone had been enough.

In any event, within a relatively short time I found myself leaving his office with a book in my hand—my first assignment as a reader for MGM—and the start of a career that would last for the next fifteen years. I went out in a daze, scarcely able to realize that I finally had what I had been seeking for six years—a job. And what a job! To my ecstatic mind then, no job could reach such a high level as editorial. And mind you, I had been willing to take work as a dishwasher and might very well have done so if the Sixth Avenue agency men hadn't spotted the softness of my hands and decided I was underqualified.

I walked home that day with my assigned book in my hand treading on air, my disappointment at the failure of Simon & Schuster to accept my novel almost forgotten. Ruby had not forgotten it, however, and came rushing home, eager and expectant, certain that I would be waving a contract in front of her and there would be another celebration.

I told her, and she did what only Ruby would have done. She flung her arms round my neck and kissed me and congratulated me as if this were even better than having a book published. We celebrated with the wine that was left over from the day before, and with candles lit on the dinner table to give a festive air to the occasion.

After dinner I got busy reading the book that had been given me.

I remember that first book. I remember too it was published by a firm named Harlequin, distinguished for its romance novels, and this was a particularly light, feathery romance that ordinarily I would not have allowed myself to read after the first page. But I had to now, and it was painful. Reading was only part of the job. In addition to a critique I had to synopsize the book, and that was even more excruciatingly painful.

I got through it, however, and reported back to the office next day. Reading my critique, which was completely negative and said precisely what I felt about such novels, Fadiman's loose, involuntary grin became even more marked. "So you didn't like it, eh?" he said. "Well, I had someone else read it and I got just the opposite report. In fact, it was highly recommended for pictures. I think she was right. I'm going to recommend it myself to Hollywood. One thing you've got to learn is to lean over backwards when you're reading for the movies. Don't look for Shakespeare. It might be literary crap, but it can make a first-rate picture. Want another book?"

I said yes. I was discouraged at having made such a bad start, but I wanted the job, so thereafter I swallowed my literary pride when I came across a novel like that first one. I learned to overlook trash in favor of what the public wanted: sickly sentiment and lots of sex.

I struggled hard those first few weeks to break myself into the job. I was what they called an "outside reader." I worked at home and was paid by the book—five dollars for novels, five for plays, two for short stories—and if I could read one book a day I could make $25 and sometimes $30 a week, which was incentive enough to keep me rushing from one assignment to another.

It went on day after day, night after night. There was little social life for us. Evenings when we might have gone visiting friends or to

a theater were spent with my nose buried in a book and Ruby tiptoe-
ing around the room so as not to disturb me. She was wonderful
about the whole thing, never complaining, and if someone should
come to visit she'd rush to the door and whisper that I was too busy
to see anyone. And when it got late in the evening and I was still im-
mersed in my book, she'd slip a cup of hot cocoa into my hand and
whisper in my ear to take a little rest.

But there was no time for rest. After I got through with my reading, which was sometimes quite late at night, I'd have to get up early
next morning to type out my synopsis and critique, with five carbon
copies, no less. Then came the big rush to collate the copies, pack
them into my briefcase together with the book, and get back to the
office as quickly as I could. There was a twenty-four-hour deadline
for every assignment.

Arriving at the office, I would generally find other readers sitting on the bench waiting their turn to go in to see the editor. They
all wore the same tired look that I had, all worn out from the daily
grind of reading and synopsizing and the rush to get here. Most of
the time we sat in silence, ignoring one another. Nevertheless I got
to know some of them. They were like me, failed writers who hadn't
yet given up and were using the reading job as a stopgap until they
finally made it.

But how much time did the job leave us to do our own writing?
There was very little. But I always found time, at least once a week in
the afternoon, to go and visit my mother.

I HAD NOT FORGOTTEN HER. I came and sat and talked with her, and
I gave her what little money I had, and she was forever grateful for
it, but especially for my coming. I would find her sitting by the window looking out as far as the basement window would permit, waiting to see me coming.

"My eyes were creeping out of my head," she would say with a little laugh that did not, however, conceal the tears in her eyes. I always came on the same day, Friday, so she knew when I was coming and had been sitting by the window since the morning.

She was in her sixties by now, but she looked much older. Her hair was gray and her face was wrinkled, and she had begun to walk with a stoop and some unsteadiness. Occasionally, I took her for a little walk to a nearby park, and I would hold her arm to give her some support.

How different this was, I sometimes thought, from other days, and my mind would go back to England, when I was a little boy and she'd take me to the market and I'd have to trot to keep up with her quick stride. There were other times, not too long before, when she'd be coming from some street market lugging two bulging shopping bags, one in each hand, her walk still vigorous.

We did not often go out. It was too tiring for her. On the way to the house I would stop off at a bakery and buy a coffee ring, and she would make a pot of tea, and we'd sit eating and drinking our tea and talk, and a little flush of happiness would come into her pallid cheeks.

I told her about my job. Her face brightened still more. "Congratulations," she said. "It sounds very important, working for the movies."

"It is," I assured her.

"But you've not given up your own writing, have you?"

"Absolutely not. I work at it just as much as before, perhaps more because now my mind's at ease over not having Ruby support me all the time."

"Ruby never minded, did she?"

"No, it meant nothing to her, and she was only too glad to have me keep on with my writing. She has a lot of faith in it."

"She's a wonderful girl." She really meant it. She had grown fond of Ruby since the first day I brought her to the house to meet her, and that fondness had increased with every visit since then. We vis-

ited as often as we could at weekends and holidays, alternating between visits to her and Ruby's mother, and whenever she saw Ruby
my mother's eyes brightened, a slight flush came into her cheeks,
and she hugged Ruby tightly.

There was little wonder about this. Ruby showed her affection
for Ma in many different ways. She would comb and brush and dress
her hair when she came, or give her a manicure, or bring her some
kind of gift, showing the attention that my mother had never received from her own daughters. I was glad that I had brought Ruby
into her life, and she was glad too. It compensated to some degree
for the loneliness and emptiness that she must have felt in those
days, for she was by herself much of the time. Sidney was in high
school, away most of the day, and he had a job after school deliver-
ing prescriptions for a drugstore and did not get home until late.

As for my father, it was the old story. That change in him had
not lasted long. He no longer stayed home and helped with some of
the household chores, or sat outside with my mother on a Saturday
night. That flash of goodness had been brief, like a sun trying to
peep out from behind storm clouds. He had reverted to his old ways,
coming and going like a boarder, the way it had been in England,
and obviously he had money to spend, because he often came home
late at night, drunk. Where his money came from was a mystery.
There was no indication that he had a job, not even the one day a
week one he claimed to have had before, although by now I knew
the truth about all that—though I had never told my mother.

The mystery was troubling my mother a great deal, and it was a
good thing that I was able to snatch those afternoons to visit her, for
she had no one else to talk to. My brothers were both unable to come
very often because of their work, and also because their wives were
unwilling to go. My sister and her husband were still in Chicago.
There was nobody except me, and there was very little I could do or
say except try to comfort her.

"Perhaps he does have a job," I said. "Where else could he be getting money from?"

"Perhaps," she said. "But he leaves the house at different times, sometimes late, sometimes early, and he comes home at different times, and then he goes out again to meet his friends on the East Side, some saloon where he does his drinking."

"Does he give you some of his money, at least?"

She gave a short, sad laugh. "Like he always did. A little bit that he takes out of his pocket, and when I tell him I can't manage the house on so little, he starts to curse. You know how he curses."

"Yes, I know," I said. "I wish I could do something, Ma." I felt sick with pity for her, and the old hatred for my father that I had grown up with flared up again, and I felt myself clenching my fists. But I knew I would have to calm myself and keep away from him. She was in no condition to suffer any kind of violence around her. Every time I saw her she had grown more and more feeble, and I knew she spent a great deal of her time in bed. Yet I felt I had to do something to help her. I gave her what money I could, telling her to hide it from him lest he spend that too on drink and, most likely, gambling. But there had to be more than that.

I didn't sleep thinking of it. I had trouble concentrating on my work. As for my own writing, that was completely pushed aside. It was a time when the happiness I could have felt being married to Ruby was clouded by worry over my mother.

Sometimes, when I was with her, I was tempted to tell her of my meeting with my grandfather in Union Square and what he had told me about her early love affair with a man named Samuel, and how my grandfather had conspired with my grandmother to trick her into marrying my father instead of Samuel. I had never told her anything at all about the meeting, because it seemed to me she had enough heartache in her life. I felt the same way about it now, but thinking of my grandfather had stirred up a suspicion in my mind as to where my father's newfound drinking money was coming from.

I remembered my promise to my grandfather to come and visit him. I had thought of it before from time to time, and I had felt guilty about not keeping my promise. But now, I thought, might be a good time to go to see him. I still had the dance ticket on the back of which I had written his address. I had kept it in a drawer of the one table in our room that served also as a desk, and I dug it out of a miscellany of items stored there and saw the address on Second Avenue scribbled in my handwriting on the back.

I waited for a slack day in my reading. I had been given two short stories to read, so I could afford to take a little time in the afternoon to go there, hoping he would be in. It was in an old tenement house in a noisy section of the downtown area. Kids were playing stickball and screaming to one another in the street. Cars were parked bumper to bumper at the curb. Bedding hung from fire escapes. I entered into a dark, smelly hallway where a row of broken mailboxes lined one wall, with bells equally broken or missing altogether underneath them. I made one out with his name along with several others on it. There was no use trying to ring the bell: this one was half pulled out from its socket.

I went up stairs whose treads were bent in the middle from years of tramping feet. Cigarette butts and chewing gum wrappers littered the dusty steps. The smells grew worse as I mounted. Some of it was food smell, cabbage predominantly, but there was also a toilet smell mingled with the mixture. At the end of each landing was a door with a red bulb glowing over it. This was the toilet that served the entire floor. I thought of all the money my grandfather had sent to his family in Chicago through the years, of all he had given away only recently, and that he should have to live in a place like this made me shake my head.

At last I came to the top floor. There was some relief to the darkness in the form of a skylight that brought some daylight to the floor. I found the door I wanted and knocked.

It was opened cautiously by an elderly woman in a sloppy housedress that showed a sagging bosom. She had a foreign accent. "Vot you vant?" she asked.

"I want to see my grandfather," I said. "I'm his grandson."

"You vas who?"

"His grandson."

"You vas his grandson? Yes, he told me you vould come. Why you don't come sooner?"

"I couldn't come sooner. I've been very busy."

"Is Yankel your father?"

"Yes."

"He come lots of times. But now he don't come no more. He vos taking care of the funeral."

"What funeral?"

"Your grandfather's. You didn't know?"

"No." I was a bit stunned. This was something I had not expected. "When did he die?" I asked.

"Oh, veeks ago. A long time now. He die in the night. I don't know for two days. He don't let me come in his room. Maybe he got things hid in his bed. Beggars make lots of money. Then I start to smell something bad, so I go in anyway and find him there in the bed. I run and tell your father in the saloon where he always goes to drink, and I tell him and he comes here and takes care of everything. He don't tell you that?"

"No."

Why should he tell us? There had been money hidden in that room, and he'd taken it. Would I tell my mother about all this? My head was in a whirl. I said, "Could I see his room?"

"Vot you vant to see his room for?"

I didn't quite know myself. But I felt I had to see it. "Just let me see it, please," I said. "I won't take more than a minute. I just want to see where my grandfather lived."

"All right," she said reluctantly. "Come in and see. I have no rented it yet, and there are still a few things there maybe you vant to take. Your father, he don't vant them. He tell me I should go pickle them. He is a bad loudmouth, your father."

I said nothing. She had opened the door wider, and I went in. The house smelled of food cooking, and it was messy. I only got a vague look at it as I followed her to one of the doors that shut off the various rooms she rented. She flung the door open and let me see the room. It was small and dark, with one window that faced a brick wall. I peered in first, then went in. There was a narrow bed, a dresser, a chair, and that was all. And he had lived here in this dark little hole for how many years? I did not know, but it had to be plenty, and in all that time, living virtually in a dark cell, he had never failed to send what must have been the bulk of the money he had made at begging to my grandmother, and after her death to his children, including my father.

What a strange man he was, I thought, and how little we really knew of him, of the depth of his generosity, the sense of responsibility to his family, the goodness that was in him. There were other things that we did not know about him. He had told me once, much to my surprise, that he read books, but I had forgotten about it until the landlady pointed out a number of books stacked in a corner on the floor for lack of shelves to put them on, apparently.

"He read a lot of books in the night," she said. "I charge him extra for the electricity. He don't care. He like books. You like books?"

"Yes," I said.

"Then you take them. Or I throw them out. I got no use for books."

I went up to them to examine them, picking up one after the other, and growing more and more amazed as I saw the authors. Dostoyevsky, Gorky, Tolstoy, Chekhov . . . all the great Russian masters. There were several by French writers, Zola, Flaubert, and English authors, Dickens, Thackeray. There had been rumors in the Chicago family of the wealth he must have, since he was able to give so much to my grandmother, and to them too, and to send us the tickets to come here. But the real wealth he had left behind was these books. I wanted them.

"I'll take them," I said to the landlady. "Do you have a bag or something I could carry them in?"

She let me have some old brown paper bags, and I stuffed the books into them. I thanked her and left hugging the bags to my sides, feeling as if I'd stumbled on buried treasure. Once on the subway, though, I began to think more soberly how I was going to explain all this to my mother: the old man's death, the money, my father's part in it, what we had been living on these past few years—this worse than anything else. I worried over the effect it would have on her, especially in her weakened condition.

I didn't have to tell her. It was told for me.

Chapter Twenty-three

ONE SUNDAY MORNING, WHEN RUBY AND I WERE STILL EATING OUR late breakfast and reading the *New York Times* at the same time, with sheets of the paper scattered on the table around us, there was a knock at the door. It was unusual for anyone to knock, because there were bells downstairs. I called out, "Who's there?"

"It's me," a voice answered. "Do you need any socks, ties, shirts?"

"No," I yelled angrily. "I don't need anything."

"I've got some very good bargains and I can let you have 'em cheap. I've got a real good buy on undershirts and shorts."

"Go away," I shouted. "I told you we don't need anything."

I got up and rushed to the door, determined to put emphasis to my words with force if necessary. I yanked the door open and there stood Uncle Barney, the family comedian, the Dwarf, a big five-cent White Owl cigar stuck in his grinning mouth.

"Uncle Barney!" I shouted, and we embraced and laughed. I

led him inside, and Ruby greeted him warmly. She had heard much about the family in Chicago from me and knew how I felt about Barney. She hastened to warm up the coffee and pour a cup for him.

"What brings you to New York?" I asked, once we were sipping our coffee.

"I came to see my father's grave," he said.

"Then you know he died," I said. I had been wondering about that, and why none of them had shown up for the funeral.

"We only found out a week ago," Barney said, and with a little twinkle in his eyes added, "It came over the grape juice vine. A drinking pal of your father's told us. He was in Chicago on what I suppose was drinking business, and he met one of my brothers in a saloon. So then we all got together and decided one of us should come here at least to pay our respects to the grave, and I was elected. Don't ask me why they picked me to go. I came in by bus this morning and decided to say hello first to my favorite nephew, and here I am."

He was a jolly fellow, Barney, forever cracking jokes in between puffs on his White Owl, and we spent a pleasant hour with him that morning over several cups of coffee before he had to leave to go up to the Bronx to see my father and mother. And if I had known what was to happen then, I might have delayed him as long as possible, for there was more to his coming than to pay respects and to visit relatives.

And there were reasons other than random choice why he had been picked to come. Of all the brothers, Barney was the least afraid of my father, and perhaps the only one among them who had been able to get along with him, so they had picked Barney to come out here to talk to him about the money they suspected my grandfather had left.

I was not there when he arrived at the old frame house in the Bronx, but Sidney, who was home at the time, gave me a good account of what happened. Both Sidney and my mother gave Barney a warm welcome, but they were afraid he had come at the wrong time to speak to my father. He was still asleep, and they explained that Saturday night was his big drinking night and he spent most of Sunday sleeping it off, and no one dared awaken him.

But Barney made light of this and, taking the cigar out of his mouth and holding it between two fingers, made a sweeping gesture. Everything was a joke to Barney and he saw nothing to be afraid of in awakening his brother. Sidney and my mother watched with considerable trepidation as Barney went to the bedroom door and flung it wide open, the cigar still held between two fingers, and shouted, "Yankel, the police are here. Don't give your right name."

My father sprang up in shock, half believing the warning was genuine, and then, seeing who was at the door, gave vent to an outburst of fury, cursing Barney and preparing to leap at his throat. But it did not last long, perhaps not surprisingly. Some canny thought may have penetrated his rage, some warning that this little dwarf of a brother was here to probe into what he did not want anyone to know, the secret he had been keeping to himself for several weeks.

"What the bloody 'ell are you doing 'ere?" he asked in a much calmer tone.

Barney had continued to grin all through the initial outburst, completely unafraid, a contrast to Sidney and my mother, who had both shrunk back in fear.

"I'm here to see you, Yankel," he said. "And our father's grave."

"Your father's grave? You couldn't come sooner? Where were you for the funeral? You couldn't come to see him buried?"

"How did we know he'd died?" Barney asked, clamping the cigar back into his mouth. "Why didn't you let us know? You kept it such a secret. What was there to hide?" His eyes twinkled a little as he spoke. Perhaps, though, there was something less amused in his tone. The twinkling eyes were fixed on my father, who had begun to bristle.

"What secret?" he said. "What the bloody 'ell are you talking about?"

As Sidney explained to me, there wasn't any argument then, and after my father had got dressed, they all sat down to the breakfast that my mother had made—though with the help of Sidney, because she was in a very feeble state and could not stand on her feet too long. When they sat down to eat they were still on good terms, and Barney was making jokes and keeping them all laughing, with even my father giving a twisted smile now and then and perhaps relieved that Barney seemed to have dropped the subject of their father and was here perhaps purely for social reasons.

But then it began, Barney puffing on the cigar and asking, "So tell me, Yankel, how did you find out that our father had died?"

"How?" My father bristled and crossed one leg over the other, as he always did when something objectionable came up and he was preparing for an argument. "I learned. Somebody told me. What the 'ell difference does it make how I learned?"

"You're right," Barney agreed. "What difference does it make? But I was just wondering—who took care of things, the funeral, the arrangements, everything that had to be done? There's more to be done for people when they die than when they're alive."

"Who took care of it?" He saw there was no way of avoiding the subject and went head-on into it, belligerent. "Who the bloody 'ell do you think took care of things? Did you? Did any of those bastards in Chicago? Not one of you ever came to see him when he was alive, so why should you come when he's dead? I used to go and see him every week."

Barney nodded. He was more serious now than he had been before. He smoked his cigar thoughtfully. "I didn't know that. I'm glad to hear it. We were always worried about Father being alone so much—"

"You're full of shit!" It burst from my father in an explosion of anger. "You never gave a good goddamn about him, any one of you."

"All right, all right . . ." Barney refused to get upset by it. He was smiling again and waving the cigar about, and my mother was sighing with relief that he hadn't taken offense. Barney went on, pacifying my father, "I'll admit that we all neglected him these past years, but so long as one of us did the right thing by him, that helps make up for what we didn't do. I'll tell them when I get home. They'll all feel better. But tell me, who paid for the funeral, the grave, everything?"

"Who paid?"

"Yes. There had to be expenses. Did he leave enough to take care of things? I should think he would. He always had money."

"You should know that," my father burst out. "You took plenty from him." He was beginning to boil up again. He knew now what Barney was getting at.

Barney did not waste too much time. He ignored the last statement and said, "It wouldn't surprise me if he had a little bundle tucked away somewhere. I hope you looked around his room carefully after he passed away to make sure there were no bankbooks or money hidden away in the mattress." He said this jestingly, eyes twinkling, sucking on the cigar, as if he had not meant it seriously.

But it did not deceive my father. He was at once belligerent, crossing his legs again, glaring across the table at Barney. "Dwarf, little shrimp, what are you trying to say? I took the money? What about our mother? She must have had a bundle, and who could have taken that except you and those other bastards in Chicago? You think I didn't know about it?"

Barney shook his head emphatically. "No, Yankel, I swear there was nothing."

"You bloody rotten liar," my father said. "You took it and shared it among yourselves and left me out. Well, what if I did the same thing? You ever hear of tit for tat? Supposing I did the same thing?

What right would you have to complain? You can go to hell, all of you."

He was practically admitting to it and taking a great deal of satisfaction in doing so, making it seem as if it had all been an act of justifiable revenge. But it was a clear enough admission, and Sidney told how then there was a sudden cry of horror from my mother, and how this seemed to whip my father into even greater fury. After a swift glance at her, he rose to his feet, seized Barney by the collar, lifted him up, and threw him out of the house.

Then he came back, hitching up his trousers and still in a rage, and turned it on my mother this time, saying, "What the bloody 'ell are you carrying on for? Is it so terrible that I took the money? Would it have been better to give it to those pigs in Chicago? Did they give me any of Mama's money? I did what was right. And whether you like it or not, you've been living off it for the past years. Even before he died he gave me something every week."

"You weren't working even then?" my mother asked tremulously, her face in her hands.

"What work? Who the bloody 'ell had work? Your money came from the streets. You might as well know it." The spittle flew out of his mouth as he spoke, and the eyes glaring at her were bloodshot. It was clear that there was guilt mixed in with his torrent of rage.

My mother's whole world must have collapsed then. She had never given up hope that she could repay my grandfather for the tickets he had sent us. She had talked to me often about it. But now she was learning that he was dead and she would never have that opportunity; not only that, but she had been living off his begging for these past two or three years, and that was a worse blow than anything else.

She was in such a state, and so weakened by it all, that Sidney had to carry her to her bed. He had no difficulty doing that; he had done it often before when she was not feeling well. He had grown into a big, husky fellow, taller even than I, and my mother must have weighed very little.

That night, Mrs. Janeski summoned me to the telephone in her apartment. It was a service she provided for her roomers. I rushed downstairs and picked up the phone.

It was Sidney, his voice not steady. "Ma's had a stroke," he said. "You'd better come."

Chapter Twenty-four

WE RUSHED UP TO THE BRONX, RUBY AND I. I HAD TRIED TO GET Ruby to stay home, but she had refused. She was as concerned as I was about my mother and wanted to be there to give whatever help she could. So I gave in and let her come, and was only too glad to have her with me. I needed her.

It was winter and a bitterly cold day, and we huddled close together as we hurried down the steps of the subway station, feeling relief as we came into the stale warmth. We were able to catch a train almost immediately, and we sat close together in a nearly empty car. It was late, around ten o'clock. Ruby took my hand and pressed it in hers, knowing how I was feeling.

Six months earlier I had done the same thing for her, given her the same comfort that she was now giving me. Her mother had died suddenly from a heart attack, and I had nursed Ruby through the days of depression that had followed, and she had been grateful for it. Now she was doing it for me, and she held my hand tightly as the train rocked and roared its way up to the Bronx.

I think I had been haunted all my life by the fear of what was happening now. It had come on me mostly when I was a child, with a dread, sinking feeling, and sometimes at night I would awaken screaming because I had dreamed that my mother had died. It would wake up the entire household, and my mother would come rushing into the bedroom and hold me tightly until I had been assured that she was still alive and with me.

Now I could feel that sinking sensation inside me. I tried to tell myself that I was older and should be able to bear up against such things, but it was there just the same, that familiar sensation of dread.

Ruby and I fought the cold once more as we got off the train and walked quickly to the old frame house that would not be much warmer than the outside.

Sidney met us at the door, and his first words confirmed my fears: "Ma's dying."

I didn't want to believe it. I pushed past him and went straight to the bedroom, with Ruby close behind me. My mother looked as if she might be sleeping. She was lying on her back, and a faint snoring came from her. But her eyes seemed open.

I bent over her and whispered, "Ma, this is Harry."

She did not answer, and Ruby's hands gently pulled me up and away from her. "She can't hear you," she whispered. "She's in a coma."

I realized it then, but was too choked to say anything. Sidney had followed us into the room. He had been alone with this for several hours. My father was not home yet from his usual visit to the saloon in downtown Manhattan.

Sidney told us he had been doing his homework in the kitchen when he heard choking sounds in the bedroom. He ran in there, and Ma seemed to be trying to tell him something but couldn't speak. Then she lost consciousness.

Sidney managed to get a neighbor to stay with her while he ran for Dr. Schwartz, who had been our doctor for years. His home and office were in an apartment house nearby. He came back with Sidney, carrying his little black bag, and it did not take long for him to examine my mother before telling Sidney that she had suffered a massive stroke. He did not advise sending her to the hospital. She could get better care here in the house, and she could be made comfortable for the little time that was left. He did not hide anything. Ma was dying.

Sidney called me, and he also called Joe and Saul, and sent a telegram to Rose in Chicago. It had been a trying time for him, alone with all this, and he was grateful that we were there. Ruby took charge at once. It was cold in the house, with little steam coming up in the radiators, and Ruby at once began to make coffee in the kitchen, while the two of us sat in the bedroom with my mother, not knowing what to do or say.

After a while Ruby called us in for the coffee, and we were sitting there drinking it, glad of its warmth, when Joe and Saul arrived. Saul immediately went into the bedroom and began to say prayers for the dying, rocking to and fro and mumbling the Hebrew words. Joe presently joined in with him, and it was in the midst of this that we heard the front door open. It was my father, and I could tell instantly from the awkward footsteps that he was drunk. The prayers halted and we all looked at one another, the same bitter thought in our minds: *Of all times for him to come home drunk. What to do with him? How to handle this?*

He made his way, staggering a little, to the bedroom door and stood looking at us. His face was a purplish color, the way it always got when he had drunk a lot, and his eyes tried to focus on the things he was seeing and hearing: my mother lying there apparently asleep, the faint snoring sound coming from her, my two older brothers standing with prayer books in their hands—and after a brief moment Saul went back to his praying, so there was that too for his befuddled brain to try to grasp.

Then he spoke thickly: "What the bloody 'ell's going on here?"

Nobody answered him, but Ruby went up to him, put an arm round him, and said gently, "Ma's had a stroke."

He looked at her. He didn't shake off her arm, as he would have with anybody else. He too in his own begrudging way had been captured by her from the very start. "What d'you mean, stroke? She's sleeping. Can't you see she's sleeping?"

"No, Dad"—she called him Dad, too, and none of us had ever called him that—"she's not sleeping. She's in a coma. She's very ill. Come with me."

He hesitated a moment longer. He looked at my mother again, as if still not believing that it was anything but sleep, then he let Ruby take him into the kitchen, where she gave him some coffee, and though it did little to sober him, he let her lead him into Sidney's bedroom, and with his clothes on he got into bed and she closed the door on him.

I was never so glad then that I had brought Ruby with me, for only she could have managed a situation that could have ended in violence if it had been left to us. The hatred that I'd always felt for him was greater that night than any time before, and I'm sure my brothers felt the same way.

We all sat up that night, sometimes in the bedroom with my mother, watching her, waiting for what we knew must happen, sometimes wandering into the kitchen to drink more coffee, and the house growing even colder than before, making it necessary for us to wear our overcoats and Ruby her raccoon coat. Ruby and I huddled close together for more warmth, and for the comfort she wanted to give me.

But one time while I sat alone beside my mother while Ruby was serving coffee to the others in the kitchen, a strange thing happened. The radiator hissed futilely, bringing no warmth into the room. Occasionally it gave a loud clanking sound, as if hammers were banging away inside to get the steam up. I kept my gaze on her and thought, *If she were just asleep, the noise would awaken her.* Then suddenly she seemed to stir a little. To my amazement, her eyes opened wider and she looked at me and smiled.

"Ma?" I whispered.

She was awake. She knew me. She whispered back, "Harry."

"Yes, it's me, Ma," I said, my heart bursting with joy. I ran to the kitchen shouting, "She's awake! She spoke to me!"

They all ran back with me. But she was no longer with us. She had sunk back into the coma. I felt bitter disappointment. The others thought I had imagined it and went back to the kitchen. I remained there for a while longer, hoping that she would awaken once more.

I was still there when gray morning came, and then I gave up. It would not happen again. But my mother clung to life as tenaciously as she had always done, much as when we were children and she had fought through all her miseries to save us from starving. It was in her yet, despite the crippling blow to her brain, the struggle to survive. She did not die that night, nor the day after, and then survived another night and day, and on that day Rose and Jim arrived. And with them—a big surprise—was Aunt Lily.

She had changed much in appearance from the time I saw her in Chicago, when she was still a radiant bride, slender and with a dark loveliness. She had grown heavy and shapeless, with a double chin and the beginning of a resemblance to my grandmother. With the loss of Phil and no other means of making a living, she had turned to nursing, and it was to be of help to my mother, whom she had always liked, that she had come with Rose and Jim.

They themselves seemed to have changed very little, Jim still warm and friendly, my sister still wearing the haughty expression on her face. But mixed with Rose's distance, and perhaps what could not have been there before, was some concern for my mother. She rushed in immediately upon arrival to look helplessly at her mother lying in the bed, and her gaze contained much of what she still could not allow herself to show. I saw Jim bend over and kiss my mother's damp brow. Rose hesitated, but she could not follow suit. She turned and went back to the kitchen.

Aunt Lily took charge immediately. She had changed into a white uniform and began the tasks that had been neglected until now with my mother, because Ruby had been unable to do them: bathing her and changing her clothes while she still remained unconscious. Dr. Schwartz had arrived with an IV to be put in, and Lily knew how to adjust it and see that it was working properly.

She was busy with this and other things when my father came into the room. He had not left the house since the night he had come home drunk, but he had scarcely spoken to anyone and had kept pretty much to himself, sitting in corners silently, and occasionally going into the bedroom to sit there for a while.

He had been asleep when Lily arrived, and his face darkened when he saw her. She belonged to the Chicago family, and he had thought he was shot of them for good when he threw Barney out. Perhaps, too, there flashed across his mind the thought that the Chicagoans were after him again about the money.

"What the bloody 'ell are you doing here?" he asked.

Lily knew him well. The greeting did not surprise her, nor did it make her angry. She remained calm and even smiled a little. "I'm here to take care of Ada," she said.

"Who needs your care?" he snarled. "Go on, pack up and get out of here, and tell them back in Chicago I don't need help from any of them."

Watching all this, I clenched my hands and got ready to interfere if he tried to do anything physical. In my mind, that he should behave in this fashion at a time like this and in front of his dying wife exceeded any of the rotten things he had done in his life before.

Luckily, it was Lily he was dealing with. With a smile she continued bathing my mother's fevered forehead and said quietly, "Yankel, keep your voice down or you'll disturb her. Even when they're lying like this in a coma they can sense unpleasant things around them. I'll leave when it's time for me to leave. But not now."

He let out a sudden roar: "Get out! Get out of my house!"

It brought the others running into the room, and it was a good thing Jim was among them, and Sidney too, for if it had gone any further I would have flown at him with my fists the way I had done once before. As it was, these two were able to get him away from the bedroom and talk him into a calmer mood. But shortly afterward he put on his overcoat and without saying anything to anyone stomped out of the house; we heard the door slam shut after him. He had gone probably to his favorite haunt, the saloon in downtown Manhattan.

Another day, another night. They all stayed, most of us sleeping on the floor covered with whatever blankets there were and our coats. There was a little warmth in the kitchen with the gas oven lit, but there was not enough room there for all of us and we were forced to use other rooms that were freezing, where the radiators had given up all pretense of bringing up steam despite their hissing and clanking.

I had gone up to the landlady to try to get her to give us a little more heat, especially under the circumstances. She still had some fear of me, still thinking I was a gangster, and when she opened the door for me it was only partially and she looked as if she might be ready to slam it shut in my face and dash into the house for protection. She nodded agreement to my request, saying, "Yes, yes, yes, I'll see what I can do. . . ."

But she did nothing, and the radiators continued to hiss and clank and give no warmth, and we sat in our overcoats shivering, taking turns to sit with my mother. When it was my turn I held her hand, as Lily had told me that it gave my mother some comfort to feel another person's hand holding hers. The hand was warm and moist. Her breathing was heavy and accompanied by the faint snoring sound. I looked down at her face. It seemed to me that there was a tightness to it, as if she might be struggling to breathe and to live.

I thought of all the times when I was a boy and had looked at her face and seen the different expressions there—so often the sadness, when she might not have wanted to live then but had forced herself to do so because of us. And there were times when her face had been very much alive, when she was sitting in her little shop surrounded by all her customers, the women who were also her friends, and how it glowed then with the pride and joy that she felt at being a queen among them.

I thought of the anxiety she had shown when one of us became ill, and the same worry that showed on her face when she stood waiting for us to come home from school, shielding her eyes from the sun with the palm of a hand, fearful that we might have been attacked by a band of Jew-hating ragamuffins. And there was laughter too on occasions when she was with one of her women friends and they were enjoying a joke of some sort.

I must have been studying her face closely all those years, because I could remember the different expressions so clearly, especially how it glowed when she talked of her one big dream, going to America. Yes, that particularly, and the joy on it when the tickets came. I could never forget that day, when all of us were a little drunk with happiness. For her, and for all of us, the dream had come true.

But had it? I glanced around at the cold, dark room, and at her lying there, and the radiator hissing futilely. Was this where the dream would end? I didn't want to believe it.

Lily was moving about softly, doing various things. Then I felt her hand on my shoulder. I looked up at her questioningly. "Harry," she said quietly, "your mother is dead."

THERE WAS THE FUNERAL NEXT day. According to Jewish law it had to take place then, not later. Saul took charge of everything. We did what he told us to do. A rabbi came to the house and said some prayers, and Saul did too, then we all joined in, mumbling words that we read in the prayer book he gave us, prayers that were for the dead, for our mother.

It was still bitterly cold and the sky was overcast. We drove out to the cemetery in the limousines the undertaker provided. A forest of gravestones stretched out as far as the eye could see. The graves were so close together that we had to be careful not to step on others as we gathered round the rectangular hole that had been dug for Ma's coffin. There were more prayers, and we all shivered as the wind struck us with a knife edge.

As the coffin was being lowered into the grave, Ruby pressed close to me and whispered, "You mustn't be afraid to cry." I wasn't. I cried a great deal. So did all the others. I didn't look at my father.

After the service was over we all started back for the limousines, careful again not to step on graves that were so close to one another they almost touched. Even in death, I thought, there is poverty. Just before we reached the gate of the cemetery something made me turn round and look. My father was still standing there near my mother's grave. He had his face in his hands and he was crying. I thought if he had ever shown any goodness, it was now.

I never saw him again after that day.

Epilogue

NOW THAT I AM WELL INTO MY NINETIES—BEING A NONAGENARIAN, they call it—I am able to look back on my life and see the whole of it spread out before me clearly in a huge panorama of events, people, places, and everything that happened to me. I am very fortunate. Age is supposed to dim memory, but mine has been sharpened to where I can see things with even greater clarity than when they actually happened.

Of all the things I look back upon, nothing touches me so deeply as the dreams my mother concocted for us, and the way they brightened our lives and gave us hope for the future during those sad days in England when all this was so badly needed. I have compared these dreams to the soap bubbles we used to blow from our clay pipes, sending them floating in the air, beautiful to look at but elusive and fragile. If you reached up and caught one in your hand, it would burst and vanish immediately. I suppose that is what happened to my mother with the biggest of all her dreams, the one that brought us to America in the summer of 1922 and to my grandmother's house in Chicago, where all the relatives had gathered to greet us.

For years before this she had written letters to them pleading with them to send us the tickets that would take us by steamship to America, believing that here in America was the better life she had always sought. Now at last we were there, and I had my first real glimpse of America through the back window of my grandmother's house. But instead of seeing the mansions, the gardens, the swimming pools, the butlers and chauffeurs and limousines that we had believed everybody had in America, I saw a back alley with garbage cans overflowing with garbage, and a big rat crawling on one of them.

And yet not even that brought complete disillusionment. After all, this was America, the land of opportunity, and times were good, and it brought the large bubble almost within my mother's grasp. My brothers and sister were working. My father was working and gave her at least a portion of his wages. There was money coming into the house, and we had a house with electric lights and a bathtub and a telephone even, but what was even more important was something my mother had promised us years ago in another dream of hers: a parlor with plush furniture and a piano.

It was almost as if she could reach up and catch the bubble and hold on to it without its bursting. But that didn't happen. The Depression came, and the poverty from which we had fled in England caught up with us here in America. The bubble burst.

The dream came completely to an end for my mother on that cold winter day in the dark basement apartment in the Bronx. It had one bit of compensation for her: It put an end to her suffering also. But for the rest of us it did not end there, and there were better times in store for all of us that would have gladdened my mother's heart.

My oldest brother, Joe, did not become the journalist that he had dreamed of becoming as a boy, but he did become a successful and profitable owner of a house remodeling business. He and his wife had one child, a girl named Rita. Saul, with his seventh-grade education, wrote two scholarly books on Jewish culture that were published, but his greatest triumph was his wife, Estelle, whom he had finally made into a religious woman, observant of all the Jewish laws and customs, attending the synagogue regularly, and considerably quieter in her dress and manner. It had been a difficult task, accompanied by much bickering, many quarrels, and a separation of several months once, but Saul had persevered and finally succeeded. They had one child, a boy named Irwin, and the good family life that Saul had always wanted.

My sister Rose never stopped affecting a haughty upper-class British accent, but she had given up her fantasies of being a duchess and seemed quite content with being the wife of a restaurant sandwich man. And although she never fully forgave my mother for taking her parlor away, her attitude toward her softened considerably in those last few days of my mother's life.

As for Sidney, he achieved one goal that my mother had for us: He became the only one in the family who went to college. He worked his way through by selling magazine subscriptions. He did that under Joe's tutelage, but became quite proficient at it, and after his graduation he became an ad salesman for a national magazine, then a successful publisher of his own magazine. But his life grew sad and difficult when his wife developed multiple sclerosis shortly after giving birth to their one child, a son named Ted. Then Sidney found himself nursing a sick woman, as he had done with my mother, only this time under even more difficult circumstances because of a baby to be cared for too. Fortunately, he had the money now to hire a housekeeper, but it was a life filled with constant worry and fear until after ten years of it his wife died.

I suppose I was the luckiest of them all—I had Ruby. People have often asked me what is the secret to my longevity. My answer is that there is no secret. There was Ruby, and the love and care she gave me in those sixty-seven years of our wonderful marriage. There is nothing else I can attribute my longevity to. In that time, too, there was added what amounted virtually to another member of our family, Aunt Lily.

She came to live in New York shortly after my mother's death and after a trip to California, where she met and married her second husband, an Italian builder named Peo—a Christian, naturally, and Italian to boot. It meant nothing, of course. He was welcomed as much into the family as Jim had been. Times had changed since the days of the invisible wall that ran down the street in England where we once lived, with Jews on one side and Christians on the other. Even my mother, had she lived, would have liked Peo and accepted him.

They came to live near us when we lived in Long Island, and to our two children, Charles and Adraenne, she was always their aunt Lil, and since Ruby and I were both then working, Lily took care of them much of the time.

It was a good life for us, and I never gave any thought to the possibility that it might end, even after my children had grown up and were married themselves and out of the house, on their own. It ended for me one gray morning in a hospital room that overlooked, of all places, Central Park, where our love had begun. Ruby died that morning of her leukemia, and I have never gotten over it.

I live alone now in a house that Ruby and I bought when we retired. It is in a quiet development restricted to adults only, and there is a lake just across the street from where I live round which Ruby and I used to walk every day, morning and evening, with her hand in mine. We'd finally come to rest on a bench facing the lake with a tree shading it that Ruby and I had planted years before as a memorial to friends who had died. On summer evenings we'd watch the sun set on the other side of the lake, the trees forming a dark, lace-like covering over the red glow in the sky, and that glow reflected in the water and turning it pink. It was very still, and we'd sit there with her hand still in mine, watching the glow gradually fade, and then we'd go home.

I cannot walk much any longer. It would not be possible for me to go round the lake. But I do manage to cross over the street to sit on that bench, alone now, watching the sunset, and sometimes I think that Ruby is still there sitting with me and I can feel her hand, soft and warm, in mine.

I think of many things then, and one of them is that all of this might have been what my mother really sought in her dream—just this quiet and peace and these beautiful surroundings, and nothing else.

Acknowledgments

My thanks are due to the following people: to Kate Elton for this second chance; to Anna Simpson for the editing that saved me from a lot of mistakes; to Robin Rolewicz for her enthusiasm and encouragement; to Charles and Adraenne for being there when I needed them and for their valuable suggestions; to Sarina Evan, who did her best for me with getting people to know me; to Bill Tiernan, for reading my manuscript and giving me some very important comments; to my caregiver, Bette, for helping me stay alive long enough to write this book; and to the many people who read *The Invisible Wall* and wrote asking for this book.

About the Author

Ninety-eight-year-old HARRY BERNSTEIN emigrated to the United States with his family after World War I. He began writing his acclaimed first book, *The Invisible Wall*, after the death of his wife, Ruby. He has also been published in "My Turn" in *Newsweek*. Bernstein lives in Brick, New Jersey, where he is working on another book.